Native American Book of the Dead

Fritz Zimmerman

Cover Design Alicia Shipley

Front Cover

1911 Photo of a Kwakiutl Indian from British Columbia Caressing a Mummy

Table of Contents

Assinboine

Origin:Montana, North Dakota, Alberta, and Saskatchewan

It is quite evident the Assiniboin, about the first years of the seventeenth century, moved northward from the densely forested region surrounding the headwaters of the Mississippi, where they had formed a division of the Yanktonai, to the vicinity of the Lake of the Woods and beyond, where they soon became allied with the Cree. They continued to move northward and westward, and by the close of the century were living in the region about Lake Winnipeg. A hundred years later they were occupying widely scattered villages near the banks of the Assiniboin and Saskatchewan Rivers. Later the region just mentioned was occupied by the northern division of the tribe, while others dominated a section of the extreme upper Valley of the Missouri.

In the year 1775 Alexander Henry reached the scattered camps of the Assiniboin. He became well acquainted with the peculiar manners and ways of life of the people, and it is evident he was a careful observer. His reference to the burial customs are here quoted at length : " With respect to the burial of the dead, if the death happen in the winter-season, and at a distance from the burial-ground of the family, the body invariably accompanies all the wanderings and journeys of the survivors, till the spring, and till their arrival at the place of interment. In the mean time, it is every where rested on a scaffold, out of the reach of beasts of prey. The grave is made of a circular form, about five feet deep, and lined with bark of the birch, or some other tree, or with skins. A seat is prepared, and the body is placed in a sitting posture, with supporters on either side. If the deceased be a man, his weapons of war, and of the chase, are buried with him, as also his shoes, and every thing for which, as a living warrior or hunter, he would have occasion, and, indeed, all his property; and I believe that those, whose piety alone may not be strong enough to ensure to the dead their entire inventory of what is supposed to be necessary for them, or is their own, are compelled to do them justice by another argument, and which is, the fear of their displeasure. A defrauded or neglected ghost, although invisible, can disperse the game of the plains or forests, so that the hunter shall hunt in vain; and, either in the chase or in the war, turn aside the arrow, or palsy the arm that draws the bow; in the lodge, it can throw a child into the fire.

"The body and its accompaniments are covered with bark; the bark with logs; and the logs with earth. This done, a relation stands up, and pronounces an eulogium on the deceased, extolling his virtues, and relating his exploits. He dwells upon the enemies whom he slew, the scalps and prisoners which he took, his skill and industry in the chase, and his deportment as a father, husband, son, brother, friend, and member of the community. At each assertion which he makes, the speaker strikes a post, which is placed near the grave; a gesture of asseveration, and which enforces the attention of the audience, and assists in counting up the points delivered. The eulogium finished, the post is painted, and on it are represented the number of prisoners taken, by so many figures of men; and of killed and scalped, by figures without heads. To these are added his badge, called, in the Algonquin tongue, a totem and which is in the nature of an armorial bearing. It informs the passing Indian of the family to which the deceased belonged. A serious duty at the grave, is that of placing food, for the use of the dead, on the journey to the land of souls. This care is never neglected, even under every disadvantage of molestation. In the neighborhood of the traders, dishes of cooked venison are very commonly placed on the graves of the long buried, and as commonly removed by Europeans, even without offense to those who placed them there. In situations of great want, I have more than once resorted to them for food." (Travels and Adventures in Canada and the Indian Territories, between the years 1760 and 1776. New York, 1809. 303-305.) On January 22, 1821, during the season of extreme cold, when the entire face of the country was covered with snow and ice, the body of an Indian was placed upon a scaffold erected in the vicinity of Brandon House, a post of the Hudson's Bay Co., erected in 1794, on the south side of the Assiniboin about 17 miles below the present Brandon.

As described by one who witnessed the simple ceremony : " I saw an Indian corpse staged, or put upon a few cross sticks, about ten feet from the ground, at a short distance from the fort. The property of the dead, which may consist of a kettle, ax, and a few additional articles, is generally put into the case, or wrapped in a buffalo skin with the body, under the idea that the deceased will want them, or that the spirit of these articles will accompany the departed spirit in traveling to another world. And whenever they visit the stage or burying-place, which they frequently do for years afterwards, they will encircle it, smoke their pipes, weep bitterly, and in their sorrow, cut themselves with knives, or pierce themselves with the points of sharp instruments." (*The Substance of a Journal during a residence at the Red River Colony. London, 1827. p. 33.*) The preceding note would conform with Henry's account already quoted, and it is quite evident that throughout the northern country the remains of those who died during the winter months, when the ground was frozen to a depth of several feet, were placed upon scaffolds. At other seasons the bodies were deposited in excavated graves. As West later states : "They have a burial ground at the Settlement, and usually put the property of the deceased into the grave with the corpse. If any remains, it is given away from an aversion they have to use any thing that belonged to their relations who have died. Some of the graves are very neatly covered over with short sticks and bark as a kind of canopy, and a few scalps are affixed to poles that are stuck in the ground at the head of several of them. You see also occasionally at the grave, a piece of wood on which is either carved or painted the symbols of the tribe the deceased belonged to, and which are taken from the different animals of the country." (Op. cit., pp. 55-56.) The " Settlement " mentioned above was that of the Red River colony, and certain of the graves described in this brief general account were probably of Cree or Sauteux Indians. The description at once suggests the photographs made by the Hind party a generation later and which are shown in Plates 2 and 3.

On April 7, 1805, the Lewis and Clark party left their winter quarters near the Mandan villages, below the mouth of Knife River, where they had arrived late in October of the preceding year. They continued to ascend the Missouri, passed the mouth of the Little Missouri, and about 20 miles beyond encountered the remains of a temporary encampment of 43 lodges, which they believed to have been occupied by a party of Assiniboin. During the days following other camps of the same tribe were discovered, and in some instances tree burials were seen near by. April 20 they had advanced to within a few miles of the mouth of White Earth River, and that day, so it is written in the journal :"In walking through the neighboring plains we found a fine fertile soil . , . Our hunters procured elk and deer which are now lean, and six beaver which are fatter and more palatable. Along the plain there were also some Indian camps; near one of these was a scaffold about seven feet high, on which were two sleds with their harness, and under it the body of a female, carefully wrapped in several dressed buffalo skins ; near it lay a bag made of buffalo skin, containing a pair of moccasins, some red and blue paint, beaver's nails, scrapers for dressing hides, some dried roots, several plaits of sweet grass, and a small quantity of Mandan tobacco. These things as well as the body itself had probably fallen down by accident, as the custom is to place them on the scaffold. At a little distance was the body of a dog not yet decayed, who had met this reward for having dragged thus far in the sled the corpse of his mistress, to whom according to the Indian usage he had been sacrificed." *(History of the Expedition under the command of Captains Lewis and Clark . . . Prepared for the press by Paul Allen. Philadelphia. 1814. 2 vols. ,I, pp. 191-192.)* It is possible the woman had died some distance from the spot where her body was discovered, it having been wrapped and placed on the sled.

Several very interesting references to the beliefs and burial customs of the Assiniboin are to be found in Maximilian's narrative. They "believe that the dead go to a country in the south, where the good and brave find women and buffaloes, while the wicked or cowardly are confined to an island, where they are destitute; of all the pleasures of life. Those who, during their lives, have conducted themselves bravely, are not to be deposited in trees when they die, but their corpses are to be laid on the ground, it being taken for granted that, in case of need, they will help themselves. Of course they are then generally devoured by the wolves, to secure them from which, however, they are covered with wood and stones. Other corpses are usually placed on trees, as among the Sioux, and sometimes on scaffolds. They are tied up in buffalo hides, and three or four are sometimes laid in one tree." *(Maximilian, Prince of Wied. Travels in the Interior of North America. London, 1843., p. 197.)* And on July 1, 1833, in the timber below Fort Union, " we found a tree, on which the corpses of several Assiniboins were deposited; one of them had fallen down, and been torn and devoured by the wolves. The blankets which covered the body were new, and partly bedaubed with red paint, and some of the branches and the trunk of the tree were colored in the same manner. Dreidoppel, who discovered this tree, took up the skull of a young Assiniboin, in which a mouse had made its nest for its young ; and Mr. Bodmer made an accurate drawing of the tree, under which there was a close thicket of roses in full blossom, the fragrant flowers of which seemed destined to veil this melancholy scene of human frailty and folly." (Op. cit., p. 205.) The sketch made by Bodmer was reproduced by Maximilian and is here given at Plate 17.

Plate 17

To paint the tree upon which the body rested was evidently an established custom among the Assiniboin who frequented the banks of the upper Missouri, and red was the color thus employed. Some miles above Fort Union, on July 13, 1833, Maximilian discovered the remains of an Assiniboin wrapped in skins, resting upon the sloping trunk of a tree, from the branches of which hung a saddle and stirrups. And most interesting is the remark, "the tree itself was painted red."

Brief references to the treatment of the sick are contained in the same journal. In one of the lodges of the Assiniboin camp, near Fort Union, a man was quite ill, medicine men were gathered around him, "singing with all their might. Many people had collected about this tent, and were peeping through the crevices. After the conjuration had continued some time, the tent was opened, and the men who had been assembled in it went away by threes, the one in the middle always stepping a little before the others, and they continued singing till they reached their own tents . . ." The following day " In the afternoon we again heard the Indian drum beating very loud in the tent of the sick man, and we went there to see their conjurations. We looked cautiously through the crevices in the tent, and saw the patient sitting on the floor, his head, covered with a small cap, sunk upon his breast, and several men standing around him. Two of the medicine men were beating the drum in quick time, and a third rattled the Quakemuha (or Shishikue), which he waved up and down. These people were singing with great effort;sometimes they uttered short ejaculations, and were in a violent perspiration; sometimes they sucked the places where the patient felt pain, and pretended they could suck out or remove the morbid matter." (Op. cit., pp. 204-205.)

Few persons were as well acquainted with the peculiar customs and understood the characteristics of the native tribes of the Upper Missouri Valley as did the great missionary Father De Smet. He traversed the country during all seasons of the year, visited the Indians in their widely scattered camps, and in many instances became their friend and comforter. In letters written just 70 years ago he made several interesting references to the burial customs of the Assiniboin with whom he came in contact, and likewise mentioned their belief of conditions as they existed after death. Writing of the burial customs, or rather of their method of disposing of the dead, he said: "The Assiniboins never bury their dead. They bind the bodies with thongs of raw hide between the branches of large trees, and more frequently place them on scaffolds, to protect them from the wolves and other wild animals. They are higher"than a man can reach. The feet are always turned to the west. There they are left to decay. When the scaffolds or the trees to which the dead are attached fall, through old age, the relatives bury all the other bones, and place the skulls in a circle in the plain, with the faces turned towards the center. They preserve these with care, and consider them objects of religious veneration. You will generally find there several bison skulls. In the center stands the medicine-pole, about twenty feet high, to which wah-kons are hung, to guard and protect the sacred deposit. The Indians call the cemetery the village of the dead. They visit it at certain seasons of the year, to converse affectionately with their deceased relatives and friends, and always leave some present." *(De Smet,Western Missions and Missionaries: A Series of Letters. New York,1863. p. 204.)*

It will prove of interest at this time to add a few words in connection with the career of that great worker among the Indians, Pere de Smet. On June 16, 1851, the young Swiss traveler Friedrich Kurz was at or near the present Omaha, when he went aboard the Missouri River packet St. Ange., Captain La Barge, bound for the upper Missouri. Kurz entered in his journal that day: "The steamer is really a hospital for victims of cholera—the sick and the dying. "The following day he wrote: "No doctor on board; two more deaths since yesterday. Evans, a professor in Geology, prepared the remedy (meal mixed with whisky) that I administered. Father Van Hocken bestows spiritual consolation. Father de Smet is, also, not well, but he is not suffering from cholera . . ." And three days later, June 21, 1851, Kurz wrote in his diary: "Pere Van Hocken dead. He died as a Christian. He had been sick only two hours. It was about 4 o'clock in the morning, when I was awakened by his calling me. I found him, half dressed, on his bed in a violent convulsion. I called Pere de Smet. We anchored in the evening and buried him by torchlight. Pere Hocken was to have gone as a missionary to the Nezperces. And I had not sketched his portrait for Pere de Smet." The following day the St. Ange passed Floyd's grave. It is interesting to find among Kurz's numerous sketches a portrait of Father de Smet made at this time, days of great anxiety to all. The sketch is reproduced in Plate 18, a. A drawing of an Assiniboin, made by Kurz at Fort Union, November 16, 1851, is given on the same plate.

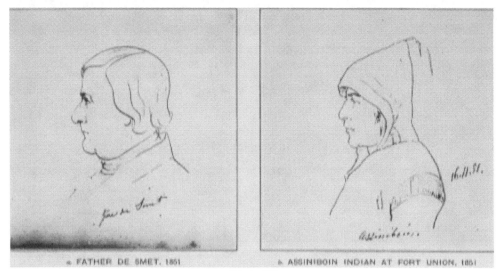

a. FATHER DE SMET, 1851   b. ASSINIBOIN INDIAN AT FORT UNION, 1851

Plate 18

The painting by Catlin, made in the vicinity of the Mandan village some years before the preceding notes by Father De Smet were prepared, and which is now reproduced in Plate 26, agrees in every detail with the Assiniboin manner of placing the skulls in a circle on the prairie, with several buffalo skulls within the circle, and with poles from which an offering was suspended. It is quite evident the customs of the two tribes were similar. Referring to other beliefs of the tribe, Father de Smet wrote: "The belief in ghosts is very profound, and common in all the tribes. Indians have often told me, seriously, that they had met, seen, and conversed with them, and that they may be heard almost every night in the places where the dead are interred. They say they speak in a kind of whistling tone. Sometimes they contract the face like a person in an epileptic fit. Nothing but the hope of gain could ever induce an Indian to go alone in a burying-ground at night. In such a case, love of gain might triumph over the fear of ghosts ; but an Indian woman would never be induced, on any condition, to enter one." This may have referred to the Mandan and other tribes of the upper Missouri, as well as to the Assiniboin. Again having in mind the Assiniboin in particular, he wrote : " The Assiniboins esteem greatly a religious custom of assembling once or twice in the year around the tombs of their immediate relatives. These sepulchres are raised on a species of scaffold, about seven or eight feet above the surface of the soil. The Indians call the dead by their names, and offer them meats carefully dressed, which they place beside them. They take care, however, to consume the best pieces themselves . . . The ceremony of burying the dead, among the Indians, is terminated by the tears, wailings, howlings, and maceration's of all present. They tear the hair, gash their legs, and at last the calumet is lighted, for this is the Alpha and Omega of every rite. They offer it to the shades of the departed, and entreat them not to injure the living. During their ceremonious repasts, in their excursions, and even at a great distance from their tombs, they send to the dead puffs of tobacco-smoke and burn little pieces of meat as a sacrifice in their memory." (Op. cit., pp. 140-141.)

Plate 26

Touching on the Assiniboin belief of existence after death. Father De Smet wrote: "In regard to the future state, they believe that the souls of the dead migrate towards the South, where the climate is mild, the game abundant, and the rivers well stocked with fish. Their hell is the reverse of this picture; its unfortunate inmates dwell in perpetual snow and ice, and in the complete deprivation of all things. There are, however, many among them who think death is the cessation of life and action, and that there is naught beyond it." (Op. cit., pp. 141-142.) Thus, like other tribes of the North, who suffered by reason of the great cold of the long winters, the Assiniboin pictured the home of the good after death in a region to the southward a region of warmth, where food was plentiful and easily secured, and where suffering was unknown.

Another version of their belief was prepared in 1837, when it was told how "The Assiniboins believe, that in another life, to obtain enduring happiness, they have to climb a very high and steep mountain, the ascent of which is so difficult and dangerous that it requires many attempts, perseverance, and great fortitude to gain the summit, but once there a delightful and boundless plain is spread before them covered with eternal verdure and countless herds of Buffalo and the other animals which they delight to hunt; and that they will find all their friends who left this life before them enjoying an uninterrupted course of happiness, dwelling in beautiful skin tents which ever appear new.

"Those who have done ill in this life and have been successful enough to gain the summit of the hill are there met by the dwellers of the happy plain, and those who knew them in this life, who bear witness against them. They are then immediately thrown down the steep and should their necks not be broken never again attempt an ascent.

"Those who have done good in this life are welcomed with unusual joy and immediately admitted to all the privileges of their never ending hunting and happiness." *(McLeod, Diary of. In Minnesota Historical Bulletin, Vol. 4. Nos. 7-8. Aug.-Nov., 1922. pp. 407-408.)*

Two views of Fort union, drawn by Kurz during the autumn of 1851, are reproduced in Plate 19. One shows the exterior, the gate open and evidently a party of hunters about to enter; the second represents the interior. The small circle above the main entrance was the position of a portrait of Chouteau. Kurz wrote in his diary September 30, 1851 : "Have been hard at work. Had to paint, from a medal, the portrait of Pierre Chouteau, Jr., in the gable over the house gallery." The date, 1851, appears in the sketch just beneath the portrait. Sketches made by Kurz at this time are shown in Plate 20. One portrait is of " Culbertson, Esq. Bourgeois of Fort Mackenzie "; another is that of the Assiniboin chief Ours fou, who frequented Fort Union during Kurz's stay.

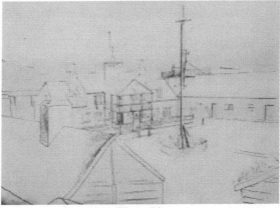

Plate 19

Plate 20

Ours fou had accompanied Culbertson to Fort Laramie to attend the great gathering of representatives of the Government and of members of many tribes, who came together during the month of September. On October 31, 1851, Kurz entered in his journal : "The unexpected often happens. Mr. Culbertson has at last arrived from Fort Laramie. We heard the glad news in the afternoon from Ours fou who had hurried on in advance to mourn with his family. Uncle Sam has appointed Ours fou chief of the Assiniboins; fate has robbed him, during his absence, of his wife—his only wife—of his son and two grandchildren. Anyone who saw this grief-stricken Chief would never speak of an Indian's lack of feeling . . . Ours fou was grieved to the soul, most profoundly affected; gazing before him in a kind of stupor, he wept silently. His hair and his body were besmeared, in token of his sorrow. And again on November 26: "Ours fou, chief of the Assiniboins, sits now beside me on the floor before the fire . . . He is uncovered; on his head, breast and legs are incisions in his skin to allow blood to flow as atonement for his deceased wife, his murdered son and beloved grandchildren." On October 27 Kurz had written : " Relatives of the three Assiniboin who were slain have planted a pole and fastened thereon two leather pouches that belonged to the dead. There for a long time they wailed and made blood-offerings by cutting their arms, cheeks, heads and legs until blood flowed. One of the dead men . . . was a son of the Assiniboin Chief Ours fou, (Mad Bear.) " The wife of Ours fou killed herself through grief and her body was " brought on a travois drawn by a horse," to Fort Union, where it was placed in a grave. Such were happenings at Fort Union during the autumn of 1851.

Sisseton Sioux

Origin: North and South Dakota, Minnesota

Continuing up the Minnesota, passing the encampments of the Mdewakanton, the Long expedition soon arrived among the Sisseton, or, rather, within the region which they claimed and occupied. But the burial customs of all the Siouan tribes then encountered in the Valley of the Minnesota were similar, and a description of one would undoubtedly have applied to all. On July 15, 1823, so the narrative of the expedition states: " we saw the remains of Indian habitations; they were deserted. Upon a scaffold, raised eighteen feet above the ground, and situated upon an elevated part of the prairie, the putrefying carcass of an Indian lay exposed to view. It had not been enclosed in a box, but merely shrouded in a blanket, which the wind and atmospheric influences had reduced to tatters. Fifteen horizontal black marks, drawn across one of the posts that supported the scaffold, designated, as we were informed by Renville, that as many scalps had been offered in sacrifice to the deceased, by those who danced at the funeral." (Keating, I, pp. 340-341.) This scaffold appears to have been unusually high, and the body was evidently less carefully prepared and wrapped than was customary. The camp and burial just mentioned stood in either Nicollet or Blue Earth County, the

Minnesota River passed between the two, and a short distance below was the mouth of Blue Earth River, the site of the present Mankato. "By the Dakotas it is called Makato Osa Watapa, which signifies 'the river where blue earth is gathered'

The mouth of the Blue Earth river is the chief residence of a tribe of the Dakotas, who call themselves the Miakechakesa, and who are generally known by the traders by the name of Sisitons" (Op. cit, pp. 34i-342.) About a half century ago Dr. C. E. McChesney, acting assistant surgeon. United States Army, prepared a most interesting account of the customs attending death and burial then prevailing among the Sisseton and closely related Wahpeton. The following quotations are made from the extended notes: "Before the year 1860 it was a custom, for as long back as the oldest members of these tribes can remember, and with the usual tribal traditions handed down from generation to generation, in regard to this as well as to other things, for these Indians to bury in a tree or on a platform, and in those days an Indian was only buried in the ground as a mark of disrespect in consequence of the person having been murdered, in which case the body would be buried in the ground, face down., head toward the south and with a piece of fat in the mouth . . . The platform upon which the body was deposited was constructed of four crotched posts firmly set in the ground, and connected near the top by cross-pieces, upon which was placed boards, when obtainable, and small sticks of wood, sometimes hewn so as to give a firm resting-place for the body. The platform had an elevation of from six to eight or more feet, and never contained but one body, although frequently having sufficient surface to accommodate two or three. In burying in the crotch of a tree and on platforms, the head of a dead person was always placed towards the south; the body was wrapped in blankets or pieces of cloth securely tied, and many of the personal effects of the deceased were buried with it ; as in the case of a warrior, his bows and arrows, war-clubs, &c., would be placed alongside of the body, the Indians saying he would need such things in the next world.

"I am informed by many of them that it was a habit, before their outbreak, for some to carry the body of a near relative whom they held in great respect with them on their moves, for a greater or lesser time, often as long as two or three years before burial. This, however, never obtained generally among them, and some of them seem to know nothing about it. It has of late years been entirely dropped, except when a person dies away from home, it being then customary for the friends to bring the body home for burial."

This was the older method of disposing of the dead, a method which had probably prevailed ever since the tribes had occupied the forest-covered region far eastward of the Valley of the Minnesota. But at the time the account was prepared, so we are told, a large proportion of the people of the two tribes had been under the direct influence of Presbyterian missionaries for a generation or longer, and as a consequence their burial customs had become somewhat changed. Few examples of the old scaffold burial were to be seen, but evidently they persisted in decorating and painting the remains as they had done through many generations. According to Doctor McChesney, the Indians with whom he came in contact disposed of their dead in the following way:

" Warrior.—After death they paint a warrior red across the mouth, or they paint a hand in black color, with the thumb on one side of the mouth and the fingers separated on the other cheek, the rest of the face being painted red. (This latter is only done as a mark of respect to a specially brave man.) Spears, clubs, and the medicine-bag of the deceased when alive are buried with the body, the medicine-bag being placed on the bare skin over the region of the heart. There is not now, nor has there been, among these Indians any special preparation of the grave. The body of a warrior is generally wrapped in a blanket or piece of cloth and frequently in addition is placed in a box and buried in a grave prepared for the purpose, always, as the majority of these Indians inform me, with the head towards the south. I have, however, seen many graves in which the head of the occupant had been placed to the east. It may be that these graves were those of Indians who belonged to the church; and a few Indians inform me that the head is sometimes placed towards the west., according to the occupant's belief when alive as to the direction from which his guiding medicine came, and I am personally inclined to give credence to this latter as sometimes occurring. In all burials, when the person has died a natural death, or had not been murdered, and whether man, woman, or child, the body is placed in the grave with the face up. In cases, however, when a man or woman has been murdered by one of their own tribe, the body was, and is always, placed in the grave with the face down head to the south, and a piece of fat (bacon or pork) placed in the mouth. This piece of fat is placed in the mouth, as these Indians say, to prevent the spirit of the murdered person driving or scaring the game from that section of country. Those Indians who state that their dead are always buried with the head towards the south say they do so in order that the spirit of the deceased may go south, the land from which these Indians believe they originally came.

Women and children.—Before death the face of the person expected to die is often painted in a red color. When this is not done before death it is done afterwards; the body being then buried in a grave prepared for its reception, and in the manner described for warrior, cooking-utensils taking the place of the warrior's weapons. In cases of boys and girls a kettle of cooked food is sometimes placed at the head of the grave after the body is covered. Now, if the dead body be that of a boy, all the boys of about his age go up and eat of the food, and in cases of girls all the girls do likewise. This, however, has never obtained as a custom, but is sometimes done in cases of warriors and women also.

The article continues and contains many interesting references to the strange and curious beliefs of the people. It tells of a custom of removing " a lock of hair from the top or scalp lock of a warrior, or from the left side of the head of a woman, which is carefully preserved by some near relative of the deceased, wrapped in pieces of calico and muslin, and hung in the lodge of the deceased and is considered the ghost of the dead person." This bundle, " the ghost," received certain offerings, was held in great reverence, and a feast would be held for it. A large proportion of the earthly possessions of an individual would be placed in the grave, some beneath and some above the body. Horses were killed on the grave of a warrior. " No food is ever buried in the grave, but some is occasionally placed at the head of it ; in which case it is consumed by the friends of the dead person."

The peculiar custom of carrying the bones of the dead from place to place, and often preserving them thus for several years before placing them in the ground, was observed by these people. As was told by Doctor McChesney: " I am informed by many of them that it was a habit, before their outbreak, for some to carry the body of a near relative whom they held in great respect with them on their moves, for a greater or lesser time, often as long as two or three years before burial. This, however, never obtained generally among them, and some of them seem to know nothing about it. It has of late years been entirely dropped, except when a person dies away from home, it being then customary for the friends to bring the body home for burial." (Op. cit., p. 109.) This curious custom has already been mentioned as prevailing among the kindred Mdwankanton. It was witnessed by Father Hennepin early in the year 1G80, and the writer, during the month of May, 1900, discovered burials of such a nature as to prove the bones to have been free from flesh when they were deposited.

The mourning ceremonies, or rather customs, were likewise described by Doctor McChesney. Referring to the days before the year 1860, about which time great changes developed in the manners and ways of life of the Sioux : "After the death of a warrior the whole camp or tribe would assemble in a circle, and after the widow had cut herself on the arms, legs, and body with a piece of flint, and removed the hair from her head, she would go around the ring any number of times she chose, but each time was considered as an oath that she would not marry for a year, so that she could not marry for as many years as times she went around the circle. The widow would all this time keep up a crying and wailing. Upon the completion of this the friends of the deceased would take the body to the platform or tree where it was to remain, keeping up all this time their wailing and crying. After depositing the body, they would stand under it and continue exhibiting their grief, the squaws by hacking their arms and legs with flint and cutting off the hair from their head. The men would sharpen sticks and run them through the skin of their arms and legs, both men and women keeping up their crying generally for the remainder of the day, and the near relatives of the deceased for several days thereafter. . . In cases of women and children, the squaws would cut off their hair, hack their person with flint, and sharpen sticks and run them through the skin of their arms and legs, crying as for a warrior." Such were probably the customs of all the related tribes living in the Valley of the Minnesota a century and more ago. *The Smithsonian Institute Bureau of Ethnology, Bulletin 83, 1927*

Gambling For The Dead's Possessions

It is not proposed to describe under this heading examples of those athletic and gymnastic performances following the death of a person which have been described by Lafitau, but simply to call attention to a practice as a secondary or adjunct part of the funeral rites, which consists in gambling for the possession of the property of the defunct. Dr. Charles E. McChesney, U.S.A., who for some time was stationed among the Wahpeton and Sisseton Sioux, furnishes a detailed and interesting account of what is called the "ghost gamble." This is played with marked wild-plum stones. So far as ascertained it is peculiar to the Sioux. Figure 33 appears as a fair illustration of the manner in which this game is played.

After the death of a wealthy Indian the near relatives take charge of the effects, and at a stated time—usually at the time of the first feast held over the bundle containing the lock of hair—they are divided into many small piles, so as to give all the Indians invited to play an opportunity to win something. One Indian is selected to represent the ghost and he plays against all the others, who are not required to stake anything on the result, but simply invited to take part in the ceremony, which is usually held in the lodge of the dead person, in which is contained the bundle enclosing the lock of hair. In cases where the ghost himself is not wealthy the stakes are furnished by his rich friends, should he have any. The players are called in one at a time, and play singly against the ghost's representative, the gambling being done in recent years by means of cards. If the invited player succeeds in beating the ghost, he takes one of the piles of goods and passes out, when another is invited to play, &c., until all the piles of goods are won. In cases of men only the men play, and in cases of women the women only take part in the ceremony.

Yankton Sioux

Origin: Wisconsin, Minnesota, and North Dakota and South Dakota.

"A century ago villages of the Yankton were situated in the vicinity of Lake Traverse, in the present Traverse County, Minn. Here the members of the Long party rested July 26, 1823. The post of the Columbia Fur Co. stood near the shore of the lake. A drawing was made by Samuel Seymour showing the wide expanse of water, the trading post, and " the Indian lodges near it, and also a scaffold, upon which the remains of a Sioux had been deposited. The horizon is bounded by a distant view of the Coteau des Prairies.The scaffold, as shown in the drawing, Plate 10, appears to be very high, and was probably similar to the one previously described as having been raised by the Sisseton farther down the river.

The various groups of Sioux encountered by Long a century ago undoubtedly held similar beliefs and followed like customs in disposing of their dead. As told in the narrative of the expedition: "The ideas of the Dakotas, respecting a future state, differ but little from those of other Indians; and we may receive them with less diffidence, as they have had but little intercourse with missionaries, whether Catholic or otherwise; still, in some of their credence's, as related to us, it was impossible not to discover a few of the doctrines of Christianity, which had probably crept in unnoticed by them. The Dakotas admit that there are in man two distinct essences, to which they respectively apply the terms of Wanare and Wahkan, which our interpreters translate by soul and spirit. They believe that after death the souls go to the Wanare Tebe, or dwelling place of the souls. That in order to reach it, they have to pass over a rock, the edge of which is as sharp as that of a knife; those who fall off go to the region of the evil spirit, where they are kept constantly chopping wood, carrying water, &e. being frequently flogged by their relentless master. Those, on the contrary, that have passed safe over the rock, have a long journey to travel ; and as they proceed, they observe the camping places of the souls that have preceded them ; at these spots fires are ready made for their accommodation; finally, they reach the habitation of Wahkan Tanka, or Great Spirit. There they find many villages of the dead ; they meet with some spirits there, who point out to them the way to the residence of their friends and relations, with whom they are reunited. Their life is an easy and blissful one, they hunt the buffalo, plant corn, &c. It is believed, that when children are on the point of death, their departed relations return from the land of souls in order to convey them thither. Women are liable to go to either of the places, but all are entitled to a situation in the land of the blessed, except such as have violated their chastity, committed infanticide or suicide. Their system of Ethics is as simple. Men are held to go to the residence of the Great Spirit if they be good and peaceable, or if they die by the hand of their enemies. If they perish in a broil with their own countrymen, their souls are doomed to the residence of the Evil Spirit." " *Narrative of an Expedition to the Source of St. Peter's River, Lake Winnepeek, Lake of the Woods, &c . . . Under the command of Stephen H. Long, Major U. S. T. E. Philadelphia, 1824. 2 vols.*

"On May 25, 1833, the steamboat Yellow Stone, on which Maximilian and the artist Bodmer were ascending the Missouri, arrived at the Sioux Agency. As they approached the agency they could see, on the hills, some burying-places of the Sioux Indians ; most of them were formed of a high platform, on four stakes, on which the corpse, sewn up in skins, lies at full length; others consisted of stakes and brushwood, like a kind of hedge, in the middle of which the deceased is buried in the ground." And they " were told that the son of a chief was buried in one of the latter, in a standing posture.

"Among the peculiar customs of the Sioux is their treatment of the dead. Those who die at home are sewed up, as I have before stated, in blankets and skins, in their complete dress, painted, and laid with their arms and other effects on a high stage, supported by four poles, till they are decomposed, when they are sometimes buried. Those who have been killed in battle are immediately interred on the spot. Sometimes, too, in times of peace, they bury their dead in the ground, and protect them against the wolves by a fence of wood and thorns. There were many such graves in the vicinity of the Sioux Agency, among which was that of a celebrated chief, Tschpunka, who was buried with his full dress and arms, and his face painted red. Very often, however, they lay their dead in trees ; and we saw, in the neighborhood of this place, an oak, in which there were three bodies wrapped in skins. At the foot of the tree there was a small shed, made of branches of poplar, which the relations had built for the purpose of coming to lament and weep over the dead, which they frequently do for several days successively. As a sign of mourning, they cut off their hair with the first knife that comes to hand, daub themselves with white clay, and give away all their best clothes and valuable effects, as well as those of the deceased, to the persons who happen to be present. The corpse of a young woman had been enveloped in skins about a week before, and placed between the branches of the oak, with six pieces of wood under it; and a little higher in the tree there was a child." Two days later, the Yellow Stone having left the agency, Maximilian wrote : "A well-known Sioux chief, called Tukan Haton, and, by the Americans, the Little Soldier, was on board with his family, intending to accompany us to Fort Pierre, on the Teton River. These Indians were in mourning for some of their relations lately deceased; their dress was, therefore, as bad as possible, and their faces daubed with white clay." *Travels in the Interior of North America. London, 1843.*

Teton Sioux

Origin: South Dakota, Minnesota

On September 26, 1804, Lewis and Clark reached the great village of the Teton, standing at the mouth of the Teton River on the banks of the Missouri. The stream to which the tribal name was applied is now known as Bad River, which flows into the Missouri at Pierre, Stanley County, S. Dakota. However, it is quite evident they had, within a comparatively short time, removed from their earlier home to the eastward, probably from the forest-covered lake region of central Minnesota.

The Teton was the largest of the several divisions of the group, and the great number of skin tipis which formed their village served to attract the attention of all. Thus, Catlin in 1832 referred to " an encampment of Sioux, of six hundred tents of skin lodges, round the Fort," but some of these may have belonged to other divisions of the Sioux who were trading or had come to trade at Fort Pierre. Fort Pierre and the surrounding encampments of Indians must have presented an animated scene when approached by a river steamboat. The various travelers were equally impressed with the view of the fort standing on the level plain near the bank of the Missouri, with the hills rising in the distance, and the intervening space usually occupied by clusters of skin-covered lodges. As Maximilian wrote when he sighted the fort on In May 30, 1833 : " Indians, on foot and on horseback, were scattered all over the plain, and their singular stages for the dead were in great numbers near the fort; immediately behind which, the leather tents of the Sioux Indians, of the branches of the Tetons and the Yanktons, stood." (Maximilian, p. 156.) A year later, when returning from the far upper waters of the Missouri, Maximilian, accompanied by the artist Bodmer, again reached Fort Pierre.

The former then recorded in his journal : " Mr. Bodmer took several views of the country, and also made a sketch of the stage of a distinguished Sioux warrior, whose remains had been brought from a great distance with much pomp, and were covered with red cloth." This is a picture of unusual interest, as it shows a body placed within a travois frame, resting upon a platform supported by four upright poles. .Undoubtedly the travois frame was the one in which it had been secured while being " brought from a great distance with much pomp."

"This is a picture of unusual interest, as it shows a body placed within a travois frame, resting upon a platform supported by four upright poles. .Undoubtedly the travois frame was the one in which it had been secured while being " brought from a great distance with much pomp." *Travels in the Interior of North America. London, 1843.*

"Culbertson visited Fort Pierre during the spring of 1850, and after mentioning the general appearance of the interesting post itself wrote in his journal: "then the Indian lodges are seen around the fort; by their irregularity of position, their conical shape and varied colors, giving life and a picturesque air to the scene; and for a couple of miles below the fort and between it and the bluffs, the whole plain is dotted with horses grazing and moving leisurely about, while the bold bluffs a mile west of the fort affords a fine back-ground for the picture. Fortunately, a most interesting and valuable account of the burial customs of the Teton, as observed by Culbertson, is contained in his journal, and is now quoted at length : "'The Fort Pierre grave yard lies about a quarter of a mile south of the fort; it is a square piece of ground which has been well fenced in but not ornamented in any way; it contains the bodies of a number of dead, both Indians and Whites the latter are in the ground and their graves are marked with wooden crosses, or with tombstones recording their names and dates of their death. The Indians however have followed their own customs in disposing of their dead, which is to place them on a scaffold about eight or ten feet from the ground. As you approach the yard coming from the fort, you see elevated on a scaffold supported by rough willow poles and now half broken down, a confused pile of old boxes of various lengths—old trunks and pieces of blankets hanging. These may seem strange things for a grave yard, but these old boxes contain the bodies of dead Indians: they were originally placed on a good scaffold and had piles of blankets wrapped around them, but the scaffold has broken down from exposure to weather and weight of the bodies, which appear to have been heaped on without order of any kind. If you look over the fence to the left of this scaffold, you will see on the ground one of these boxes which has probably fallen down and broken and there the bones lay exposed, except the skull which perhaps has been buried by some friend of the deceased; if you look a little more closely you will see lying with the bones, a dark looking object about three inches broad and perhaps fifteen long, tied around with a string: this is some tobacco given to the dead to smoke in the other world; they always place with their dead almost every article of common use, for their benefit in the other world : blankets, sometimes as many as twenty, the best the parties can afford—tobacco, sugar, coffee, molasses, kettles of mush and other things of use. These remain undisturbed until they decay, or are destroyed by the weather or wolves. On the east side is a scaffold put up a few months since; the box is a rough one, daubed with black paint, and is surrounded by several old trunks, that were the property of the old squaw who rests within. On the opposite side is another scaffold, on which is placed the body of a man who died not many months since; you can see the scarlet blanket through the large cracks in this rude coffin. It appears to me, that this method of burial originated in a desire to protect the bodies from the wolves, more than in any of their religious opinions: they frequently bury the bones, after the flesh has decayed entirely. On a large tree, a little above the fort, is a body which must have a great pile of blankets on it, from the size." A few days later, just before leaving Fort Pierre on the steamboat El Paso; to ascend the Missouri to and beyond Fort Union, Culbertson entered in his journal : "Before one of the lodges near where the feast was held, was the body of a little girl who had died yesterday; it was wrapped in a blue blanket, and was to be placed on the scaffold as soon as the coffin should be finished. I did not see the ceremony of conveying it to the tomb, or rather, to its resting place, but it was probably done in a very simple manner, as I was told that the burying of the dead, except braves, is left principally to the squaws. Blankets and food are placed on the scaffold for their use in the other world; the family of the deceased mourn very much, and if others aid them in this sad work, they expect pay and are sure to get it."

The winter following Culbertson's visit to the upper Missouri Valley was cold and severe. About the middle of January a large party of Indians, with several white men, all from Fort Pierre, were overtaken by the blizzard and 30 of the former are said to have lost their lives. The bodies of the Indians were later carried to the fort where " a few boxes " were provided for them and they were then placed " on scaffolds in their own cemetery." The following summer cholera raged in the vicinity of Fort Pierre, and on July 4 of that year, 1851, the Swiss artist Kurz made an interesting sketch of the fort from the river side, probably from the upper deck of the steamboat in which he was ascending the Missouri. The dreaded cholera caused many deaths among the Indians, whose remains were evidently placed upon scaffolds in the cemetery near the fort. In that most interesting autobiography from which the preceding quotation was made, that of the" Canadian trader, Louis D. Latellier, is an account of the death and burial of an Indian whose tipi stood near the fort. It reads: "Another death occurred and it was the son of the Iron Horse, a chief of the Sioux nation. In singing he gave up the last breath. In his death there was nothing strange but its funeral interested me the most. After having made the coffin and covered it with scarlet cloth and placed the defunct in it, old Francois L'Alsatien came up to the tepee with his heavy old two-wheeled cart that had never been painted and covered with dry mud. A large bull covered with a rawhide harness was hitched to this cart. We loaded the coffin into the cart and started for the Indian cemetery, Francois standing by the side of his cart driving his old bull, old Henrie Picotte, a partner of the P. Chouteau Fur Company, and myself following behind the cart, two squaws, hired by the relatives of the defunct to do the crying part of the ceremony at the cemetery under the scaffold at the cemetery were following behind us, laughing and chattering while walking up slowly for it was a very hot afternoon. . . . We arrived at the scaffolding cemetery. The scaffold of this dead Indian was already up. It was four posts set in the ground, about five feet high, a fork at each end, in which two cross bar^ were tied. We put the coffin on top, the bow and arrows of the defunct on top of the coffin, and tied the whole to the post, also a long pole with the American flag unfurled. Our ceremony was over. It was already dark with low black clouds hanging over our heads, peals of thunder and lightning was playing in the distance, and we was one mile from the fort. We started in a hurry for home. The two squaws took their positions under the coffin and began their wild crying and loud screams. Before we reached the fort the thunder and lightning with a torrent of rain was rushing all round yet we could hear the crying of the squaws. They were doing it loud and fine, to please their friends, who had hired them for that purpose."

Miss Densmore, in her most interesting and valuable work on Teton Sioux music, gave various songs associated with the treatment of the sick. " No one attempted to treat the sick unless he had received a dream telling him to do so, and no one ever disregarded the obligations of such a dream." *In Fifth Annual Report of the Smithsonian Institution. Washington. 1851.*

Origin South Dakota, Montana

The Sichangu or Brules, when mentioned by Lewis and Clark in 1804, occupied both banks of the Missouri, in the vicinity of the White and Teton Rivers, the central portion of the present State of South Dakota. They moved westward, as did the kindred tribes, and by 1860 roamed over the region of the Big Horn, Rosebud, and Tongue Rivers, and often pitched their camps on the banks of Powder River, within the southeastern section of the present State of Montana.

A daughter of Spotted Tail, one of the greatest of the Brule chiefs, died early in 1866, while the village was encamped on Powder River. It had been her wish to be buried at Fort Laramie," up on the hill, near the grave of Old Smoke, a distant relative and a great chief among the Sioux in former years." Fort Laramie was 260 miles southward from the camp on Powder River. "When her death took place, after great lamentations among the band, the skin of a deer freshly killed was held over the fire and thoroughly permeated and creosoted with smoke. Ah-ho-appa was wrapped in it, and it was tightly bound around her with thongs,so that she was temporarily embalmed."Runners were sent forward to Fort Laramie to make known the coming of the party. "The landscape was bleak and frozen and the streams were covered with ice, and the hills speckled with snow. The trail was rough and mountainous. The two white ponies of Ah-ho-appa were tied together, side by side, and the body placed upon them. . . For nearly a week of the trip there was a continual sleet. The journey lasted fifteen days, and was monotonous with lamentations. "When the Indians arrived at the bank of the river, some 2 miles from the post, they were met by troops to serve as escort to the fort." The next day a scaffold was erected near the grave of Old Smoke. It was made of tent poles twelve feet long, embedded in the ground and fastened with thongs, over which a buffalo robe was laid, and on which the coffin was to be placed. To the poles of the scaffold were nailed the heads and tails of the two white ponies, so that Ah ho-appa could ride through the fair hunting-grounds of the skies. A coffin was made and lavishly decorated. The body was not unbound from its deer-skin shroud, but was wrapped in a bright red blanket and placed in the coffin." The ceremony was attended by officers and troops from the post, and the chaplain assisted, but Spotted Tail "wanted his daughter buried Indian fashion, so that she would go not where the white people went, but where the red people went." The coffin was carried to the hill, near the grave of Old Smoke, and soon "each of the Indian women came up, one at a time, and talked to Ah-ho-appa; some of them whispered to her long and earnestly, as if they were by her sending some hopeful message to a lost child. Each one put some little remembrance in the coffin ; one put a little looking-glass, another a string of colored beads, another a pine cone with some sort of an embroidery of sinew in it. Then the lid was fastened on and the women took the coffin and raised it and placed it on the scaffold. The Indian men stood mutely and stolidly around looking on, and none of them moved a muscle or tendered any help. A fresh buffalo skin was laid over the coffin and bound down to the sides of the scaffold with thongs. The scaffold was within the military square, as was also the twelve-pound howitzer. The sky was leaden and stormy, and it began to sleet and grow dark. At the word of command the soldiers faced outward and discharged three volleys in rapid succession. They and their visitors then marched back to the post. The howitzer squad remained and built a large fire of pine wood, and fired the gun every half-hour all night, through the sleet, until daybreak." *In Collections of the Kansas State Historical Society, 1913-1914, Vol. XIII. Topeka, 1915.*

Fort Laramie was one of the most important posts in the great western country. A photograph of the post, showing the group of buildings, made in 1868, is reproduced in Plate 12, and in Plate 13 is shown one of the log structures at the fort, " Brown's Hotel," as it appeared at the same time.

Plate 12

From the very beginning the fort was a gathering place for traders and Indians, later to become a resting place for emigrants on their slow, toilsome journey to the region beyond the mountains. It was likewise visited by some seeking knowledge of the ways of life of the people of the wilderness, Indians and whites, and it is quite evident many interesting and remarkable scenes were witnessed both within and without the walls of this crude frontier structure. It stood in the midst of a region roamed over by several hostile tribes, enemies of each other, and all of whom were treacherous in their dealings with the whites. Many who died when encamped near the fort were buried near by. Others who died at a distance were carried by their friends and placed in the cemetery near the fort, as was the body of Ah-ho-appa, the daughter of Spotted Tail, during the early part of the year 1866.

Plate 13

Just 20 years before, late in the spring of 1846, Francis Parkman and his companions spent some days at Fort Laramie during their adventurous journey through the Indian country. He saw the curious scaffolds scattered over the prairie in the vicinity of the fort, and wrote in his narrative: "As we were looking, at sunset, from the wall, upon the wild and desolate plains that surround the fort, we observed a cluster of strange objects, like scaffolds, rising in the distance against the red western sky. They bore aloft some singular-looking burdens; and at their foot glimmered something white like bones. This was the place of sepulture of some Dakota chiefs, whose remains their people are fond of placing in the vicinity of the fort, in the hope that they may thus be protected from violation at the hands of their enemies. Yet it has happened more than once, and quite recently, that war parties of the Crow Indians, ranging through the country, have thrown the bodies from the scaffolds, and broken them to pieces, amid the yells of the Dakotas, who remained pent up in the fort, too few to defend the honored relics from insult. The white objects upon the ground were buffalo-skulls, arranged in the mystic circle, commonly seen at Indian places of sepulture upon the prairie." *Parkman, The California and Oregon Trail. New York, 1849.*

Parkman mentioned the death of an Indian woman, a member of a small party moving from their village to a camp some miles away. She was very ill, and early in the day, when the party was preparing to proceed on their journey, "she was lifted into a *travail.* Later in the day she failed rapidly, and soon" lay dead in the basket of the vehicle." This was quite similar, undoubtedly, to the beautiful example shown in Plate 7. The relatives of the woman were required by custom to secure "valuable presents, to be placed by the side of the body at its last resting-place," and two members of the party immediately set forward to obtain the necessary and desired objects. "It was very late and quite dark when they again reached the lodges. They were all placed in a deep hollow among the dreary hills. Four of them were just visible through the gloom, but the fifth and largest was illuminated by the ruddy blaze of a fire within, glowing through the half-transparent covering of raw-hides. There was a perfect stillness as they approached. The lodges seemed without a tenant. Not a living thing was stirring,—there was something awful in the scene. They rode up to the entrance of the lodge, and there was no sound but the tramp of their horses. A squaw came out and took charge of the animals, without speaking a word. Entering, they found the lodge crowded with Indians; a fire was burning in the midst, and the mourners encircled it in a triple row. Room was made for the new-comers at the head of the lodge, a robe spread for them to sit upon, and a pipe lighted and handed to them in perfect silence. Thus they passed the greater part of the night. At times the fire would subside into a heap of embers, until the dark figures seated around it were scarcely visible; then a squaw would drop upon it a piece of buffalo-fat, and a bright flame instantly springing up, would reveal on a sudden the crowd of wild faces, motionless as bronze. The silence continued unbroken . . . they placed the presents they had brought near the body of the squaw, which, most gaudily attired, remained in a sitting posture in one of the lodges. A fine horse was picketed not far off, destined to be killed that morning for the service of her spirit, for the woman was lame, and could not travel on foot over the dismal prairies to the villages of the dead. Food, too, was provided, and household implements, for her use upon this last journey." (Parkman, pp. 165-167.) The father of the squaw was " Mahto-Tatonka, who had transmitted his names, his features, and many of his characteristic qualities, to his son." Later, while at the camp, so Parkman wrote : "For several nights ... we could hear wild and mournful cries, rising and dying away like the melancholy voice of a wolf. They came from the sisters and female relatives of Mahto-Tatonka, who were gashing their limbs with knives, and bewailing the death of" the squaw (p. 188). And soon again, when the people of the village had come together, " Mahto-Tatonka and his brothers took no part in this parade, for they were in mourning for their sister, and were all sitting in their lodges, their bodies bedaubed from head to foot with white clay, and a lock of hair cut from each of their foreheads." (Op. cit., pp. 195-196.)

Unfortunately, and it is certainly to be regretted, Parkman did not witness the actual disposition of the remains, the placing of the body on the scaffold, and the sacrifice of the horse. The various customs mentioned were probably those of all the Siouan tribes of the region.

It is quite evident numerous platforms, supporting the remains of the dead, were erected in many trees in the vicinity of Laramie. But the trees, of sufficient size, were scattered and much of the region was barren and open, with scant timber, affording little protection to man or beast. Fortunately, several very interesting and undoubtedly very characteristic views of tree burials near Laramie are preserved. Two photographs made during the year 1868 are reproduced in Plate 14. It is interesting to see the large tree in Plate 14.

Plate 14

The photograph reproduced in Plate 15 has not been identified. It may, however, have been made near Laramie. This is of special interest, as the platform supporting the body or bodies is resting partly on the branches of the tree and partly on a stout post placed in an upright position. This is rather a combination of scaffold and tree burial.

A communication addressed by W. J. Cleveland, of the Spotted Tail Agency, Nebr., to Doctor Yarrow, gave a remarkably valuable and interesting account of the burial customs of the Brules. It serves to verify, as well as to make more clear, certain statements made by other writers which have been quoted. Cleveland wrote in part: "Though some few of this tribe now lay their dead in rude boxes, either burying them when implements for digging can be had, or, when they have no means of making a grave, placing them on top of the ground on some hill or other slight elevation, yet this is done in imitation of the whites, and their general custom, as a people, probably does not differ in any essential way from that of their forefathers for many generations in the past. In disposing of the dead, they wrap the body tightly in blankets or robes (sometimes both), wind it all over with thongs made of the hide of some animal, and place it, reclining on the back at full length, either in the branches of some tree or on a scaffold made for the purpose. These scaffolds are about eight feet high, and made by planting four forked sticks firmly in the ground, one at each corner, and then placing others across on top, so as to form a floor, on which the body is securely fastened. Sometimes more than one body is placed on the same scaffold, though generally a separate one is made for each occasion. The Indians being in all things most superstitious, attach a kind of sacredness to these scaffolds and all the materials used on or about the dead. This superstition is in itself sufficient to prevent any of their own people from disturbing the dead, and for one of another nation to in any wise meddle with them is considered an offense not too severely punished by death.

"The same feeling also prevents them from ever using old scaffolds or any of the wood which has been used about them, even for firewood, though the necessity may be very great, for fear some evil consequences will follow. It is also the custom, though not universally followed, when bodies have been for two years on the scaffolds to take them down and bury them under ground." Continuing, the account tells of the work of the women and in this respect agrees with the narrative of the burial of Ah-ho-appa, as told on a preceding page. To again quote: "All the work about winding up the dead, building the scaffold, and placing the dead upon it is done by women only, who, after having finished their labor, return and bring the men, to show them where the body is placed, that they may be able to find it in future. Valuables of all kinds, such as weapons, ornaments, pipes, &c., in short, what ever the deceased valued most highly while living, and locks of hair cut from the heads of the mourners at his death, are always bound up with the body. In case the dead was a man of importance, or if the family could afford it, even though he were not, one or several horses (generally, in the former case, those which the departed thought most of) were shot and placed under the scaffold ... A body is seldom kept longer than one day, as besides the desire to get the dead out of sight, the fear that the disease which caused the death will communicate itself to others of the family causes them to hasten the disposition of it as soon as they are certain that death has actually taken place."

The friends and relatives of the deceased, those who would mourn his death, expressed their grief in various ways, and " in uttering the most heartrending, almost hideous wails and lamentations, in which all join until exhausted," Others would " cut themselves in various places, generally in the legs and arms, with their knives or pieces of flint, more commonly the latter, causing the blood to flow freely over their person." After death the mourners would not touch food until after the burial of the body. The remaining property of the deceased would be given away; often the lodge would become the possession of some woman who assisted in the burial ceremony. "The custom of placing food at the scaffold also prevails to some extent. If but little is placed there it is understood to be for the spirit of the dead, and no one is allowed to touch it. If much is provided, it is done with the intention that those of the same sex and age as the deceased shall meet there and consume it. If the dead be a little girl, the young girls meet and eat what is provided; if it be a man, then men assemble for the same purpose. The relatives never mention the name of the dead.

The curious and strange custom of preserving a small quantity of the hair of the deceased, wrapped and bound in cloth or skins, and which was termed "the ghost," as mentioned in the preceding notes on the Sisseton and Wahpeton, was likewise observed among the Brules. In the article written from the Spotted Tail Agency, some time before the year 1879, it was told that " another custom though at the present day by no means generally followed, is still observed to some extent among them. This is called wanagee yuha'pee^ or ' keeping the ghost.' A little of the hair from the head of the deceased being preserved is bound up in calico and articles of value until the roll is about two feet long and ten inches or more in diameter, when it is placed in a case made of hide handsomely ornamented with various designs in different colored paints. "When the family is poor, however, they may substitute for this case a blue or scarlet blanket or cloth. The roll is then swung lengthwise between two supports made of sticks, placed thus X in front of a lodge which has been set apart for the purpose. In this lodge are gathered presents of all kinds, which are given out when a sufficient quantity is obtained. It is often a year and sometimes several years before this distribution is made. During all this time the roll containing the hair of the deceased is left undisturbed in front of the lodge. The gifts as they are brought in are piled in the back part of the lodge, and are not to be touched until given out. No one but men and boys are admitted to the lodge unless it be a wife of the deceased, who may go in if necessary very early in the morning. The men sit inside, as they choose, to smoke, eat, and converse. As they smoke they empty the ashes from their pipes in the center of the lodge, and they, too, are left undisturbed until after the distribution. When they eat, a portion is always placed first under the roll outside for the spirit of the deceased. No one is allowed to take this unless a large quantity is so placed, in which case it may be eaten by any persons actually in need of food, even though strangers to the dead. When the proper time comes the friends of the deceased and all to whom presents are to be given are called together to the lodge and the things are given out by the man in charge. Generally this is some near relative of the departed. The roll is now undone and small locks of the hair distributed with the other presents, which ends the ceremony." The article continues and sheds additional light on the beliefs of the people respecting wanagee yuhapee. It was sometimes repeated, in which event it was regarded "as a repetition of the burial or putting away of the dead." The lodge in which the presents were kept, and where the roll was suspended, was considered in the light of a sacred spot until after the distribution of the material. No friend or relative desired to possess anything that had belonged to the deceased. Much was deposited with the body, and much was given away. " They have no idea of a future life in the body, but believe that after death their spirits will meet and recognize the spirits of their departed friends in the spirit land." *A Further Contribution to the Study of the Mortuary Customs of the North American Indians. In First Annual Report Bureau of Ethnology, 1879-1880. Washington, 1881.*

Such were the strange beliefs of this roving people of the prairies. Through the kindness of Francis La Flesche I am able to give a reproduction of a sketch made by Miss Alice C. Fletcher of a death scene among the Brules, on Rosebud Reservation, S. Dakota The scene, or rather ceremony, was witnessed by Miss Fletcher during her first journey into the Indian country and is dated October 18, 1881. In her journal the ceremony was thus described.

" On the morning of October 18, 1881, a Sioux Indian died suddenly. The nearest of kin goes out of the door and calls : 'A forerunner has gone to the spirit land, come and meet him.' His best horse is shot as soon as possible. The wives open their packs and empty their store of calicos, beadwork, &c., these are thrown on the railing beside the tent.

"The man held the drum of the Fox club. He belonged also to the Omaha club. His horse lay dead as in the sketch. The row of heads were men of the Omaha club, these chanted long and low, the death song. His dog came out, these men shot it. It turned and cried piteously. It ran up the hill and there died. One of the men dragged it down and it lay as in the sketch. The tent was open. There was some sort of feather ornament hanging over his head. This was his war bonnet. The calicos and bead work hanging on the railing were distributed among the members of the club and the women. The women relatives cut their hair and placed it on the body—this is buried with the person. I saw all the household utensils being carried away. Nothing will be left in the tent.

" Just before the man called out the gifts of horses, I noticed a man clad in a light blanket lean over the dead man and paint his face red and yellow. When this was done he called out the horses given away. The man was buried in the afternoon, his knife, pistol, drum and bow put with him."

The horse was later dragged to the place of burial while the dog furnished food for a feast. The preceding is one of the most interesting accounts of a death scene among the Siouan tribes ever prepared, and being accompanied by a drawing adds greatly to its importance. *The Smithsonian Institutes Bureau f Ethnology, Bulletin 83 1927*

Origin: Kansas, Missouri

The Kansa, of all the Siouan tribes, reared and occupied the greatest variety of habitations. The earth-covered lodge, the skin tipi, and the frail structure of bark and mats, were made and used by different bands at different times. Their burial customs were more uniform, and evidently they disposed of their dead with very little ceremony. As stated by one well acquainted with the manners and customs of the Kansa : " The female relatives of the deceased take the entire charge of the dead, prepare the body for burial, dig the grave, take the body to the place of interment, and bury it without the presence of any men." And " if the deceased was a brave or a hunter his gun, saddle, bridle, blankets and other articles, supposed to be necessary for his use in the spirit world, were placed in the grave with his body, and his best horse strangled to death over his grave and left lying on it. For three nights succeeding his burial a light was kept burning at the head of his grave to give light to the soul on its passage to the Indian land of plenty and happiness, the happy hunting-ground, and for the same length of time food was placed at the head of the grave, upon which he, in some mysterious way, was supposed to feed until he reached his new and eternal home." (*Spencer, The Kaw or Kansas Indians. In Transactions of the Kansas State Historical Society, 1907-1908. Topeka, 1908. p. 378.*)

The preceding agrees with another account, one referring to a particular settlement : "The Kaws, while living at their old village near Manhattan, buried their dead in graves on the bottom land near the village, leaving no permanent markings of any kind which might lead to the identification of the spot. In later years, stones were heaped over the graves, to protect the bodies from wolves. Often a horse was killed over the spot, whose spirit was supposed to convey that of the departed to the happy hunting grounds." *(Griffing,Committee on Explorations. In Transactions of the Kansas State Historical Society, 1903-1904, Vol. VIII. Topeka, 1904. pp.134-135.)*

A remarkably interesting and full account of the various ceremonies and customs of the Kansa, following the death of a member of the tribe, was given by Frederick Chouteau, who had been in contact with the people since the early years of the last century. To quote from the notes which were prepared in 1880 : "When a member of a family dies, a warrior of the band to which the family belongs is chosen to make propitiation with the Great Spirit. He smears his face with mud and ashes, goes out in the morning to a high, lonely place, and sits there all day, crying and moaning, and blowing smoke toward heaven; eating and drinking nothing from morning till night. This he does every day for a month. The warrior then takes a body of warriors, sometimes to the number of 100, and goes out on a war expedition against some hostile tribe. If he is successful in taking scalps or stealing ponies he returns, and the widow can put aside her mourning and is at liberty to marry again.

"If a woman dies, the husband selects the one to make propitiation ; the father, if a child dies.

"The idea which this superstition embodies is, that the affliction which the Kaws have been made to suffer has been an act indicating the displeasure of the Great Spirit, and intended to humble the tribe in respect to its standing with the Great Spirit, as between the Kaws and a hostile tribe. The sacrifice which the hostile tribe (against which the incursion is made) has been made to suffer in this way results in placing the Kaw family, and the band to which it belongs, on an equal footing before the Great Spirit with the hostile tribe which had not suffered the infliction imposed by the Great Spirit by the hand of death. . . At the same time that the chosen warrior is performing his acts of mourning, the members of the family of the deceased, every morning just at break of day, go through similar mourning exercises at their lodge." *(Reminiscences of Frederick Chouteau. In Transactions of the Kansas State Historical Society. Vol. VIII, 1903-4. Topeka, 1904, Adams, p. 429.)*

Chouteau arrived among the Kansa during the autumn of 1825; six years before, about midsummer of 1819, the Long expedition reached the same region and came in contact with some members of the tribe. A brief reference to the vague beliefs of the people is given in the narrative of the expedition: "When a man is killed in battle the thunder is supposed to take him up, they do not know where. They seem to have vague notions of the future state. They think that a brave warrior, or good hunter, will walk in a good path; but a bad man or coward will find a bad path. Thinking the deceased has far to travel they bury with his body, moccasins, some articles of food, &c. to support him on the journey. Many persons, they believe, have become reanimated, who had been, during their apparent death, in strange villages; but as the inhabitants used them ill they returned. They say they have never seen the Master of Life, and therefore cannot pretend to personify him; but they have often heard him speak in the thunder; they wear often a shell which is in honor, or in representation of him, but they do not pretend that it resembles him, or has anything in common with his form, organization, or dimensions." And, as was the custom among other tribes, "After the death of the husband the widow scarifies herself, rubs her person with clay, and becomes negligent of her dress until the expiration of a year, when the eldest brother of the deceased takes her to wife without any ceremony, considers her children as his own, and takes her and them to his house ; if the deceased left no brother, she marries whom she pleases." *(James, Account of an Expedition from Pittsburgh to the Rocky Mountains, performed in the years 1819 and 1820. Philadelphia, 1823. 2 vols. I, pp. 124-126.)*

Missouri

Unfortunately, the Missouri had lost their strength as a tribe before the region which they had occupied was traversed by the several expeditions sent out by the Government soon after the transfer of Louisiana to discover the tribes of the newly acquired Territories. On June 13, 1804, the Lewis and Clark party, ascending the Missouri River, reached the site of the great Missouri village between two creeks on the north bank of the Missouri, about 5 miles below the mouth of Grand River. Evidently it must have been a very large and important village only a few years before, as at that time, June, 1804, it consisted of "a feeble remnant of about thirty families." Not many years elapsed before the remnant of this once important tribe sought refuge among the kindred Oto, then established west of the Missouri, and eastward from the villages of the Pawnee. The two tribes—Missouri and Oto—continued to dwell together, and later occupied a reservation in southern Gage County, Nebraska.

Dr. W. C. Boteler, stationed at the Oto Indian Agency before the year 1880, prepared an account of the burial customs of the two tribes with whom he came in such close contact. The customs, so he wrote, revealed little change through the contact of the Indians with the whites. "The Otoe and Missouri tribes of Indians are now located in southern Gage County, Nebraska, on a reservation of 43,000 acres, unsurpassed in beauty of location, natural resources, and adaptability for prosperous agriculture."

The narrative begins with telling how, even before life is extinct and while the person is still capable of understanding what is being done, he or she is dressed in the best clothes and most elaborate ornaments obtainable. This is usually done by women of the tribes, following the wishes of the person. "It is customary for the dying Indian to dictate, ere his departure, the propriety or impropriety of the accustomed sacrifice. In some cases there is a double and in others no sacrifice at all. The Indian women then prepare to cut away their hair; it is accomplished with scissors, cutting close to the scalp at the side and behind.

"The preparation of the dead for burial is conducted with great solemnity and care. Bead-work the most ornate, expensive blankets and ribbons comprise the funeral shroud. The dead, being thus enrobed, is placed in a recumbent posture at the most conspicuous part of the lodge and viewed in rotation by the mourning relatives previously summoned by a courier, all preserving uniformity in the piercing screams which would seem to have been learned by rote.

"An apparent service is then conducted. The aged men of the tribe, arranged in a circle, chant a peculiar funeral dirge around one of their number, keeping time upon a drum or some rude cooking utensil." Some would dance within the circle, to drive away the evil spirit. This would be followed by feasting, at which time "All who assemble are supplied with cooked venison, hog, buffalo, or beef, regular waiters distributing alike hot cakes soaked in grease and coffee or water, as the case may be."

Near the conclusion of the feast the bereaved family would often receive gifts from their friends," such as calico in bolt, flannel cloth, robes, and not infrequently ponies or horses." The body was then conveyed to the grave, on the back of a horse but in more recent times in a wagon, and "before the interment of the dead the chattels of the deceased are unloaded from the wagons or unpacked from the backs of ponies and carefully arranged in the vault-like tomb. The bottom, which is wider than the top (graves here being dug like an inverted funnel), is spread with straw or grass matting, woven generally by the Indian women of the tribe or some near neighbor. The sides are then carefully hung with handsome shawls or blankets, and trunks, with domestic articles, pottery, & c., of less importance, are piled around in abundance. The sacrifices are next inaugurated. A pony, first designated by the dying Indian, is led aside and strangled by men hanging to either end of a rope. Sometimes, but not always, a dog is likewise strangled, the heads of both animals being subsequently laid upon the Indian's grave. The body, which is now often placed in a plain coffin, is lowered into the grave, and if a coffin is used the friends take their parting look at the deceased before closing it at the grave. After lowering, a saddle and bridle, blankets, dishes, &c., are placed upon it, the mourning ceases, and the Indians prepare to close the grave. It should be remembered, among the Otoe and Missouri Indians dirt is not filled in upon the body, but simply rounded up from the surface upon stout logs that are accurately fitted over the opening of the grave. After the burying is completed, a distribution of the property of the deceased takes place, the near relatives receiving everything from the merest trifle to the tent and horses, leaving the immediate family, wife and children or father out-door pensioners." A small fire was then kept burning at the grave for four days and four nights and, according to their belief, " at the expiration of this time the Indian arose, and mounting his spirit pony^, galloped off to the happy hunting-ground beyond." *(Yarrow, A Further Contribution to the Study of the Mortuary Customs of the North American Indians. In First Annual Report Bureau of Ethnology, 1879-1880. Washington, 1881. pp. 96-97.)*

The preceding is one of the most interesting and complete accounts known of the ceremonies attending death and burial of a member of a tribe of this Siouan group. It reveals few, if any, changes from the old customs of the tribes as a result of contact with the whites. The objects which were deposited in the graves with the bodies were necessarily in some instances different from those used in earlier days. Guns were probably substituted for the more primitive bows and arrows, and plain coffins took the place of more elaborate wrapping in robes and blankets. But the ceremonies remained unchanged. *The Smithsonian Institution Bureau of Ethnology, Bulletin 83, 1927.*

Omaha

Origin: Iowa, Nebraska, Prehistoric origin in the Ohio Valley presently known as the Ohio Hopewell mound builders.

Interesting accounts of the burial and mourning customs of the primitive Omaha, as witnessed more than a century ago, are contained in the narrative of the Long expedition to the Rocky Mountains. To quote from the narrative: "When an Omaha dies, his kinsmen and friends assemble around his body, and bewail their loss with loud lamentation, weeping, and clapping of hands . . . They suffer the deceased to remain but a short time previously to interment, and often bear the body to the grave, before the warmth of vitality is entirely dissipated. The body is enveloped in a bison robe, or blanket, which is secured by a cord. It is then carried to the grave on the shoulders of

31

two or three men, and followed by the greater portion of the mourners, without any order. The grave is an oblong square, of sufficient length, and four or five feet deep. The body is placed in the grave, and with it a pair or two of moccasins, some meat for food, and many little articles and comforts, the gifts of affection, to be used on the long journey which the deceased is supposed to be about to perform, in order to arrive at the Wa-nocha-te, or town of brave and generous spirits. The grave is then filled with earth, and a small tumulus is raised over it, proportioned in magnitude to the dignity of the deceased. The relatives bedaub their persons with white clay, scarify themselves with a flint, cut out pieces of their skin and flesh, pass arrows through their skin, and if on a march, they walk barefoot at a distance from their people, in testimony of the sincerity of their mourning.

" For a considerable time, they nightly visit the grave of the deceased, to lament over it. A sorrowing relative may be seen, of a bleak wintry night, bending over the grave, clad in a scanty robe, which scarcely conceals the middle of the back, as an additional self-punishment and unequivocal manifestation of grief.

"For the death of a brave warrior, or of a chief, the lamentation is more general, and many of those, who visit the body previous to its removal, present to it blankets, bison robes, breech-cloths, and moccasins, which are sometimes thus accumulated in considerable numbers; of these presents, part is retained by the orphans, if any, but the greater number is entombed with the body. Over the grave

of a person of this description, a kind of roof or shelter is constructed, of pieces of wood reared against each other, and secured at top, then sodded over with grass sod.

"The season prescribed by custom for mourning, is a period of from seven to twelve months; during this time the violent expressions of their grief gradually diminish, and towards the expiration of the allotted season, the state of mourning is only manifested by the coating of white clay, and even this, like the black apparel of civilized mourners, is at length dispensed with, -and with the same decorous gradation." (*James, Account of an Expedition from Pittsburgh to the Rocky Mountains, performed in the years 1819 and 1820. Philadelphia, 1823. 2 vols.,I pp. 281-282.*)

A woman, when her husband died, would usually give away practically all her possessions, then leave the village, and erect a small structure of grass and bark in which she would dwell apart from her friends for a period of six months or even a year. During this time she would cut off her hair and inflict other forms of self punishment.

Referring to the Omaha's belief of conditions after death, the narrative relates that " This people believe firmly in an existence after death, but they do not appear to have any definite notions, as to the state in which they shall be. And although they say that many reappear after death, to their relatives, yet such visitants communicate no information respecting futurity. They consist of those only who have been killed, either in battle with an enemy, or in quarrels with individuals of their own nation, and their errand is to solicit vengeance on the perpetrators of the deed." And, continuing, " They say that after death, those who have conducted themselves properly in this life, are received into the Wa-noch-a-te,

or town of brave and generous spirits; but those who have not been useful to the nation, or their own families, by killing their enemies, stealing horses, or by generosity, will have a residence prepared for them in the town of poor and useless spirits; where, as well as in the good towns, their usual avocations are continued." (Op. cit., pp. 267-268.)

Plate 21 a

The great chief Blackbird, who lived and died before the Lewis and Clark expedition ascended the Missouri, was buried on the summit of the river cliffs, not far from the Omaha village. Catlin's very graphic sketch of the grave and of the surroundings is reproduced in Plate 21, a. The original picture is in the United States National Museum.

A view of the cliff and grave, looking from the Missouri, made by Bodmer in 1833, is given in Plate 22.

A group of more recent scaffold burials is shown in Plate 23, but unfortunately the date of the photograph has not been ascertained.

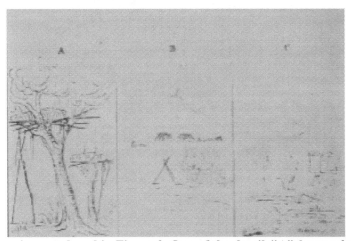

One of Catlin's illustrations is reproduced in Figure 3. One of the details "A" shows what he in 1832 designated as the usual form of Omaha burial.

Romantically conceived, and carried out to the fullest possible extent in accordance with the *ante mortem* wishes of the dead, were the obsequies of Blackbird, the great chief of the Omahas. The account is given by George Catlin: [Footnote: Manners, Customs, &c., of North American Indiana, 1844, vol. ii, p. 5]

Blackbird's grave is on the on the crest of the distant bluff.

"He requested them to take his body down the river to this his favorite haunt, and on the pinnacle of this towering bluff to bury him on the back of his favorite war-horse, which was to be buried alive under him, from whence he could see, as he said, 'the Frenchmen passing up and down the river in their boats.' He owned, amongst many homes, a noble white steed, that was led to the top of the grass- covered hill, and with great pomp and ceremony, in the presence of the whole nation and several of the far-traders and the Indian agent, he was placed astride of his horse's back, with his bow in his hand, and his shield and quiver slung, with his pipe and his medicine bag, with his supply of dried meat, and his tobacco-pouch replenished to last him through the journey to the beautiful hunting grounds of the shades of his fathers, with his flint and steel and his tinder to light his pipes by the way; the scalps he had taken from his enemies' heads could be trophies for nobody else, and were hung to the bridle of his horse. He was in full dress, and fully equipped, and on his head waved to the last moment his beautiful head-dress of the war-eagles' plumes. In this plight, and the last funeral honors having been performed by the medicine-men, every warrior of his band painted the palm and fingers of his right hand with vermilion, which was stamped and perfectly impressed on the milk-white sides of his devoted horse. This all done, turfs were brought and placed around the feet and legs of the horse, and gradually laid up to its sides, and at last over the back and head of the unsuspecting animal, and last of all over the head and even the eagle plumes of its valiant rider, where all together have smoldered and remained undisturbed to the present day."

Figure 7, after Schoolcraft, represents an Indian burial-ground on a high bluff of the Missouri River.

Osage

Origin: Arkansas, Oklahoma, Kansas, and Missouri. Prehistoric origin in the Ohio Valley presently known as the Ohio Hopewell mound builders.

   Two and one-half centuries ago, when Pere Marquette floated down the Mississippi, past the mouth of the Missouri, he learned of the Osage whose villages stood to the westward. They evidently at that time dominated a large part of the rough, broken region of the Ozarks, a region where game was abundant ; where the many streams of clear water teemed with fish; where the wants and requirements of a native tribe were readily satisfied. Thus by the latter part of the seventeenth century the Osage were well established in what was to them a

35

comparatively new home, as few generations had passed since their migration from the eastward, from their old villages in the valley of the Ohio.

There is reason to believe the Osage and Quapaw after their movement from the eastward maintained more closely their old manners and ways of life than did the remaining three tribes of the related group, who, pushing onward to the plains, were compelled to adopt new customs.

The Osage place their dead in graves, and in many instances the excavations were quite shallow, many having been discovered on high points in the Ozarks covered with large quantities of rock which had been gathered from the surrounding surface. As related in one early narrative, when referring to the Osage in particular: "At, or soon after burial, the relations of the deceased sometimes cover the grave with stones, and for years after, occasionally resort to it, and mourn over or recount the merits and virtues of its silent tenant." *(Memoirs of a Captivity among the Indians of North America. London,*
1823. Hunter, p. 309.)

Burials covered with irregular heaps of stones are to be found on the summits of cliffs in many parts of the Ozarks. The bodies, in many instances, had been placed in very shallow excavations, often appearing to have been not more than a few inches deep, and then covered with stones gathered from the surrounding surface. What proportion of these numerous graves may be justly attributed to the
Osage is an unsolved question, but undoubtedly the great majority were reared over the dead of this tribe. The Gasconade River is a typical Ozark stream, usually with a high cliff on one side and low ground on the other. A view of the Gasconade near Arlington, Phelps County, Mo., made many years ago, is reproduced in Plate 25, h. Many small heaps of stones, covering graves in which the human remains were scarcely discernible through decay, were encountered on the highest points of the cliffs shown in this picture. These were probably Osage burials of some generations ago; certainly not later than the beginning of the last century. Burials in various caves in the same region may likewise have been made by the Osage.

Plate 25

Osage graves as they appear in an old cemetery near Pawhuska, Okla., are shown in Plate 25, a. The burials seem to have been made near the brow of a cliff", extending along the edge. These were similar to the graves on the Ozark cliffs in the valley of the Gasconade.

The actual ceremony enacted at the time the body was placed in the grave was probably quite simple, but later and for many days they expressed their sorrow by rising early in the morning and "crying " near the grave. This strange and curious custom attracted the attention of many who came in contact with the people a century and more ago.

During the early part of April, 1811, a number of lodges of the Little Osage stood near the right bank of the Missouri, in the vicinity of Fort Osage, which stood a short distance northeast of the present town of Independence, Jackson County, Mo. Bradbury, then ascending the Missouri with a party of traders, reached the fort on April 8, 1811.

He visited the native village and was interested in the unusual custom of the Osage already "mentioned. To quote from his journal : " I inquired of Dr. Murry concerning a practice which I had heard prevailed amongst the Osage, of rising before day to lament their dead. He informed me that such was really the custom, and that the loss of a horse or a dog was as powerful a stimulus to their lamentations as that of a relative or friend; and he assured me, that if I should be awake before day the following morning, I might certainly hear them. Accordingly on the 9th I heard before day that the howling had commenced ; and better to escape observation, I wrapped a blanket around me, tied a black handkerchief on my head, and fastened on my belt, in which I stuck my tomahawk, and then walked into the village. The doors of the lodges were closed, but in the greater part of them the women were crying and howling in a tone that seemed to indicate excessive grief. On the outside of the village I heard the men who Dr. Murry had informed me always go out of the lodges to lament. I soon came within twenty paces of one, and could see him distinctly, as it was moonlight: he also saw me and ceased, upon which I withdrew. I was more successful with another, whom I approached nearer unobserved. He rested his back against the stump of a tree, and continued for about twenty seconds to cry out in a loud and high tone of voice, when he suddenly lowered to a low muttering, mixed with sobs : in a few seconds he again raised to the former pitch." *(Travels in the Interior of America, in the years 1809, 1810, and 1811. Liverpool, 1817.Bradbury, pp. 39-40.)*

The preceding notes refer to the old villages which stood south of the Missouri. About the beginning of the last century a large part of the Great Osage, led by their chief, Big Track, moved southward to the valley of the Arkansas, where they were later visited by many travelers and missionaries. During the summer of 1819, while ascending the Arkansas River, Nuttall encountered the first of the Osage villages about 60 miles from the mouth of the Verdigris. Another settlement was situated some 60 miles away. Both were probably quite large and interesting groups. Nuttall was attracted by their strange wailing, and on August 4, 1819, wrote : "This morning, about day-break, the Indians, who had encamped around us, broke out into their usual lamentations and complaints to the Great Spirit. Their mourning was truly pathetic, and uttered in a peculiar tone. Amongst those who first broke forth into lamentation, and aroused the rest to their melancholy orisons, was the pious Ta-lai. The commencing tone was exceeding loud, and gradually fell off into a low, long continued, and almost monotonous base. To this tone of lamentation was modulated, the subject of their distress or petition. Those who had experienced any great distress or misfortune, previously blackened their faces with coal, or besmeared them with ashes." *(A Journal of Travels into the Arkansa Territory during the year 1819.*

Philidelphia, 1821. Nuttall, p. 190.) And referring to certain beliefs of the same people: "Although they generally believe in the immortality of the soul, they have no steady and distinct conception of a state of reward and punishment. The future state, believed to be but little different from that which they now enjoy, is alike attainable by every hunter, and every warrior. It is on a conviction of this belief, that the implements of war, and the decorations and utensils employed by the living, are entombed with the dead." (Op. cit., p. 195.)

A very good account of the manners and ways of life of the Osage, probably written by an officer of the Army, but unfortunately not signed, appeared in the *American Turf Register and Sporting Magazine, Volume VI, No. 9, May, 1835.* The communication was in the form of a letter, dated Fort Gibson, March, 1835. A part of the article is of special interest at this time. It reads : "Over the dead body of a relative, they frequently vow to mourn a certain number of months or years; which they religiously perform. They give away, while in mourning, all their ornaments and good clothing, retaining only rags; put mud upon the heads, cut off locks of the hair, if women, and allow it to grow, if men; pay no attention to personal appearance, and disfigure themselves by inflicting wounds; and every morning, an hour or two before day-dawn, raise a song of lamentation for the departed. The mud is renewed daily for three months;and during this period they do not bathe, nor is any food eaten by the head of a lodge—parent for a child, a child for a parent; a husband for a wife, a wife for a husband—while the sun is above the horizon; but the children are allowed to eat at noon: at the setting of the sun the mourners hail his departure, which allows them to refresh nature. At the expiration of three months they apply the mud, and mourn (or cry, as it is termed,) every four alternate days, until the expiration of their vows, or their grief subsides. They sometimes mourn for three years . . . The effect produced in the darkness of the night, when awakened from a deep slumber, by the voices of perhaps a hundred persons of both sexes who are addressing the deity, and the spirits of the dead, is, in the highest degree, impressive."

An interesting account of the beliefs of the Osage was printed several years before Nuttall's journey. The notes are brief but concise, and among them is a reference to their belief in a future state after death. "They believe, if they are faithful to their nation and kind to their relatives, good warriors and good hunters, that when they die, they shall go to a most delightful country, which abounds in game; where there will be perpetual day; a bright sun and clear sky; when they will meet their old friends; and where they will enjoy every pleasure they were fond of here, without interruption. But that those who are bad here, especially those who are ungrateful to the aged, when they die, will go to a place of punishment, where they will suffer the severest privations, and be denied every thing that was pleasant or desirable in this life. But the traders say, it is with great difficulty they can be prevailed upon to converse at all on these subjects." *(A Topographical Description of the State of Ohio, Indiana Territory, and Louisiana. Boston, 1812. Cutler, p. 119.)* The Osage were evidently at that time little influenced by their contact with Europeans, and the work just quoted continues to say : "The French made repeated attempts to introduce Missionaries among them, but they could not succeed."

Although the French did not meet with much success in their endeavors to send missionaries among the Osage, others were more fortunate in later years, and missions were established. Interesting references to the manners and ways of life of the people are contained in letters written from the missions. Naturally, the writers of the letters had intercourse with the Indians in a different manner than did the traders and casual visitors to their villages, and were able to observe more closely and more clearly certain customs of the people. Father Bax, Avho wrote to Father De Smet from the Osage " Village of St. Francis Hieronymo, June 10th, 1850," told of the death of an Indian convert. He wrote in part : "The consoling death of this Indian was followed by a most distressing scene. I had never witnessed demonstrations of sorrow so profound. The men, throwing off that stoical indifference which appears to be so natural to them, heaved deep sighs and shed torrents of tears; the women, with disheveled hair, shrieked and gave all signs of a despair over which reason cannot predominate. I buried the Indian, on the following day, in accordance with the ritual of the Church." Thus men, as well as women, were wont to express their grief at the death of one of their number. This would agree with Bradbury's account of the scene which he witnessed at the Osage camp on the bank of the Missouri during the spring of 1811.

Father Bax had more to say about the actions of the Osage in the presence of one who they believed was about to expire. The father was called from the mission to the village. This was during the autumn of 1848. He told how, "Arriving at the village at midnight, I found the lodge filled with women and children, crying and singing the Indian death-song. I besought them to conclude these lugubrious accents, and approached the sick woman, extended on a buffalo-hide, and scarcely covered with some tattered blankets. She was unconscious." He remained through the night. Later, "the women and the children recommenced their frightful clamor; the dogs of the wigwam passed back and forward over me with such steady regularity, that it would have been quite impossible to me to count the number of visits. About daylight, the patient began to give some signs of life; but she could not yet speak. As soon as she had recovered her senses entirely, I made her a short exhortation. She appeared attentive, and gave signs of real joy. I baptized her, and departed." *(Western Missions and Missionaries: A Series of Letters. New York,1863.De Smet, pp. 364-365.)* Such were the labors of a missionary among a scattered tribe.

A more general account, but no less interesting, begins by stating that it was the custom of the Osage to bury their dead as did other tribes. As it was also the custom of many tribes to mourn their dead, "yet the Osages are by far the most accomplished mourners of them all." And the narrative continues:
"Being once encamped near a party of them, I was awakened at the dawn of day by the most doleful, piteous, heart-rending howls and lamentations. The apparently distressed mourner would cry with a protracted expiration till

38

completely out of breath. For some instants he seemed to be in the very last agonies : then he would recover breath with a smothered gurgling inspiration : and thus he continued for several minutes, giving vent to every variety of hideous and terrific sounds. Looking around, I perceived the weeper standing with his face towards the faint gleam which flitted from the still obscured sun. This was perhaps his idol; else he was standing thus because his deceased relation lay in that direction. A full ' choir ' of these mourners (which is always joined by the howls and yelps of their myriads of dogs), imparts the most frightful horror to a wilderness camp." *(Commerce of the Prairies. New York, 1844. 2 vols. Gregg, II, p. 303.)*

Ponca

Origin: Nebraska, South Dakota, Prehistoric origin in the Ohio Valley presently known as the Ohio Hopewell mound builders.

The Ponca and Omaha were formerly closely united, forming practically one tribe, few generations having passed since they became separated. Within historic times their villages resembled one another, and their customs and ways of life did not differ. They followed the same manner of disposing of their dead.

Unfortunately, very little can be found in the early narratives concerning the burial customs of the people. However, they were probably quite simple.

On May 12, 1833, the steamboat Yellow Stone then ascending the Mississippi, arrived " in the vicinity of Basil Creek, where the Puncas formerly dwelt, numbers of whose graves are seen upon the hills." *(Maximilian, Travels in the Interior of North America. London, 1843. p. 140.)*

Plate 24a

Plate 24b

Interesting photographs of Ponca burials are shown in Plate 24. Unfortunately, the history of the pictures is not known.

Oto

Origin: Missouri and Nebraska. Prehistoric origin in the Ohio Valley presently known as the Ohio Hopewell mound builders.

On July 21, 1804, the Lewis and Clark party reached the mouth of the Platte, at which time the Oto were living on the south side of the stream some 10 leagues above its confluence with the Missouri.

Six days later, while ascending the Missouri, they arrived at a point a short distance above Papillion Creek, not far from the present city of Omaha, and there, so they wrote, "we saw and examined a curious collection of graves or mounds, on the south side of the river. Not far from a low piece of land and a pond, is a tract of about two hundred acres in circumference, which is covered with mounds of different heights, shapes, and sizes; some of sand, and some of both earth and sand; the largest being nearest the river. These mounds indicate the position of the ancient village of the Ottoes, before they retired to the protection of the Pawnees." *(Lewis and Clark, History of the Expedition under the command of Captains Lewis and Clark . . . Prepared for the press by Paul Allen. Philadelphia. 1814. 2 vols. I, p. 35.)* Although the statement is not very clear, it is quite evident the party discovered a group of large mounds, formed by the falling of earth lodges, and likewise encountered the cemetery which belonged to the once flourishing village.

The graves were indicated by small mounds of earth, probably protected in various ways.

Sometime during the winter of 1851-52 a German traveler named Mollhausen became separated from his companions and lost on the snow and ice covered prairies of Nebraska. He reached a small encampment of Oto and remained with them until their return to the permanent village situated near the angle " formed by the Nebraska and Missouri." At that time, so he wrote, "We passed the burial place of the Ottoes just before we descended into the valley, and shortly afterwards came to the village. The first consisted of a number of hillocks enclosed by rough palings, and decorated with sticks with little bits of colored stuff and feathers fluttering from them." *(Mollhausen, Diary of a Journey from the Mississippi to the Coasts of the Pacific. London, 1858. 2 vols. I, pp. 210-211.)*

A brief but clear and concise account of an Oto burial, one which explains the origin of the small mounds of earth, was prepared by a missionary to the tribe, September 3, 1836: "Iskutupe, son of Jokdpedied, died last night—he has been ill ten or fifteen days. Was under the care of Otoe physicians. Several times sent him coffee and bread. Twice by request gave him purgative medicine. His illness was ague and fever—at last fever only. He died immediately after coming out of their steaming house. This morning visited the house of mourning. It was painful to witness the wailings of these heathens. They weep as they have no hope. They say their friend is lost. Some old men who had killed their enemies and stolen horses, gave to the spirit of the deceased the virtue of these deeds of bravery that it might go happy to the world of spirits. For this gift the old men received presents of cloth. Wailing continued among the relatives till 11 o'clock a. m., at which time two persons took the body of the deceased, which was wrapped in a skin and blanket, and bore it slung on a pole, to the grave. After the body followed the relatives bearing articles and provisions for the deceased to be interred with the body. The body was placed in a sitting posture one or two feet under ground, with a covering of poles, mats, and earth. The relatives buried the body; none others except myself and wife were present." *(Merrill, Extracts from the diary of Rev. Moses Merrill, a missionary to the Otoe Indians from 1832 to 1840. In Transactions and Reports of the Nebraska State Historical Society, Vol. IV. Lincoln, 1892. p. 176.)*

The missionary whose description of a burial among the Oto has just been given left an equally interesting account of the treatment of a wounded man. This was prepared May 15, 1834, and reads: "There is a class of men here called Washwahe, or medicine men. They are men advanced in life, and are the physicians of the tribe. Today they had much to do for the wounded Ioway man before spoken of. I was permitted to witness only the closing exercises. The medicine men were sitting on one side of the lodge, and the sick man, naked, sitting upon the other side. When I entered the lodge the old men were singing, aided with beating of the drum, sound of rattles and small wind instruments. After the lapse of a few minutes, they commenced dancing around the poor man, who was no doubt expecting to derive great benefit from these exercises. Near the sick man were placed several dishes with water. Whether or not this water was supposed to possess some peculiar virtue I do not know. But as they danced around, they took this water in their mouths, and occasionally would spurt it upon the head of the sick man. These exercises continued half an hour after I entered the lodge. The spectators then dispersed and I followed them." He also witnessed the manner of treating a small child: "I saw one of these medicine men perform the operation of cupping on an infant at the breast. The incisions were made with a large penknife and the blood drawn with the mouth. This operation was performed four several times in succession on different parts of the body amidst the shrieks of the infant babe." (Op. cit., p. 167.)

Otoe Sioux Burial Mounds with cists

The first to which attention is directed is interesting as resembling cist-burial combined with deposition in mounds. The communication is from Prof. F. W. Putnam, curator of the Peabody Museum of Archaeology, Cambridge, made to the Boston Society of Natural History, and is published in volume XX of its proceedings, October 15, 1878:

"…He then stated that it would be of interest to the members, in connection with the discovery of dolmens in Japan, as described by Professor Morse, to know that within twenty-four hours there had been received at the Peabody Museum a small collection of articles taken from rude dolmens (or chambered barrows, as they would be called in England), recently opened by Mr. E. Curtiss, who is now engaged, under his direction, in exploration for the Peabody Museum.

"These chambered mounds are situated in the eastern part of Clay County, Missouri, and form a large group on both sides of the Missouri River. The chambers are, in the three opened by Mr. Curtiss, about 8 feet square, and from 4-1/2 to 5 feet high, each chamber having a passage-way several feet in length and 2 in width leading from the southern side and opening on the edge of the mound formed by covering the chamber and passage-way with earth. The walls of the chambered passages were about 2 feet thick, vertical, and well made of stones, which were evenly laid without clay or mortar of any kind. The top of one of the chambers had a covering of large, flat rocks, but the others seem to have been closed over with wood. The chambers were filled with clay which had been burnt, and appeared as if it had fallen in from above. The inside walls of the chambers also showed signs of fire. Under the burnt clay, in each chamber, were found the remains of several human skeletons, all of which had been burnt to such an extent as to leave but small fragments of the bones, which were mixed with the ashes and charcoal. Mr. Curtiss thought that in one chamber he found the remains of 5 skeletons and in another 13. With these skeletons there were a few flint implements and minute fragments of vessels of clay.

"A large mound near the chambered mounds was also opened, but in this no chambers were found. Neither had the bodies been burnt. This mound proved remarkably rich in large flint implements, and also contained well-made pottery and a peculiar "gorget" of red stone. The connection of the people who placed the ashes of their dead in the stone chambers with those who buried their dead in the earth mounds is, of course, yet to be determined."

It is quite possible, indeed probable, that these chambers were used for secondary burials, the bodies having first been cremated.

In the volume of the proceedings already quoted the same investigator gives an account of other chambered mounds which are, like the preceding, very interesting, the more so as adults only were inhumed therein, children having been buried beneath the dwelling-floors.

Oglala Sioux

Origin: Nebraska

"On July 2, 1849, they crossed the South Fork of the Platte, and to quote from the journal : "About one and a half miles above the crossing a new Indian lodge was seen standing entirely alone. A fact so unusual excited our curiosity : upon going to the place, it was found to contain the body of an Indian (probably a chief) raised upon a low platform or bier, surrounded by all the implements

believed by these simple children of the forest to be necessary for his use in the spirit-land. The lodge was carefully and securely fastened down at the bottom, to protect its charge from the wolves. It was an affecting spectacle. We had observed yesterday, on the opposite side of the river, a number of Indian lodges, pitched on the bank; but the total absence of any living or moving thing about them induced us from curiosity to pay them a visit. In order to do this it was necessary to cross the river, here nearly a mile in breadth, with a strong, rapid current, The passage of the stream was made with great difficulty, swimming and wading, with the treacherous sands and swift water, but reaching the shore. I put on my moccasins, and, displaying my wet shirt, like a flag, to the wind, we proceeded to the lodges which had attracted our curiosity. There were five of them, pitched upon the open prairie, and in them we found the bodies of nine Sioux, laid out upon the ground, wrapped in their robes of buffalo-skin, with their saddles, spears, camp kettles, and all their accouterments, piled up around them. Some lodges contained three, others only one body, all of which were more or less in a state of decomposition. A short distance apart from these was one lodge which, though small, seemed of rather superior pretensions, and was evidently pitched with great care. It contained the body of a young Indian girl of sixteen or eighteen years, with a countenance presenting quite an agreeable expression: she was richly dressed in leggings of fine scarlet cloth, elaborately ornamented; a new pair of moccasins, beautifully embroidered with porcupine quills, was on her feet, and her body was wrapped in two superb buffalo-robes worked in like manner.

She had evidently been dead but a day or two; and to our surprise a portion of the upper part of her person was bare, exposing the face and part of the breast, as if the robes in which she was wrapped had by some means been disarranged, whereas all the other bodies were closely covered up. ... I subsequently learned that they had all died of the cholera, and that this young girl, being considered past recovery, had been arrayed by her friends in the habiliments of the dead, enclosed in the lodge alive, and abandoned to her fate—so fearfully alarmed were the Indians by this, to them, novel and terrible disease. "*An Expedition to the Valley of the Great Salt Lake of Utah. Philadelphia, 1855.*

Mandan Sioux

Origin: North Dakota

The French-Canadian trapper Le Rave arrived at the mouth of the Osage, on the banks of the Missouri, October 7, 1801. Later the same month he was taken captive by a band of Indians, by whom he was conducted northward up the Missouri. Early in June, 1802, he reached the Mandan villages. The lower town, the one standing farther clown the Missouri, was first reached, and in his narrative he wrote : "Here a sight, new to me, and exceedingly disagreeable, arrested my attention as soon as I came in view of the village. This was their manner of depositing the bodies of the dead. Immediately after my arrival I had an opportunity of witnessing the funeral ceremonies practiced by these people, which was in the following manner: A dead body was brought out of a hut, and laid on the ground before it, dressed in its best apparel, and wrapped in a buffalo robe. The relations and principal part of the people of the village, assembled around it. A fire was then made, and the sacred stem, or pipe, was brought and lighted. The deceased having been a warrior, an eulogy of considerable length was pronounced by his brother, in which he impressed on their minds, the great importance which the deceased man had been to their nation; rehearsed his war exploits, and concluded by urging all to follow his example, and to become of equal usefulness to their tribe. Then they would be sure of following and becoming companions of him, and all the other great warriors, which had died before, in the world of spirits. After this address was closed, provisions were brought out, consisting of boiled dog's flesh, of which the company just tasted, and then a bowl full of it was presented to the dead man. He was then taken up by four men and carried outside of the village, just into the edge of the woods, and placed on a stage which had been previously erected, about ten feet high. The bowl of food was brought and set by his head, and his arms and accouterments laid by his side. In this manner their dead are deposited, and are never buried. The wife and relations of the deceased made the most violent and dreadful howling, tearing their hair, and appearing to be in the deepest anguish, under the loss they had sustained." *(Le Raye, Journal of, In Cutler. pp. 181-182.)*

Little more than two years were to pass after the visit by Le Raye before the arrival of the Lewis and Clark expedition among the Mandan. On October 26, 1804, the latter party reached the first of the two occupied villages, Matootonha, a short distance below the mouth of Knife River, on the bank of the Missouri. Kagohami, or Little Raven, had been declared second chief of the village, and he often visited at the winter encampment of the expedition situated near the native village. And in the journal, dated February 20, 1805, is a brief reference which tells that : " Kagohami came down to see us early his village is afflicted by the death of one of their eldest men, who from his account to us must have seen one hundred and twenty winters. Just as he was dying, he requested his grandchildren to dress him in his best robe when he was dead, and then carry him on a hill and seat him on a stone, with his face down the river towards their old villages, that he might go straight to his brother who had passed before him to the ancient village under ground." (*Lewis and Clark, History of the Exi^edition under the command of Captains Lewis and Clark . . . Prepared for the press by Paul Allen. Philadelphia 1814. 2 vols. I, p. 163.)* The sites of the old Mandan villages had already been passed by the party while ascending the Missouri. They were nine in number, two having stood on the east or left bank of the Missouri and seven on the opposite side. Evidently all were occupied as late as the year 1760, this being the information recorded in 1804. A brief reference to the curious beliefs of the Mandan was written in the journal on December 4, 1804. " Their belief in a future state is connected with this tradition of their origin: the whole nation resided in one large village under ground near a subterraneous lake a grape-vine extended its roots down to their habitation and gave them a view of the light some of the most adventurous climbed up the vine and were delighted with the sight of the earth, which they found covered with buffalo and rich with every kind of fruits returning with the grapes they had gathered, their countrymen were so pleased with the taste of them that the whole nation resolved to leave their dull residence for the charms of the upper region; men, women, and children ascended by means of the vine; but when half the nation had reached the surface of the earth, a corpulent woman who was clambering up the vine broke it with her weight, and closed upon herself and the rest of the nation the light of the sun. Those who were left on earth made a village below where we saw the nine villages; and when the Mandans die they expect to return to the original seats of their forefathers; the good reaching the ancient village by means of the lake, which the burden of the sins of the wicked will not enable them to cross." (Op. cit.,p. 139.)

The group of ancient villages had probably been occupied through many generations, and sufficient time had elapsed since their founding to let them be considered the first home of the nation on earth. Here they were undoubtedly living in 1738, when visited by La Verendrye and his French and Indian companions.

The many scaffolds standing in the vicinity of the Mandan villages were mentioned by Brackenridge, who spent July 4, 1811, among these interesting people. He wrote : "On a visit to the village, I saw a great number of small scaffolds scattered over the prairie, on which human bodies were exposed. The scaffolds are supported with four forks, and sufficiently large to receive one or two bodies. They are covered with blankets, cloth of different colors, and a variety of offerings. In this they are different from the Arkansas, who bury their dead as we do." *(Brackenridge, Views of Louisiana ; together with a Journal of a voyage up the Missouri River, in 1811. Pittsburgh, 1814.p. 261.)*

Maximilian left Fort Clark, near the lower of the two Mandan villages, on the steamboat Assiniboin, bound for the upper waters of the Missouri, June 19, 1833. By 10 o'clock that morning they were approaching "Ruhptare, the second Mandan village, on the south bank, "where, so Maximilian wrote :" all the inhabitants, in their buffalo dresses, were collected on the bank, and some had taken their

station on the tops of their huts to have a better view:the whole prairie was covered with people, Indians on horseback, and horses grazing. In the low willow thickets on the bank, the brown, naked children were running about ;all the men had fans of eagles' feathers in their hands. The village was surrounded with a fence of palisades; and, with its spherical clay huts, looked like a New Zealand Hippah. Here, too, there were high poles near the village, on which skins and other things were hung, as offerings to the lord of life, or the sun, and numerous stages for the dead were scattered about the prairie." *(Maximilian, Travels in the Interior of North America. London, 1843. p. 177.)* Maximilian returned to the Mandan towns later in the year and subsequently wrote an interesting account of the manners and ways of life of the people. The customs of the Mandan and of their neighbors were evidently quite similar. Thus Maximilian wrote concerning the ceremonies attending death and burial among the two tribes: "When a Mandan or Manitari dies, they do not let the corpse remain long in the village ; but convey it to the distance of 200 paces, and lay it on a narrow stage, about six feet long, resting on four stakes about 10 feet high, the body being first laced up in buffalo robes and a blanket. The face, painted red, is turned towards the east. A number of such stages are seen about their villages, and, although they themselves say that this custom is injurious to the health of the villages, they do not renounce it. On many of these stages there are small boxes, containing the bodies of children wrapped in cloth or skins." And, continuing, Maximilian wrote : "They believe that every person has several spirits dwelling in him; one of these spirits is black, another brown, and another light-colored, the latter of which alone returns to the lord of life. They think that after death they go to the south, to several villages which are often visited by the gods ; that the brave and most eminent go to the village of the good, but the wicked into a different one ; that they there live in the same manner as they do here, carry on the same occupations, eat the same food, have wives, and enjoy the pleasures of the chase and war. Those who are kind-hearted are supposed to make many presents and do good, find everything in abundance, and their existence there is dependent on their course of life while in the world. Some of the inhabitants of the Mandan villages are said not to believe all these particulars, and suppose that after death they will live in the sun or in a certain star."

The peculiar mourning customs of the Mandan were next considered by the same careful observer, who related how "They mourn for the dead a whole year; cut off their hair, cover their body and head with white or grey clay, and often, with a knife or sharp flint, make incisions in their arms and legs in parallel lines, in their whole length, so that they are covered with blood. For some days after death the relations make a loud lament and bewailing. Often a relative, or some other friend, covers the dead, as they express it: he brings one or two woolen cloths, of red, blue, white, or green color, and, as soon as the body is laid on the stage, mounts upon the scaffolding, and conceals the body beneath the covering. A friend who will do this is, in token of respect, presented, by the family of the deceased, with a horse. If it is known beforehand that a person intends doing this honor to the dead, a horse is at once tied near the stage, and the friend, having performed this last office, unties the animal and leads it away. If a Mandan or Manitari falls in battle, and the news of his death reaches the family, who are unable to recover the body, a buffalo skin is rolled up and carried to the village. All those who desire to lament the deceased assemble, and many articles of value are distributed among them. The mourners cut off their hair, wound themselves with knives, and make loud lamentations. Joints of the fingers are not cut off here, as among the Blackfeet, as a token of mourning, but as signs of penance and offering to the lord of life and the first man." *(Maxmilian, Travels in the Interior of North America. London, 1843. pp. 392-393.)* The strange method of preserving the skulls and arranging them close together on the prairie, as was recorded by Catlin, was witnessed by Maximilian and Bodmer. The former described the custom in his narrative while the latter made one or more interesting drawings of the unusual sight thus presented. Evidently Catlin had understood more clearly the reason for these groups than did Maximilian, who did not offer any explanation but merely described briefly what he saw. "The Mandans have many other medicine establishments in the vicinity of their villages, all of which are dedicated to the superior powers. Mr. Bodmer has made very accurate drawings of those near Mih-Tutta-Hang-Kush, one of which consists of four poles placed in the form of a square; the two foremost have a heap of earth and green turf thrown up round them, and four buffalo skulls laid in a line between them,while twenty-six human skulls are placed in a row from one of the stakes at the back to the other; some of these skulls are painted with a red stripe. Behind the whole a couple of knives are stuck into the ground, and a bundle of twigs is fastened at the top of the poles with a kind of comb, or the teeth of a rake, painted red. (Pl. 27.) The Indians repair to such places when they desire to make offerings or put up petitions; they howl, lament, and make loud entreaties, often for many days together, to the lord of life, which the French Canadians call weeping, though no tears are shed." (Op. cit., p. 381.) Another drawing was made at the same time. This was supposed to represent " a couple of human figures, very clumsily made of skins," which were attached to poles, "representing, as we were told, the sun and moon, probably the lord of life and the old woman who never dies."

George Catlin [Footnote: Hist. N. A. Indians, 1844, I, p. 90.] describes what he calls the "Golgothas" of the Mandans: "There are several of these golgothas, or circles of twenty or thirty feet in diameter, and in the center of each ring or circle is a little mound of three feet high, on which uniformly rest two buffalo skulls (a male and female), and in the center of the little mound is erected 'a medicine pole,' of about twenty feet high, supporting many curious articles of mystery and superstition, which they suppose have the power of guarding and protecting this sacred arrangement.

"Here, then, to this strange place do these people again resort to evince their further affections for the dead, not in groans and lamentations, however, for several years have cured the anguish, but fond affection and endearments are here renewed, and conversations are here held and cherished with the dead. Each one of these skulls is placed upon a bunch of wild sage, which has been pulled and placed under it. The wife knows, by some mark or resemblance, the skull of her husband or her child which lies in this group, and there seldom passes a day that she does not visit it with a dish of the best-cooked food that her wigwam affords, which she sets before the skull at night, and returns for the dish in the morning. As soon as it is discovered that the sage on which the skull rests is beginning to decay, the woman cuts a fresh bunch and places the skull carefully upon it, removing that which was under it.

Mandan Indian Golgatha

"Independent of the above-named duties, which draw the women to this spot, they visit it from inclination, and linger upon it to hold converse and company with the dead. There is scarcely an hour in a pleasant day but more or less of these women may be seen sitting or lying by the skull of their child or husband, talking to it in the most pleasant and endearing language that they can use (as they were wont to do in former days), and seemingly getting an answer back."

From these accounts it may be seen that the peculiar customs which have been described by the authors cited were not confined to any special tribe or area of country, although they do not appear to have prevailed among the Indians of the northwest coast, so far as known.

Origin: North Dakota, South Dakota, Wisconsin, and Minnesota.

"Saturday, May 26, 1900, the writer was in camp on the northeastern shore of Mille Lac, Minn. A short distance down the lake shore was a large group of artificial mounds, 127 in number, some of which were 10 feet in height and 60 feet in diameter, although the great majority were much smaller. This was undoubtedly the site of a Sioux village of two and one-half centuries ago, and the mounds were the burial places of the dead. It was an interesting site, typical of others throughout the region, all of which were worthy of careful examination. Two of the mounds were excavated and in the first a single stone implement was discovered, but no trace of bones. The second mound was about 3 feet in height and 15 feet in diameter and proved of much interest. Resting upon or near the original surface were parts of four skeletons. In every case the long bones of the arms and legs had been placed together, with a skull resting upon the bundle thus formed. There were four such bundles which were discovered in the relative positions as indicated in the accompanying sketch. (Fig. 1.) In one instance two small ribs and two vertebrae were found in contact with the long bones, and one flint knife and a single fragment of pottery were discovered in the earth between the human bones, but no other objects were recovered from the mound. All material of a perishable nature had long ago decayed and disappeared, and undoubtedly the bones, when they were placed upon the ground to be covered with earth, were wrapped in skins, bags, or robes, possibly decorated with embroidery of quills. The bones remain but they will soon have vanished, leaving no trace of the burials.

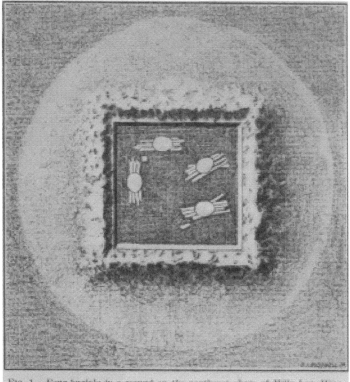

Fig. 1.—Four burials in a mound on the northeast shore of Mille Lac, Minn.

Figure 1

Early in the spring of the year 1680 Father Louis Hennepin while ascending the Mississippi was taken captive by a Sioux war party. They continued up the river, thence through the dense forests to their village situated on the shore of a small lake only a short distance south of Mille Lac. While at the village Father Hennepin saw much to interest him and fortunately his notes were preserved. He referred to the strange custom of the people in caring for and carrying about with them the bones of their relatives. He wrote regarding a certain member of the tribe :"This wily savage had the bones of some important deceased relative, which he preserved with care in some skins dressed and adorned with several rows of black and red porcupine quills; from time to time he assembled his men to give it a smoke, and he made us come several days in succession to cover the deceased's bones with goods, and by a present wipe away the tears he had shed for him, and for his own son killed by the Miamis. To appease this captious man, we threw on the bones of the deceased several fathoms of French tobacco, axes, knives, beads, and some black wampum bracelets." Soon after reaching the village of their captors Hennepin wrote : "Aquipaguetin's son, who called me his brother, paraded about with our brocade chasuble on his bare back, having rolled up in it a dead man's bones, for whom these people had a great veneration."

It is reasonable to suppose the bones of their relatives, so carefully preserved and cared for, would later be buried. Undoubtedly the four distinct bundles of bones discovered in the mound at Mille Lac had been preserved and carried about, wrapped in decorated skins, before they were placed upon the ground to be covered with a mass of earth.

The Mdewakanton removed from the vicinity of Mille Lac to the banks of the Mississippi, below the Minnesota, where they were living when visited by American explorers during the early part of the nineteenth century.

During the early summer of 1823 Major Long's party started from Fort Crawford to trace the course of the Minnesota River, then known as the St. Peters, in which undertaking they were quite successful. Some members of the party went overland to Fort Snelling, situated at the mouth of the Minnesota, and others accompanied the boat used in conveying supplies to that post. On June 29 the latter party reached "Wapasha's village," and during the afternoon of July 1 were at "the Redwing village." The following day they passed the mouth of the St. Croix and not far away went ashore to examine an Indian cemetery. It stood on the bank of the river," but elevated above the water's level; it exhibits several scaffolds, supporting coffins of the rudest form; sometimes a trunk, (purchased from a trader,) at other times a blanket, or a roll of bark, conceal the bodies of the deceased. There were, also, several graves, in which are probably deposited the bones, after all the softer parts have been resolved into their elements, by long exposure to the atmosphere." Later in the day they arrived at Fort Snelling. The cemetery just mentioned belonged to the village of Kaposia, where Little Crow was chief, a village of much importance in its time.

The several villages on the banks of the Mississippi below Fort Snelling: always proved places of interest to the traveler, as they did to Latrobe just 90 years ago, when he wrote: "We passed more than one permanent village of the Sioux, now all deserted ; the houses were made of rude poles covered with pieces of oak-bark, and swarmed with fleas, numerous as the dust. In their vicinity were seen the dead bodies of their chiefs, wasting in the air, enclosed in rude wooden cases, elevated upon scaffolds raised eight or ten feet above the surface." This was during the autumn, and the Indians were evidently on their fall hunt, seeking buffalo on the prairie lands to the west and south or in the valley of the St. Croix.

A later and more complete account of the cemetery at Kaposia has been preserved. It refers to conditions at that most interesting village during the spring of 1849, at which time it had a population of about 300, and consisted of some 40 lodges, with two frame houses, one occupied by a missionary, the other by a teacher. On May 17 of that year, " On the high bluffs in the rear of their village, several flags, affixed to long poles, were seen floating in the wind. Beneath these flags, erected on scaffolds about ten feet high, were the bodies of deceased Indians in coffins, covered with white or red cloth. This custom of elevating their dead on scaffolds originated, probably, in the difficulty of burying their dead during the winter. The bodies of those who died during that season of the year were preserved until spring for interment, and were erected on scaffolds to preserve them from the reach of wolves. It has grown into a custom, so that now the bodies of those who request it are elevated on scaffolds at other seasons of the year. A half-breed Indian informed me, that Indians dread to have the heavy earth press upon their breasts; they prefer to have their bodies elevated in a conspicuous place, where they can have a view of all that is transpiring around them. In a few months the bodies are, in ordinary cases, taken down and buried. Sometimes, however, they are left on the scaffold several years, especially those of persons of distinction in the tribe." A few days later Seymour again visited the village of Kaposia, and in describing the cemetery wrote : "Ascending the high bluff which overhangs the village, I examined their burial-ground, which occupies the summit. The first object that attracted my attention was a small boulder, painted red, and encircled by offerings, which the friends of deceased persons had made to this idol; a dead eagle, a dead dog, an arrow, etc., were among the offerings. If any one is in want of articles thus offered to their idols, it is regarded as lawful to take them, provided others, of equal value, are left in their stead." And describing the burials them selves: "Attached to the poles, upon which some of the coffins are suspended, are bunches of hair, resembling a scalp. I supposed that these were placed here to commemorate the exploits of the deceased. I was informed, however, that they were torn by mourners from their own heads, in testimony of their grief. The bodies, when buried, are protected by a tight paling closing over them, like a double roof. This is necessary to prevent the shallow graves from being dug up by the wolves.

"Mourners, during occasional paroxysms of grief, resort to the graves of their friends, and vent their sorrow in loud, doleful, and hideous wailings."

The expedition led by Long arrived at Fort Snelling July 2, 1823, and after a brief rest began to ascend the Minnesota. They soon passed Taoapa, better known as Shakopee's village, and later reached the small Indian settlement called by them Weakaote. Though small and deserted it proved an interesting site. It "consisted of two lodges and the ruins of a third, near which were two scaffolds. On these scaffolds, which are from eight to ten feet high, corpses were deposited in a box made from part of a broken canoe. Some hair was suspended, which we at first mistook for a scalp; but our guide informed us that these were locks of hair torn from the heads by the relations, to testify their grief. In the center, between the four posts which supported the scaffold, a stake was planted in the ground ; it was about six feet high, and bore an imitation of human figures, five of which had a design of a petticoat, indicating them to be females, the rest, amounting to seven, were naked, and were intended for male figures. Of the latter, four were headless, showing that they had been slain; the three other male figures were unmutilated, but held a staff in their hand, which, as our guide informed us, designated that they were slaves. The post, which is an unusual accompaniment to the scaffold that supports a warrior's remains, does not represent the achievements of the deceased, but those of the warriors that assembled near his remains, danced the dance of the post, and related their martial exploits. A number of small bones of animals were observed in the vicinity, which were probably left there after a feast celebrated in honor of the dead. The boxes in which the corpses were placed are so short that a man could not lie in them extended at full length, but in a country where boxes and boards are scarce, this is overlooked. After the corpses have remained a certain time exposed, they are taken down and interred. Our guide, Renville, related to us, that he had been a witness to an interesting, though painful circumstance, that occurred here. An Indian who resided on the Mississippi, hearing that his son had died at this spot, came up in a canoe, to take charge of the remains, and convey them down the river to his place of abode; but, on his arrival, he found that the corpse had already made such progress towards decomposition, as rendered it impossible for it to be removed. He then undertook, with a few friends, to clean off the bones; all the flesh was scraped off and thrown into the stream; the bones were carefully collected into his canoe, and subsequently carried down to his residence."

The statement by Renville, as given above, tends to add value to certain passages in Carver's curious work. He claimed to have spent the winter of 1766-67 among the Sioux, then occupying villages on the banks of the Minnesota, and wrote : " I left the habitations of these hospitable Indians the latter end of April 1767; but did not part from them for several days, as I was accompanied on my journey by near three hundred of them, among whom were many chiefs, to the mouth of the River St. Pierre. At this season these bands annually go to the Great Cave ... to hold a grand council with all

the other bands; wherein they settle their operations for the ensuing year. At the same time they carry with them their dead for interment bound up in buffaloes skins." He had already mentioned the cave, placing it about 30 miles below the Falls of St. Anthony, and wrote : "The Indians term it Wakon-teebe, that is, the Dwelling of the Great Spirit." And, "At a little distance from this dreary cavern is the burying place of the several bands of the Naudowessie Indians: though these people have no fixed residence, living in tents, and abiding but a few months in one spot, yet they always bring the bones of their dead to this place; which they take the opportunity of doing when the chiefs meet to hold their councils." The remains would first be disposed of and the council would then be held.

The spot thus described so many years ago had probably not changed in appearance when painted by Eastman nearly a century later. Eastman's painting, as engraved by J. Andrews and reproduced by Schoolcraft, is here given as Plate 9. The view from the Mississippi shows the high bluff with its summit plateau covered with burials. This, according to Schoolcraft, was the burial place for the people of the three Mdewakanton villages, all of which were situated a few miles distant.

Plate 9

Some 14 years after the Long expedition another explorer, in the same region, recorded a similar experience. On April 14, 1837, McLeod entered in his diary: "Embarked at sun raise in a canoe with Indians and squaws who are going down to where the St. Peters joins the Mississippi at Fort Snelling. Have for company 10 Indians and squaws in three canoes. These people have in one of their canoes the bodies of two of their deceased relatives which they intend carrying to a lake near the Mississippi more than 100 miles from this. In many instances these people bring the bodies of their friends much farther when it is the wish of the dying person to be deposited in a particular place." They were probably bound for the burial ground mentioned by Schoolcraft, not to a lake as mentioned.

Twelve years after Major Long's party ascended the Mississippi, and passed the several important native settlements before reaching the mouth of the St. Peters, or Minnesota River, the English geologist, Featherstonhaugh, traversed the same region. On September 7, 1835, he arrived at the village of the great chief Wapasha, on the bank of the Mississippi, in the present Wabasha County, Minn. The village at that time "consisted of twelve large oblong wigwams, or teepees, covered in with bark, and two round lodges, made with poles and covered with skins." He witnessed a peculiar form of mourning practiced by the people of the village and likewise visited their cemetery. His narrative continued : "As we approached the prairie, a great number of men came to the landing-place, painted in the most hideous manner, one-half of their faces being rubbed over with a whitish clay, and the other side all begrimed with charcoal; not that they were going to war, but because they were in mourning for the wife of a chief of the second class, who had recently died." And "near the village several death-scaffolds were erected, formed of four poles each, about eight feet high, with a floor made by fastening shorter poles to them about seven feet from the ground, and the frail structure shored up by another pole extending to the ground. Upon this floor a rude coffin was placed, containing the body, and from one end of the scaffold a sort of bunting was flying, to denote the rank of the individual . . . An old squaw was standing near the scaffold of the defunct lady, howling in a most extraordinary manner. Around these scaffolds were numerous inferior graves, some of them containing full-length corpses, and others only the bones of the dead after they have remained too long on the scaffolds to hold together."

Later, before passing the mouth of the St. Croix, he encountered a number of Indians, among whom "There was a frightful-looking old squaw, with a little boy, a youth about twenty, with strings of wampum hanging from his forelocks, and his face all begrimed with charcoal, whilst his sister, a tolerable-looking young squaw, about nineteen, had only a black grimy spot on each cheek. The journey they were upon was connected with the death of a relative, and the party had gone into cheap mourning, which, nevertheless, amongst these simple and rude people, is the symbol of wounded affections." And quite similar to this was a reference made by the wife of Capt. Seth Eastman to an old Indian whom she saw at Fort Snelling. He was an old man, so she wrote, "in mourning, and he looked particularly *en dishabille*, his clothing (and there was little of it) was dirty in the extreme. His face he had painted perfectly black; his hair he had purposely disarranged, to the greatest degree. Thus he presented a striking contrast to the elaborately adorned warriors around him."

Hidasta Sioux

Origin: They once lived in semipermanent villages on the upper Missouri River between the Heart and the Little Missouri rivers in what is now North Dakota.

The Hidatsa, neighbors of the Mandan, at the beginning of the nineteenth century occupied villages on the banks of

Knife River, at and above its junction with the Missouri. The manners and customs of the two tribes were quite similar. Le Raye, who arrived among the Mandan early in the month of June, 1802, and who left such an interesting account of the burial customs of that people, wrote on the 13th of the same month concerning the Hidatsa:"They were formerly more numerous, but the small pox has made its ravages among them. These people deposit their dead in the same manner as the Mandans, but at a greater distance from their villages." *(Le Raye, Journal of. In Cutler. pp. 183-184.)* The distance of the scaffolds from the villages was told by Bradbury, who visited the Hidatsa just nine years after Le Raye. He told of arriving on the river bank " opposite to the third village of the Minetaree or Gros Ventres Indians, as the night was closing in. On arriving, some Indians came down to the bank of the river opposite to us, and immediately ran back to the village. In a few minutes we saw them returning along with six squaws, each of whom had a skin canoe on her back, and paddle in her hand." *(Bradbury, Travels in the Interior of America, in the years 1809, 1810, and 1811. Liverpool, 1817.p. 139.)* Thus they were ferried across the river, they and their saddles in the bull boats and the Indians driving the horses. The squaws received "three balls and three loads of powder for each man, being the price of ferriage." On June 24, 1811, Bradbury, being at the Hidatsa village, wrote : "passed through a small wood, where I discovered a stage constructed betwixt four trees, standing very near each other, and to which the stage was attached, about ten feet from the ground. On this stage was laid the body of an Indian, wrapt in a buffalo robe. As the stage was very narrow, I could see all that was upon it without much trouble. It was the body of a man, and beside it there lay a bow and quiver with arrows, a tomahawk, and a scalping knife. There were a great number of stages erected about a quarter of a mile from the village, on which the dead bodies were deposited,which, for fear of giving offense, I avoided; as I found, that although it is the custom of these people thus to expose the dead bodies of their ancestors, yet they have in a very high degree that veneration for their remains which is a characteristic of the American Indians."

It is interesting to know that scaffolds for the dead were erected in the midst of the timber, "a small wood," and evidently the bodies were placed in the branches of trees. However, the latter may not have been of sufficient size to have sustained the weight and bulk.

When the Hidatsa were visited by Maximilian, during the year 1833, they were living on the banks of Knife River, a few miles distant from the Mandan villages. He described the burial customs of the two tribes as being similar, as already mentioned, but later referred to the Hidatsa and told how "The Manitaries always lay their dead upon stages or scaffolds. As the lord of life is displeased when they quarrel and kill each other, those who do so are buried in the earth, that they may be no longer seen. In this case a buffalo's head is laid upon the grave, in order that the buffalo herds may not keep away, for, if they were to smell the wicked, they might remove and never return. The good are laid upon stages, that they may be seen by the lord of life." *(Maximilian, Travels in the Interior of North America. London, 1843.pp. 404—405.)*

Many Hidatsa removed from their old habitat on Knife River about the year 1845 to the vicinity of Fort Berthold, on the bank of the Missouri some 60 miles above the site of old Fort Clark. Culbertson stopped at the new village on June 13, 1850, and observed that " on the plane near the fort is the burying place, studded with many scaffolds on which the dead are placed, and also many graves in which they have been buried. Many of the scaffolds were partly broken down and had deposited their burdens on the ground where they lay exposed unsightly and forbidding. A number of skulls were kicking about the ground." (Culbertson, p. 118.) And three years later, on October 9, 1853, another party " arrived at Fort Berthold about sunset," and received many " visits from the Gros Ventres." The earth lodges were described, and the journal continues : " These Indians, in common with some other tribes, have a peculiar method of disposing of the bodies of their dead. They are placed upon a scaffold six or eight feet above the ground, enveloped in all the blankets, robes, &c., which belonged to them when alive, with a supply of food, arrows, moccasins, &c., for the use of the deceased in the happy hunting-grounds. The last resting-place of the Indian is as sacred to his friends as the white man's tomb, and Avhoever should disturb it in any way would expose himself to an Indian's vengeance." *(Saxton, Journal. In Reports of Explorations and Surveys to Ascertain the Most Practicable and Economical Route for a Railroad from the Mississippi River to the Pacific Ocean . . . 1853-1854. Vol. I. Washington, 1855. pp. 263-268.)*

Morgan visited the village of the Hidatsa and Mandan at Fort Berthold during his trip through the Upper Missouri Valley in 1862, and fortunately left an interesting, though brief, account of the burials in the vicinity of the settlement. He referred to the village and said in part: "It is situated upon a bluff at a bend in the river in a situation precisely similar to that of the old Mandan village, but upon the north-east side of the Missouri. It contains about the same number of houses, of the same design, and is surrounded, except on the bluff, with a wall of wooden pickets set close together vertically in the ground, and rising to a height of ten or twelve feet, with two or three gateways or openings."The groups of burials were evidently some distance away from the village, on the open prairie. His narrative continued: "Back of the village, about half a mile in the prairie, was the field of scaffolds. They were thickly studded together, about two hundred in number, and some of them containing more bodies than one. Four posts or poles are set in the ground, about eight feet high, with stringers and cross pieces resting in forks, upon which a flooring of smaller poles is placed, all of which are secured with raw hide strings. This is covered with a buffalo robe. The body dressed and painted, and wrapped in blankets, red or blue, is then placed upon the scaffold and lashed to it with strips of raw hide. One partially uncovered, showed the head resting on a pillow, the arms crossed on the breast, and a pipe of catlinite with a long wooden stem, laid by his right side, resting on the shoulder. At the foot of the body was a detached bundle . . . lashed to the scaffold." *(Morgan, The Stone and Bone Implements of the Arickarees. In Twenty-first Annual Report of the Regents of the University of the State of New York, Albany, 1871.p. 45.)*

In the year 1877 the three tribes, Hidatsa, Mandan, and Arikara, occupied an extensive and permanent village in the vicinity of Fort Berthold, on the bank of the Missouri River. The village consisted of many earth lodges, the older form of structures, but there were numerous cabins similar to those erected by the pioneers from the East. At that time (1877) Matthews wrote: "On the prairie, a short distance behind the village, are scattered around the scaffolds and the graves whereon and wherein are deposited the dead. Formerly, all who died in the village were placed on scaffolds, as is the custom with most of the Missouri Valley tribes ; but the practice of burying in the ground, after the manner of the Europeans and Arickarees, is gradually becoming more common; and every year the scaffolds decrease, and the graves increase in number. When at a distance from their village on their hunts, if encamped in the neighborhood of timber, they lay the corpses in the branches of the trees instead of building scaffolds." *(Matthews, Ethnography and Philology of the Hidatsa Indians. In Miscellaneous Publications, No. 7, United States Geological and Geographical Survey. Washington, 1877. p. 9.)* The preceding notes evidently referred to the three tribes, but it is doubtful if any scaffolds were erected by the Arikara. Now writing about the Hidatsa in particular, Matthews continued: "Their faith concerning a future life is this: When a Hidatsa dies, his shade lingers four nights around the camp or Village in which he died, and then goes to the lodge of his departed kindred in the Village of the Dead. When he has arrived there, he is rewarded for his valor, self-denial, and ambition on earth by receiving the same regard in the one place as in the other; for there, as here, the brave man is honored and the coward despised. Some say that the ghosts of those who commit suicide occupy a separate part of the village, but that their condition differs in no wise from that of the others. In the next world, human shades hunt and live on the shades of buffalo and other animals that have here died. There too there are four seasons, but they come in an inverse order to the terrestrial seasons. During the four nights that the ghost is supposed to linger near his former dwelling, those who disliked or feared the deceased, and do not wish a visit from the shade, scorch with red coals a pair of moccasins, which they leave at the door of the lodge. The smell of the burning leather, they claim, keeps the ghosts out but the true friends of the dead man take no such precautions." And "they believe in the existence and visibility of human and other ghosts, yet they seem to have no terror of graveyards and but little of mortuary remains." (Op. cit., p. 49.)

Another account, referring to the same people in the same village, was prepared about this time. It will serve to supplement the notes by Doctor Matthews, previously quoted. The account was prepared by E. H. Alden, Indian agent at Fort Berthold, and states that "The Gros Ventres and Mandans never bury in the ground, but always on a scaffold made of four posts about eight feet high, on which the box is placed, or, if no box is used, the body wrapped in red or blue cloth if able, or, if not, a blanket or cheapest white cloth, the tools and weapons being placed directly under the body, and there they remain forever, no Indian ever daring to touch one of them. It would be bad medicine to touch the dead or anything so placed belonging to him. Should the body by any means fall to the ground, it is never touched or replaced on the scaffold. As soon as one dies he is immediately buried, sometimes within an hour, and the friends begin howling and wailing as the process of interment goes on, and continue mourning day and night around the grave, without food sometimes three or four days. Those who mourn are always paid for it in some way by the other friends of the deceased, and those who mourn the longest are paid the most. They also show their grief and affection for the dead by a fearful cutting of their own bodies, sometimes only in part, and sometimes all over their whole flesh, and this sometimes continues for weeks. Their hair, which is worn in long braids, is also cut off to show their mourning. They seem proud of their mutilations. A young man who had just buried his mother came in boasting of, and showing his mangled legs." *(Yarrow, A Further Contribution to the Study of the Mortuary Customs of the North American Indians. In First Annual Report Bureau of Ethnology, 1879-1880. Washington, 1881.p. 161.)*

Hidasta village

The first is by Dr. W. Mathews, U. S. A., [Footnote: Ethnol. and Philol. of the Hidatsa Indians. U.S. Geol. Surv. of Terr., 1877, p. 409] and relates to the Hidatsa:

"When a Hidatsa dies his shade lingers four nights around the camp or village in which he died, and then goes to the lodge of his departed kindred in the 'village of the dead.' When he has arrived there he is rewarded for his valor, self-denial, and ambition on earth by receiving the same regard in the one place as in the other, for there as here the brave man is honored and the coward despised. Some say that the ghosts of those that commit suicide occupy a separate part of the village, but that their condition differs in no wise from that of the others. In the next world human shades hunt and live in the shades of buffalo and other animals that have here died. There, too, there are four seasons, but they come in an inverse order to the terrestrial seasons. During the four nights that the ghost is supposed to linger near his former dwelling, those who disliked or feared the deceased, and do not wish a visit from the shade, scorch with red coals a pair of moccasins which they leave at the door of the lodge. The smell of the burning leather they claim keeps the ghost out; but the true friends of the dead man take no such precautions."

Hidasta lodge

From this account it will be seen that the Hidatsa as well as the Algonkins and Mexicans believed that four days were required before the spirit could finally leave the earth. Why the smell of burning leather should he offensive to spirits it would perhaps be fruitless to speculate on.

Quapaw

Origin: Arkansas, Missouri, Mississippi, and Tennessee. Prehistoric origin in the Ohio Valley presently known as the Ohio Hopewell mound builders.

The Quapaw of two and a half centuries ago, living in their native state, followed the customs of the kindred Osage and expressed their grief by howling and moaning, long after the death of the individual. And it is possible that, like the Osage, they chose the early hours of the day for the ceremony. It is also evident that they had two or more ways of disposing of their dead. The remains of the principal men of a village were placed in " lofty Coffins," a statement which at once suggests a form of tree or scaffold burial. All others were probably placed in ordinary graves. Similar methods of disposing of their dead were followed by the Algonqian tribes of Virginia at the time of the settlement of Jamestown, but among them the bodies of the chief men were wrapped and placed on platforms erected within a mat covered structure termed by the early writers a "temple." A structure of this nature may have stood in every village, as did the "bone houses" among the Choctaw. *The Smithsonian Institution Bureau of Ethnology, Bulletin 83, 1927*

Crow

Crow Indian Grave

Origin: Wyoming, through Montana and into North Dakota

It is evident the common form of burial among the Crows, as among the kindred Hidatsa, was to place the body, properly wrapped, upon a scaffold erected some feet above the ground. Photographs made in the vicinity of the Crow Agency which stood on the Yellowstone, near Shields River, during the summer of 1871, show the large scaffolds on which were placed two or more bodies. This custom of putting more than one body on a scaffold seems to have been contrary to the general practice of the people farther down the Missouri. The photograph is reproduced in Plate 30

Plate 30

The Crows expressed their grief by cutting and gashing their bodies, but probably to no greater extent than did other tribes of the Missouri Valley. One account states that " Long Hair cut off a large roll of his hair; a thing he was never known to do before." *(Beckwourth, The life and adventures of James P. Beckwourth. mountaineer, scout, pioneer, and chief of the Crow Nation of Indians. Written from his own dictation by T. D. Bonner. London, 1892. p. 223.)*

Photographs of various forms of Crow burials, as they appeared between 30 and 40 years ago, are shown in Plates 31, 33, 34, and 35. These represent the scaffold burials soon after death and the graves in which the bones were placed after the scaffolds had fallen through decay. A photograph of the old Crow, Iron Bull, is shown in Plate 32, and his grave in Plate 31, b. He died in 1884 and probably his body was first placed upon a scaffold, there to remain some months until it fell to the ground, after which the bones were collected and deposited in the grave.

Iron Bull

Iron Bull's Grave

It is evident that under certain conditions the Crows placed the remains of their dead in tipis, a custom which has already been noted among the Oglala. A remarkable example of this form of burial was witnessed by Col. P. W. Norris in]876, and was given by Yarrow. (Op. cit., p. 163.) It reads: "The lodge poles enclosed an oblong circle some 18 by 22 feet at the base, converging to a point at least 30 feet high, covered, with buffalo-hides dressed without hair except a part of the tail switch, which floats outside like, and mingled with human scalps. The different skins are neatly fitted and sewed together with sinew, and all painted in seven alternate horizontal stripes of brown and yellow, decorated with various life-like war scenes. Over the small entrance is a large bright cross, the upright being a large stuffed white wolf-skin upon his war lance, and the cross-bar of bright scarlet flannel, containing the quiver of bow and

58

arrows, which nearly all warriors still carry, even when armed with repeating rifles. As the cross is not a pagan but a Christian (which Long Hair was not either by profession or practice) emblem, it was probably placed there by the influence of some of his white friends. I entered, finding Long Horse buried Indian fashion, in full war dress, paint and feathers, in a rude coffin, upon a platform about breast high, decorated with weapons, scalps, and ornaments. A large opening and wind-flap at the top favored ventilation, and though he had lain there in an open coffin a full month, some of which was hot weather, there was but little effluvia; in fact, I have seldom found much in a burial-teepee, and when this mode of burial is thus performed it is less repulsive than natural to suppose."

Plate 34 . Lodge removed and poles placed beneath scaffold

Plate 33 Scaffold Burial

Plate 35 a. Tree burial near Fort Keogh, Montana

Plate 35 b. Body of Child wrapped and in crotch of tree on bank of the Big Horn

Plate 33. Surface burial

One of the most carefully described scenes of mourning at the death of a chief of the Crows is related in the life of Beckwourth, [Footnote: Autobiography of James Beckwourth, 1856, p. 260.] who for many years lived among this people, finally attaining great distinction as a warrior. "I dispatched a herald to the village to inform them of the head chief's death, and then, burying him according to his directions, we slowly proceeded homewards. My very soul sickened at the contemplation of the scenes that would be enacted at my arrival. When we drew in sight of the village, we found every lodge laid prostrate. We entered amid shrieks, cries, and yells. Blood was streaming from every conceivable part of the bodies of all who were old enough to comprehend their loss. Hundreds of fingers were dismembered; hair torn from the head lay in profusion about the paths, wails and moans in every direction assailed the

60

ear, where unrestrained joy had a few hours before prevailed. This fearful mourning lasted until evening of the next day...."A herald having been dispatched to our other villages to acquaint them with the death of our head chief and request them to assemble at the Rose Bud in order to meet our village and devote themselves to a general time of mourning there met in conformity with this summons over ten thousand Crows at the place indicated. Such a scene of disorderly vociferous mourning no imagination can conceive nor any pen portray. Long Hair cut off a large roll of his hair, a thing he was never known to do before. The cutting and hacking of human flesh exceeded all my previous experience; fingers were dismembered as readily as twigs, and blood was poured out like water. Many of the warriors would cut two gashes nearly the entire length of their arm, then separating the skin from the flesh at one end, would grasp it in their other hand and rip it asunder to the shoulder. Others would carve various devices upon their breasts and shoulders and raise the skin in the same manner to make the scars show to advantage after the wound was healed. Some of their mutilations were ghastly and my heart sickened to look at them, but they would not appear to receive any pain from them.

East Coast and Gulf Coast Sioux

The Monacan

Origin: Half of Virginia, including almost all of the Piedmont region and parts of the Blue Ridge Mountains.

During the autumn of the year 1608 a party of the colonists from Jamestown, led by Capt. Newport, ascended the James to the Falls, the site of the present city of Richmond, and leaving their boats, continued westward "into the Land called the Monscane." This was the territory of the Monacan, a Siouan people who were ever enemies of the Powhatan tribes of the tidewater region, which extends eastward from the line of the Falls to the Atlantic. Moving westward from the Falls the party discovered the Monacan villages of Massinacak and Mowhemenchouch. Although the eastern boundary of this tribal territory was so clearly defined its western limits are not known, but at some time it undoubtedly extended westward to the mountains beyond the Jackson Valley. The Rivanna was near the center of this region, and at or near the mouth of this stream, on the left bank of the James, in the present Fluvanna County, Virginia, was one of the most important Monacan towns, Rassawck. as indicated on the map prepared by Capt. John Smith.

An Indian village seldom remained for many years on a given spot, its position being shifted back and forth, as certain causes made necessary ; therefore, it is more than probable that remains of an old settlement encountered on the river bank some 3 miles above Columbia indicate the site of Rassawck during some period of its existence. Traces of the town were exposed by the great freshet of 1870, and "when the water receded it was found that fully four feet of the surface had been removed, revealing not less than 40 or 50 ' fireplaces scattered at intervals, generally 30 to 40 feet apart. Lying among the ashes and burned earth, or scattered close about, were many burned stones, fragments of pottery, animal bones, mostly broken, some of them calcined, arrowheads, great quantities of chips and broken arrows, and other indications of a former Indian town. . . . Scattered between the fire beds were the graves, readily distinguished by the darker color of the earth. They were circular, or nearly so, about 3 feet in diameter, and none of them more than 18 or 20 inches deep. One contained the skeletons of a woman and a child, one of a man and a woman, a few those of two women, but most of them disclosed the remains of only one individual in each. . . . More than 25 graves were carefully examined, but no relics were found in any of them ; if anything had been buried with the bodies, it was of a perishable nature." *(Fowke, Archeological Investigations in James and Potomac Valleys. Bulletin 23. Bureau of Ethnology. Washington, 1894. (1), p. 13.)*

The valley of the James is rich in evidence of the days of Indian occupancy, and of the many sites which have been discovered one of the most interesting and extensive stood on the bank of the stream near Gala, in the present Botetourt County. Many human remains have been recovered from the site, and it has been estimated that about 200 skeletons were encountered while constructing the railway which traversed the ancient settlement. Some of the bodies had been placed extended, others were closely flexed. Many pits were discovered, some quite shallow, others several feet in depth, all filled with camp refuse, like the great mass by which the site was covered. *(Fowke, op. cit.)*

There was evidently a great similarity between the two settlements just mentioned. It appears that no burial place was set apart away from the habitations, but that the graves were made at intervals between the fire beds, or the caches which originally served for the storage of food supplies. In this southern country the fires were probably made outside the dwellings, in which circumstance the latter must necessarily have stood between the fire beds. Therefore the burials were made either just outside the habitations or, following the custom of the Creeks, which is doubtful, the dead may have been placed in graves excavated beneath the floors of the homes of the living. However this may have been, the burial customs of the occupants of these settlements on the banks of the James differed greatly from those of the people who, at one time, lived just northward, in the valley of the Rivanna. But, as will be shown later, there was a great similarity between the appearance of the site at Gala, with its numerous pits, and various ancient villages in Ohio.

To return to the valley of the Rivanna, on the map made by Capt. Smith, as already mentioned, Rassawck is indicated, and beyond it toward the north is another town, *Monassukapanough* not far from a stream evidently intended to represent the Rivanna. The valley may have been comparatively thickly peopled during precolonial times, as it was well adapted to the wants and requirements of the native inhabitants, but before the close of the seventeenth century the number had become greatly reduced, and about the year 1730, when white settlers entered the region, only a few Indians lived in or frequented the present county of Albemarle. In 1735 a grant of 600 acres of land was made to one Thomas Moorman; the land laid on the right, or south, bank of the Rivanna, and included the "Indian Grave low grounds." This is a rich area of many acres, but subject to overflow. It is directly north of the University of Virginia. "Indian Grave " referred to a burial mound which stood on the lowland just south of the Rivanna. In this connection it is interesting to know that the term "Indian grave," often heard in the South, referred to a mound, a communal grave or burial, and not to a single grave containing the remains of one person. The mound near the bank of the Rivanna was examined and described by Jefferson a few years before the Revolution. Monticello, the home of Jefferson, was only a few miles away to the southeast. Regarding this most interesting work Jefferson wrote:

"It was situated on the low grounds of the Rivanna, about two miles above its principal fork, and opposite to some hills, on which had been an Indian town. It was of a spheroidical form, of about forty feet diameter at the base, and had been of about twelve feet altitude, though now reduced by the plough to seven and a half, having been under cultivation about a dozen years. Before this it was covered with trees of twelve inches diameter, and round the base was an excavation of five feet depth and width, from whence the earth had been taken of which the hillock was formed. I first dug superficially in several parts of it, and came to collections of human bones, at different depths, from six inches to three feet below the surface. These were lying in the utmost confusion, some vertical, some oblique, some horizontal, and directed to every point of the compass, entangled, and held together in clusters by the earth. Bones of the most distant parts were found together; as, for instance, the small bones of the foot in the hollow of a skull, many skulls would sometimes be in contact, lying on the face, on the side, on the back, top or bottom, so as, on the whole, to give the idea of bones emptied promiscuously from a bag or basket, and covered over with earth, without any attention to their order. The bones of which the greatest numbers remained, were skulls, jaw-bones, teeth, the bones of the arms, thighs, legs, feet, and hands. A few ribs remained, some vertebrae of the neck and spine, without their processes, and one instance only of the bone which serves as a base for the vertebral column. The skulls were so tender, that they generally fell to pieces on being touched. The other bones were stronger. There were some teeth which were judged to be smaller than those of an adult; a skull, which, on a slight view, appeared to be that of an infant, but it fell to pieces on being taken out, so as to prevent satisfactory examination; a rib, and a fragment of the under-jaw of a person about half grown; another rib of an infant; and part of the jaw of a child, which had not yet cut its teeth. This last furnishing the most decisive proof of the burial of children here, I was particular in my attention to it. It was part of the right half of the under jaw. The processes, by which it was articulated to the temporal bones, was entire ; and the bone itself firm to where it had been broken off, which, as nearly as I could judge, was about the place of the eye-tooth. Its upper edge, wherein would have been the sockets of the teeth, was perfectly smooth. Measuring it with that of an adult, by placing their hinder processes together, its broken end extended to the penultimate grinder of the adult. This bone was white, all the others of a sand color. The bones of infants being soft, they probably decay sooner, which might be the cause so few were found here. I proceeded then to make a perpendicular cut through the body of the barrow, that I might examine its internal structure. This passed about three feet from its center, was opened to the former surface of the earth, and was wide enough for a man to walk through and examine its sides. At the bottom, that is, on the level of the circumjacent plain, I found bones; above these a few stones, brought from a cliff a quarter of a mile off, and from the river one-eighth of a mile off; then a large interval of earth, then a stratum of bones, and so on. At one end of the section were four strata of bones plainly distinguishable; at the other, three; the strata in one part not ranging with those in another. The bones nearest the surface were least decayed. No holes were discovered in any of them, as if made with bullets, arrows, or other weapons. I conjectured that in this barrow might have been a thousand skeletons. . . . Appearances certainly indicate that it has derived both origin and growth from the accustomary collection of bones, and deposition of them together ; that the first collection had been deposited on the common surface of the earth, a few stones put over it, and then a covering of earth, that the second had been laid on this, had covered more or less of it in proportion to the number of bones, and was then also covered with earth; and so on." *(Jefferson, Notes on the State of Virginia. Philadelphia, 1788. (1), pp. 103-106.)* From the statement by Jefferson it is evident the mound had been greatly reduced by the plow at the time of his examination, and the reduction of several feet in height, as indicated would' have undoubtedly removed one or more strata of human remains. Such a mass of bodies, or rather parts of bodies, probably represented an accumulation during several generations. It must have been a place of renown among the ancient inhabitants of the valley of the Rivanna, and this may have been the site of the town of *Monassukepanough.* That it was an important place is indicated by another statement by Jefferson (op. cit.), who, when writing of mounds in general, but of the " Indian grave" in particular, said : "But on whatever occasion they may have been made, they are of considerable notoriety among the Indians; for a party passing, about thirty years ago, through the part of the country where this barrow is. went through the woods directly to it, without any instructions or inquiry, and having staid about it some time, with expressions which were construed to be those of sorrow, they returned to the high road, which they had left about half a dozen miles to pay this visit, and pursued their journey." This visit probably took place about the time the land was granted to the settlers, and the Indians who so well knew of the situation of this burial place must have been some who had formerly lived in the near-by Village.

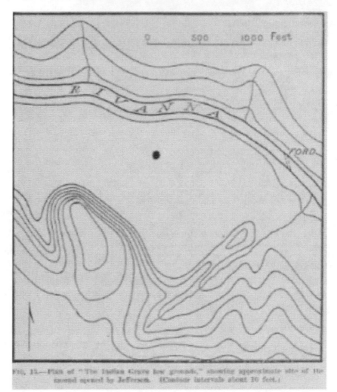

FIG, 15.—Plan of "The Indian Grave low grounds," showing approximate site of the mound opened by Jefferson. (Contour intervals about 10 feet.)

A plan of this interesting area is given in figure 15, the approximate site of the "Indian grave " being indicated by the heavy dot. In plate 14 are shown several views of the same area. Looking northward across the Rivanna, the sites of the village and ancient mound are visible on the level lowland, just before reaching the first line of trees which stands along the right bank of the river. The second, b, is looking northwestward, along the cliffs which bound the lowland, and c shows the Rivanna in front of the land once occupied by the native village. At the present time the surface upon which the settlement stood is covered by nearly 3 feet of alluvium, deposited by the waters of the Rivanna during freshets. During recent years, floods have several times cut into this upper stratum, and when the waters receded various objects of Indian origin were discovered, thus proving the location of a native town. And it is said that within a century other Indians stopped here, a site known to them, while moving from place to place, but who they were, or whence they came, may never be revealed.

a. LOOKING NORTHWARD

b. THE CLIFFS

c. THE RIVANNA PASSING THE "LOW GROUNDS"
SITE OF MOUND OPENED BY JEFFERSON

Another great burial place, evidently similar to the "Indian grave," stood on the right bank of the Rapidan about 1 mile east of the boundary between Orange and Greene Counties, Virginia, and in an air line about 15 miles from the latter. A great part of the structure had been washed away by the river, which, having formed a new channel, reached to the base of the mound, a part being undermined and carried away by the current. It was estimated to have been originally not less than 12 feet in height, and the diameters of its base were probably about 50 and 75 feet. When the remaining portion was examined, many strata of bones were encountered, mingled and confused, all ages being represented. "While some of the remains were in a fair state of preservation others were reduced to a powder." Numerous small deposits of human bones almost destroyed by fire were scattered through the mound. When found in the bone beds, they seemed to have been placed at random, but when found with the remains of not more than 2 or 3 skeletons they formed a thin layer upon which the latter rested." Pits were encountered beneath the mound, these evidently having been prepared before the superstratum was formed. These were of two forms: " One class was excavated to a depth of 2 feet in the soil, with a diameter varying from 4 to 5 feet; the others did not exceed a foot in depth, and all were somewhat less than 4 feet across. The deeper one contained usually 3 layers of decomposed bones

65

at intervals of about 10 inches; in the shallower there was in most cases only a single layer, at the bottom, though in a few a second deposit had been made a few inches above the first. The bones in some of the graves appeared to have been placed in their proper position; but it was impossible to ascertain with certainty whether such was the case. One of the deeper pits had its bottom and sides lined with charcoal; none of the others had even this slight evidence of care or respect. . . . No relics of any sort were deposited with the bones; a rough mortar, 2 arrowheads, and some fragments of pottery were found loose in the debris. . . . It is impossible to accurately estimate the number of skeletons found in this mound; but there were certainly not fewer than 200, and there may possibly have been 250. These figures will represent, approximately, one-fourth of the entire number deposited, if the statements as to the original size of the mound be correct." (Fowke, (1), pp. 33-3G.)

Jefferson failed to mention pits beneath the mound examined by him, and they may or may not have existed; nevertheless the great similarity of the two mounds makes it certain they were erected by people possessing the same burial customs. Both were on the right banks of the streams, and they undoubtedly indicated the positions of two ancient Monacan settlements which may have been occupied at the time of the coming of the colonists to Jamestown in 1607.

The visit of Indians to the mound on the Rivanna, some years after the adjoining village had been abandoned, as told by Jefferson, is most interesting, but other similar instances are known. In a letter to the Bureau of Ethnology about the year 1890 the late W. M. Ambler, of Louisa County, Virginia, mentioned a burial mound on the bank of Dirty Swamp Creek, in that county, and said in part: "I was told by Abner Harris, now deceased, that some Indians from the southwest visited this mound many years ago. They left their direct route to Washington at Staunton, and reached the exact spot traveling through the woods on foot. This has made me suppose that this mound w^as a noted one in Indian annals."

Another visit by some remnant of a native tribe to an ancient burial place has been recorded. This was on the lowlands near the bank of the Cowpasture, or Wallawhutoola River, in Bath County, Virginia, on the lands of Warwick Gatewood. The account, as preserved, reads: "Some years since, Col. Adam Dickinson, who then owned and lived on the land, in a conversation I had with him, related to me that many years before that time, as he was sitting in his porch one afternoon, his attention was arrested by a company of strange-looking men coming up the bottom lands of the river. They seemed to him to be in quest of something, when, all at once, they made a sudden angle, and went straight to the mound. He saw them walking over it and round and round; seeming to be engaged in earnest talk. After remaining a length of time, they left it and came to the house. The company, I think he told me, consisted of ten or twelve Indians; all young men except one, who seemed to be borne down with extreme old age. By signs they asked for something to eat; which was given them; after which they immediately departed." *(Montanus, Series of articles in the Virginia Historical Register, Vol. III, 1870 (1), pp. 91-92.)*

With three distinct accounts of visits by parties of Indians to their ancient burial places—and it is plausible to consider the different journey's to have been undertaken by some whose forefathers were buried in the mounds—it is to be regretted that apparently no attempt was made to ascertain the name of the tribe to which the several groups belonged or whence they came. But only those whose
ancestors lay in these great tribal burial places would have retained the traditions of the sites, and these and no others would have made pilgrimages to their tombs. And so it is evident that descendants of the once numerous Monacan were living in Piedmont Virginia within a century, and still retained knowledge of the locations of their ancient settlements with their near-by cemeteries. Now all have passed away.

It is more than probable that other mounds once standing in this part of Virginia, similar to the one examined by Jefferson, have been entirely destroyed and no record of their existence preserved, and were it not for Jefferson's own account that most interesting example would have suffered a like fate. But burial places of this form may not have existed over a very wide region. One was formerly standing some 3 miles north of Luray, near the bank of Pass Run, in Page County, Virginia. It had been reduced by the plow from an original height of between 8 and 9 feet to about one third of that elevation. The remaining portion of the mound when examined revealed great quantities of human remains, some of which were cremated, all greatly decayed. Graves were encountered beneath the original surface upon which the structure was raised. Some burials were covered by stones. Various objects of native origin were associated with the burials. *(Fowke, Archaeological Investigations in James and Potomac Valleys. Bulletin 23. Bureau of Ethnology. Washington, 1894. (1), pp. 49-53.)*

A similar burial place, estimated to have contained at least 800 skeletons, or remains of that number of individuals, stood about 2 miles northwest of Linville, near the bank of Linville Creek, in Rockingham County, Virginia. This likewise had been greatly reduced by cultivation, and "over the entire surface of the mound, to a depth of six inches, there is not so much as a space three inches square that did not contain fragments of bone which had been dragged down from the top by cultivation" (Fowke, op. cit.) Another stood about 5 miles above the mouth of the Bullpasture, in Highland County, Virginia. "For forty years human bones and teeth have been plowed out every time the mound was cultivated," but from the remaining part of the mound " the remains of between seventy-five and one hundred skeletons were exhumed." (Fowke, op. cit.) A mound in which the bodies were less compactly deposited stood on Hayes Creek, in Rockbridge County, Virginia. *(Valentine Museum, (1).)*

Referring to the native tribes of this part of Virginia Mooney has written : "The history of the Monacan tribes of Virginia belongs to two distinct periods, the colonization period and the colonial period. By the former we may understand the time of exploration and settlement from the first landing of the English in Virginia to the expeditions of Lederer and Batts, in 1670 and 1671, which supplied the first definite information in regard to the country along the base of the mountains. Under the colonial period we may include everything else, as after the Revolution the small remnant incorporated with the Iroquois in Canada virtually disappeared from history. Up to 1670 the Monacan tribes had been but little disturbed by the whites, although there is evidence that the wars waged against them by the Iroquois were keeping them constantly shifting about. Their country had not been penetrated, excepting by a few traders, who kept no journals, and only the names of those living immediately on the frontiers of Virginia were known to the Whites. Chief among these were the Monacan proper, having their village a short distance above Richmond. In 1670 Lederer crossed the country in a diagonal line from the present Richmond to Catawba River, on the frontiers of South Carolina, and a year later a party under Batts explored the country westward across the Blue Ridge to the headwaters of New River. Thence forward accounts were heard of Nahyssan, Sapona, Totero, Occaneechi, and others consolidated afterwards in a single body at the frontier, Fort Christanna, and thereafter known collectively as Saponi or Tutelo. The Monacan proper form, the connecting link between the earlier and the later period. The other tribes of this connection were either extinct or consolidated under other names before 1700, or were outside of the territory known to the first writers. For this reason it is difficult to make the names of the earlier tribes exactly synonymous with those known later, although the proof of lineal descent is sometimes beyond question." *(Mooney, Certain Aboriginal Mounds of the Georgia Coast In (Journal Academy of Natural Sciences, Vol. XI. Philadelphia, IS97.(1), pp. 2.5-26.)*

Thus it will be understood that although Piedmont Virginia was the home of many related tribes, all of whom may have belonged to the Siouan linguistic family, Sufficient information is not available to make it possible to designate the habitat of each tribe, and thereby identify the occupants of a village when a near-by burial place was created The ancient burial places which have been encountered scattered over this region reveal something of the customs of the people, and indicate the final disposition of the remains of the dead, but practically nothing is known of the ceremonies which attended death and burial. Mooney, when summarizing Lederer's rather vague narrative, said: "They had a strict marriage and kinship system, based on this clan division, with descent in the female line. . . . Even in death this division was followed out and separate quarters of their burial places were assigned to each of the four clans. The dead were wrapped in skins of animals and buried with food and household properties deemed necessary for the use of the ghost in the other world. When a noted warrior died, prisoners of war were sometimes killed at the grave to accompany him to the land of the dead. Their spirit world was in the west, beyond the mountains and the traditional western ocean." *(Mooney, (1), p. 33.)*

It is not known to which of the tribes Lederer referred in particular, but there is a possibility of its having been applicable to all the Siouan groups with whom he came in contact while crossing the central Piedmont country. He mentioned four gentes, therefore it would be expected that the ancient cemeteries, of whatever form they were, contained burials in that number of groups (*Lederer, The discoveries of . . . in three several marches. London, 1672. (1))*, but at the present time it would be impossible to distinguish any such division.

Origin: South Carolina

Siouan tribes extended southward into the central portions of the present State of South Carolina, and the Santee were undoubtedly members of this linguistic family. One of their villages probably
stood on the shore of Scott Lake, in the valley of the Santee about 9 miles southwest of Summerton, Clarendon County. Here, near the shore of the lake, is a conical mound of earth, and scattered over the surrounding area are many fragments of pottery and other traces of an Indian settlement, but the surface has been modified by the waters of the Santee during periods of flood, and consequently the greater part of the surface as it was at the time of Indian occupancy has been washed away or covered by alluvium. This site is, in a direct line, a little more than 60 miles northwest of Charleston, and the village may have been one visited by Lawson during the first days of January, 1701. The mound may have been the one referred to by Lawson, who, after mentioning his meeting with the Santee, continued: "Near to these Cabins are several tombs made after the fashion of the Indians; the largest and chiefest of them was the sepulchre of the late Indian king of the Santees, a man of great power, not only amongst his own subjects, but dreaded by the neighboring nations for his great valor and conduct, having as large a prerogative in his Way of ruling as the present king I now spoke of.

"The manner of their interment is thus: A mole or pyramid of earth is raised, the mole thereof being worked very smooth and even, sometimes higher or lower, according to the dignity of the person whose monument it is. On the top there is an umbrella, made ridge-ways, like the roof of an house; this is supported by nine Stakes or small posts, the grave being about 6 to 8 foot in length, and four foot in breadth; about it is hung gourds, feathers, and other such like trophies, placed there by the dead man's relations, in respect to him in the grave. The other part of the funeral rites are thus: As soon as the party is dead, they lay the corpse on a piece of bark in the sun, seasoning or embalming it with a small root beaten to powder, which looks as red as vermillion ; the same is mixed with bear's oil to beautify the hair. . . . After the carcass has laid a day or two in the Sun, they remove it and lay it upon crotches cut on purpose for the support thereof from the earth ; Then they anoint it all over with the fore-mentioned ingredients of the powder of this root and bear's oil. When it is so done, they cover it over very exactly with bark of the pine or cyprus trees, to prevent any rain to fall upon it, sweeping the ground very clean all about it. Some of the nearest kin brings all the temporal estate he was possessed of at his death, as guns, bows, arrows, beads, feathers, match-coat, etc. This relation is the chief mourner, being clad in moss, and a stick in his hand, keeping a mournful ditty for three or four days, his face being black with the smoke of pitch pine mingled with bear's oil. All the while he tells the dead Man's relations, and the rest of the spectators who that dead person was, and of the great feats performed in his lifetime; all of what he speaks, tending to the praise of the defunct. As soon as the flesh grows mellow, and will cleave from the bone, they get it off, and burn it, making all the bones very clean, then anoint them with the ingredients aforesaid, wrapping up the skull (very carefully) in a cloth artificially woven of possum's hair, (These Indians make girdles, sashes, garters, etc., after the same manner) The bones they very carefully preserve in a wooden box. every year oiling and cleaning them; by this means preserve them for many ages, that you may see an Indian in possession of the bones of his grandfather, or some of his relations of a larger antiquity. They have other sorts of tombs, as where an Indian is slain, in that place they make a heap of stones, (or sticks where stones are not to be found) to this memorial every Indian that passes by adds a stone to augment the heap, in respect to the deceased hero." *(Lawson, The History of Carolina. London. 1714. reprint Charlotte, 1903. (1), pp. 9-10.)*

The preceding account treated of the Santee, with whom Lawson came in contact soon after starting on his memorable journey through the wilds of Carolina, but later in his history he presented a more general description of the burial customs of the native tribes of the region, and fortunately recorded many interesting details. The greater the man in life, the more elaborate was his burial. "The first thing which is done is to place the nearest relations near the corpse, who mourn and weep very much, having their hair hung down their shoulders, in a very forlorn manner. After the dead person has laid a day and a night in one of their hurdles of canes, commonly in some out-house made for that purpose, those that officiate about the funeral go into town, and the first young men they meet withal that have blankets or match coats on, whom they think fit for their turn, they strip them from their backs, who suffer them to do so without any resistance. In these they wrap the dead bodies, and convey them with two or three mats which the Indians make of rushes or cane; and last of all they have a long web of woven reeds, or hollow canes, which is the coffin of the Indians, and is brought around several times and is tied fast at both ends, which indeed looks very decent and well. Then the corpse is brought out of the house into the orchard of peach-trees, where another hurdle is made to receive it, about which comes all the relations and nation that the dead person belonged to, besides several from other nations in alliance with them; all which sit down on the ground upon mats spread there for that purpose."

Then various persons gathered about the body and would tell of his very many acts of bravery, speak of his greatness while living, and extol his virtues, and "At last the corpse is brought away from that hurdle to the grave, by four young men, attended by the relations, the King, old Men and all the nation. When they come to the sepulchre, which is about six foot deep, and eight foot long, having at each end, (that is, at the head and foot) a light-wood or pitch-pine fork driven close down the sides of the grave, firmly into the ground; (these two forks are to contain a ridge-pole, as you shall understand presently) before they lay the corpse into the grave they cover the bottom two or three times over with bark of trees, then they let down the corpse with two belts, that the Indians carry their burdens withal very leisurely upon the said barks; then they lay over a pole of the same wood, in the two forks, and having a great many pieces of pitch-pine logs, about two foot and a half long, they stick them in the sides of the grave down each end, and near the top thereof, where the other ends lie on the ridge-pole, so that they are declining like the roof of a house. These being very thick placed they cover them (many times double) with bark; then they throw the earth thereon, that came out of the grave, and beat it down very firm, by this means the dead body lies in a vault, nothing touching him; so that when I saw this way of burial, I was mightily pleased with it, esteeming it very pleasant and decent, as having seen a great many Christians buried without the tenth part of that ceremony and decency. Now when the flesh is rotten and moulder'd from the bones they take up the carcass and clean the bones, and joint them together; afterwards they dress them up in pure white dressed deer-skins, and lay them amongst their grandees and Kings in the Quiogozon, which is their royal tomb or burial-place of their Kings and War-Captains. This is a very large magnificent cabin, (according to their building) which is raised at the public charge of the Nation, and maintained in a great deal of form and neatness. About seven foot high is a floor or loft made, on which lie all their princes and great men, that have died for several hundred years, all attired in the dress I have before told you of. No person is to have his bones lie here and be thus dressed, unless he gives a round sum of their money to the rulers, for admittance. If they remove never so far, to live in a foreign country, they never fail to take all these dead bones with them, tho' the tediousness of their short daily marches keeps them never so long on their journey. They reverence and adore this Quiogozon, with all the veneration and respect that is possible for such a people to discharge, and had rather lose all than have any violence or injury offer'd thereto. These savages differ some small matter in their burials; some burying right upwards, and otherwise, . . . Yet they all agree in their mourning, which is to appear every night at the sepulchre, and howl and weep in a very dismal manner, having their Faces dawb'd with light-wood soot, (which is the same as Lamp-Black) and Bears Oil. ... If the dead person was a grandee, to carry on the funeral ceremonies, they hire people to cry and lament over the dead body." *(Lawson, (1), pp.106-109.)*

Santee platform mound from the Mississippian Culture (1000-1500 AD) on Lake Marion (formerly the Santee River). Photo from Wikipedia

A cemetery and village site which may be attributed to one of the Siouan tribes stand near the bank of Yadkin River, a short distance from the village of East Bend, Yadkin County, North Carolina. The cemetery, which was examined by Capt. R. D. Wainwright, occupies the north end of a low ridge, and many graves have been exposed or washed away by the waters of the Yadkin. The majority of skeletons appear to have been flexed. As described, " these skeletons were found within a few feet of each other and all nearly on the same level, about four feet below the original surface. In nearly every case, at the same level and very close to the burial, were the remains of a fire. In these remains were found tortoise shells, bones of the deer, and often fragments of pottery discolored by the action of the fire." Many implements and ornaments were found associated with the burials. These included stone celts and one of iron, and shell and copper beads of different forms, while resting upon one skeleton was a copper ornament 4 inches in diameter and perforated through the center. Pieces of galena were met with in different burials. Pipes of stone and some of pottery were likewise found. The area adjoining the cemetery was evidently occupied by the village, and many objects of stone and copper, fragments of pottery vessels, beads, and broken pipes are found scattered about, "and in every direction calcined stones are plentiful." This was evidently the site of an important town of two centuries or more ago.

In the far southeastern section of the region once occupied by Siouan tribes, in Duplin County, North Carolina, are several burial mounds which may have been erected by these people long before the coming of the colonists to the Cape Fear. The mounds were carefully examined some years ago by the late Dr. J. A. Holmes, and one in particular recalls the burial mounds of Piedmont Virginia, likewise attributed to a Siouan tribe. This stood about one half mile southwest of the court house at Kenansville, Duplin County, on a dry, sandy ridge. When examined it was only 3 feet in height and 35 feet in diameter. Its height was probably much reduced since erection. It was found to contain 60 burials, and with few exceptions the skeletons had been closely flexed. "In a few cases the skeletons occurred singly, while in other cases several were found in actual contact with one another; and in one portion of the mound, near the outer edge, twenty-one skeletons were found placed within a space of six feet square. Here, in the case last mentioned, several of the skeletons lay side by side, others on top of
these, parallel to them, while still others lay on top of and across the first. When one skeleton was located above another, in some cases the two were in actual contact, in other cases they were separated by one foot or more of soil.

Many fragments of pottery, and small pieces of charcoal were scattered throughout the mound. No implements of any form were found. Near the skull of one skeleton
were discovered about seventy-five small shells, Marginella roscida, which had served as beads. The apex of each one had been ground off obliquely so as to leave an opening passing through the shell from the apex to the anterior canal." *(Sprunt, Cape Fear Chronicles. Raleigh, 1914. (1).)* As stated above, this mound is suggestive of others discovered northward in Piedmont Virginia.

Their early ancestors were the Siouan-speaking Santee Indians in South Carolina. The Santee River in that state was named after them. Two thousand years ago, some of them migrated into the Ohio Valley, where they built burial mounds and earthworks and would be known as the Hopewell mound builders.

One of the tributaries of the Santee River is the Wateree River where these Hopewell mounds and earthwork were found and reported in *"Ancient Monuments of the Mississippi Valley 1848."*

It is unquestionable that the race of the mounds occupied a portion of the State of South Carolina; and although the traces of their occupation are far from abundant, they are still sufficiently numerous to deserve notice. The only reliable information we have concerning them, is contained in a MS. letter from William Blanding, M. D., late of Camden, South Carolina, a gentleman distinguished for his researches in natural history, to Samuel George Morton, M. D., of Philadelphia, the eminent author of *"Crania Americana,"* by whose permission it is embodied in this connection. The observations of Dr. Blanding were confined to a section of the valley of the Wateree river, embracing about twenty-five miles in the immediate vicinity of Camden, and mainly included in the Kershaw district.

"The first monument deserving of notice is 'Harrison's Mound' (A in the Map). It is the highest in position of any on the river, and is situated on the west side of the same, in the Fairfield district. It is about four hundred and eighty feet in circumference at the base, fifteen feet high, and has a level area one hundred and twenty feet in circumference at its summit.

"The next relic of antiquity is the 'Indian Mortar,' (B in the Map,) in the Kershaw district. It is a regular bowl-shaped excavation in a solid block of granite, holding upwards of half a bushel, and is evidently the work of art. It was used as a mortar by the early settlers, and is still devoted to the same purpose. The part of the rock projecting out of the ground is equivalent to eight or ten tons.

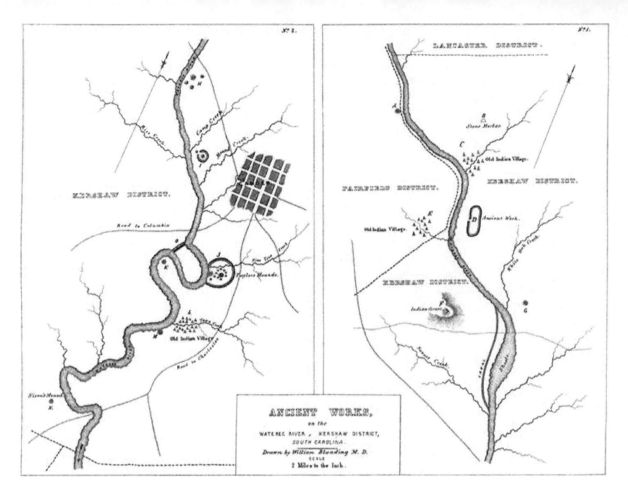

"Next is an old Indian town or camp near the mouth of Beaver creek (C in the Map). A little below the mouth of the creek is an old fortification, of oblong form, consisting of a wall and ditch (D in the Map). The embankment is now not more than three feet high above the level of the plain. The ditch is distinct. Nearly opposite this work, on the west side of the river, are the traces of an old Indian village, remarkable for its arrow-heads, fragments of pottery, etc.

"Proceeding down the river, we come to a point near the head of the canal, where the land rises to the extraordinary height of five hundred feet, forming a long, narrow hill. Upon the point of this hill nearest the river, stands what is called the 'Indian Grave' (F in the Map). It is composed of many tons of small round stones, weighing from one to four pounds each. The pile is thirty feet long from east to west, twelve feet broad, and five feet high, so situated as to command an extensive view of the adjacent country, stretching as far as Rocky Mount, twenty miles above, and for a long distance below on the river. It may be suggested that this is the elevated burial-place of some great chief, or that it was designed as some sort of an observatory. The Catawba Indians can give no account of it, nor will they venture a conjecture as to its purposes. A mound, G, is situated opposite this stone heap, on the other side of the river. The 'shoals' in the immediate vicinity seem to have been a favorite haunt of the ancient and more recent races. Here to this day is to be found an abundance of fish and game, and the vicinity is marked by numerous aboriginal relics. Here also is the highest boundary of the long-leaved pine, and the limit of the alluvial region. Below, the river becomes sluggish, and during high water leaves its banks and spreads over large tracts of land.

"The mound next below, H, was two hundred and fifty feet in circumference at the base, seventy-five feet at the top, and thirteen feet high. It was situated about a hundred yards from the river on lands subject to overflow. Three other small mounds surrounded it. In 1826 it was leveled, and the material used for manuring the adjacent lands. A part of the treasures which it contained were saved, but the rest are scattered or destroyed. The mound presented, upon excavation, a succession of strata, varying in thickness from six inches to one foot, from top to base. First vegetable loam, then human and animal bones, followed by charcoal of reeds, vessels of clay and fragments of the same, (some holding not more than one pint,) arrow-heads and stone axes, then earth, etc., alternately. In one small vessel was found a tag or needle made of bone, supposed to have been used in making dresses. Near it was found the skeleton of a female, tolerably entire, but which fell in pieces on exposure. A stratum of dark-colored mould was mixed with these articles; perhaps decomposed animal matter. The superstructure of the mound was the alluvial loam, and constituted tolerable manure. It was mixed with great quantities of mica, some pieces three or four inches square. Marine shells, much decomposed, were found in this as in other mounds, mixed with the bones, from top to bottom.

"Descending the river, near Mound creek, we come to a large mound, I, enclosed in a circle, and accompanied by a smaller one. It is perhaps the largest and most perfect on the river. It is five hundred feet in circumference at the base, two hundred and twenty-five feet in circumference at the summit, and thirty-four feet high,—slightly oblong. It is covered with stumps, briars, etc., having recently been brought under cultivation. In April last, while ploughing over the small mound, an urn was discovered, a sketch of which is enclosed. It holds forty-six quarts, or nearly twelve gallons. It had a cover fitting closely over the body for about six inches; this was broken by the plough. The vessel was curiously ornamented, and is probably the largest ever discovered in the valley. It contained a number of large shell beads, much decomposed, about the size and shape of nutmegs. It also contained another article of the same material, about the size of a man's palm, a quarter of an inch thick, and carved in open work; probably designed for suspension around the neck as a badge or ornament. The ditch around this mound is slight.

"Still further down the river, upon the opposite side, and some distance south of the road from Camden to Columbia, is the most remarkable ancient work in the valley (O). It is called the 'Indian Ditch.' It occurs at the great bend of the river, and consists of an embankment and ditch carried across the isthmus, cutting off, and, with the river, enclosing some hundreds of acres of fine alluvial land. It is about *one mile in length*, and the circuit of the river from one end to the other is between three and four miles. Twenty-one years ago, when 1 first visited it, this ditch was about eight feet deep and the wall of corresponding dimensions: a primitive forest was then growing upon its southern portion, but it is now all under the plough and fast disappearing. The bank is *exterior* to the ditch, which circumstance seems to conflict with the notion that the work was constructed for defense. It has been suggested, but with no good reason, that it was designed for a '*cut off*" or artificial channel for the river. Whatever its purpose, it was a great undertaking for a rude or savage people.

"On the opposite side of the river, about two hundred yards below the mouth of Pine-tree creek, is a group of mounds, surrounded by a low embankment (J). One of them has been nearly washed away by the river, and the others have been much reduced by cultivation. The largest is yet twelve or fifteen feet high, with a very wide base. From these mounds are disclosed arrow-heads, axes, urns, and other vestiges of art, accompanied by human bones and the bones of wild animals, and marine shells, all much decayed. As the water washes away the side of the mound on its bank, charcoal, urns, bones, etc., in successive strata, are exposed; as though it had constituted a cemetery, receiving deposits from time to time, from its commencement to its completion. The strata vary in thickness from six to eighteen inches, and are mixed with much mica, sometimes in large plates. It was long under cultivation in corn, then indigo, and in 1806, when I first saw it, in cotton, which is still cultivated on it. On the large mound stood the overseer's house; around it, on the smaller piles, were the negro quarters.

"In the bend of the river nearly opposite the south end of the 'Indian Ditch,' is a mound, perhaps fifteen feet high (K). Little is known respecting it, having been for many years the site of an overseer's house. I obtained a circular stone, with concave sides and finely polished, which had been found here, also two large urns, one holding twelve, the other twenty quarts, with a number of other aboriginal relics. At the mouth of Town creek, some distance below, there was formerly, no doubt, an Indian town or camp, (L,) judging from the quantity of relics found here. A very fine description of clay is found at this spot, which is resorted to by the Catawba Indians every spring and autumn, for the purpose of manufacturing pottery from it.

"Boykin's mound (M) is one mile lower down the river upon the same bank. It is now nearly washed away by the river. Twenty years ago, when I first saw it, large trees covered it, and it was entire. Four years afterwards I visited it, when only about one third remained, which on the side next the river beautifully exhibited the various strata composing it. It had the usual layers of earth, pottery, charred reeds, etc. Some few of the vases were entire, containing fragments of bones, and were well arranged in tiers, one above the other.

"Last of the series is Nixon's mound (N). It is much reduced, and is not now more than ten feet high. From this to the sea I know of no similar relics. Paint hill and Kirkwood, in the neighborhood of Pine-tree creek, must have been much frequented, judging from the numerous relics occurring on and around them; the former for its pure water, the

latter for its fine clay. Hobkirk's hill, near Camden, abounds in aboriginal relics. I have procured several large pipes from these localities, all of which exhibit a skill in workmanship surpassing that of the present race. The entire section in which the above remains occur is exceedingly fertile, and capable of sustaining a large agricultural population."
Ancient Monuments of the Mississippi Valley 184

The Biloxi and Pascagoula

Biloxi Origin: Gulf Coast near Biloxi Mississippia
Pascagoula:Indians lived in southwestern Alabama and southeastern Mississippi

The "Siouan Tribes of the East," whose burial customs so far as known are detailed on the preceding pages, were carefully studied some years ago, at which time all available notes were gathered and presented in a single volume. *(Mooney, The Siouan Tribes of the East. Bulletin 22, Bureau of Ethnology,Washington, 1894.)* A few years before the preparation of this most interesting- bulletin a discovery of the greatest importance was made by another member of the bureau staff, Mr. Gatschet, who, while engaged in Louisiana in 1886, discovered a small band of Biloxi, some of whom spoke their old language, which Gatschet soon found was Siouan. The Biloxi therefore belonged to the great Siouan family, and the neighboring Pascagoula were probably of the same stock. These were among the first of the native tribes encountered by the French in 1699, and, fortunately, a sketch of their burial customs has been preserved. The account was written by a French officer about the year 1730, and, as quoted by Swanton, reads *(Dorsey and Swanton, A Dictionary of the Biloxi and Oto Languages. Bulletin 47, Bureau of American Ethnology. Washington, 1912. , p. 7) :*

" The Pascagoulas and the Biloxis never inter their chief when he is dead, but they have his body dried in the fire and smoke so that they make of it a veritable skeleton. After having reduced it to this condition they carry it to the temple (for they have one as well as the Natchez) and put it in the place occupied by its predecessor, which they take from the place which it occupied to place it with the bodies of their other chiefs in the interior of the temple, where they are all ranged in succession on their feet like statues. With regard to the one last dead, it is exposed at the entrance of the temple on a kind of altar or table made of canes and covered with a very fine mat worked very neatly in red and yellow squares with the skin of these same canes. The body of the chief is exposed in the middle of this table upright on its feet, supported behind by a long pole painted red, the end of which passes above his head and to which he is fastened at the middle of the body by a creeper. In one hand he holds a war club or a little ax, in the other a pipe, and above his head is fastened, at the end of the pole which supports him, the most famous of all the calumets which have been presented to him during his life. It may be added that this table is scarcely elevated from the earth half a foot, but it is at least six feet wide and ten long. It is to this table that they come every day to serve food to the dead chief, placing before him dishes of hominy, parched or smoke-dried grain, etc. It is there also that at the beginning of all the harvests his subjects offer him the first of all the fruits which they can gather. All of this kind that is presented to him remains on this table, and as the door of the temple is always open, as there is no one appointed to watch it, as consequently whoever wants to enters, and as besides it is a full quarter of a league distant from the village, it happens that there are commonly strangers—hunters or savages—who profit by these dishes and these fruits, or that they are consumed by animals. But that is all the same to these savages. ... It is also before this table that during some months the widow of the chief, his children, his nearest relations, come from time to time to pay him a visit and to make him a speech as if he were in a condition to hear . , . they always end their speech by telling him not to be angry with them, to eat well, and that they will always take good care of him." *(Dumont, Memoires historiques sur la Louisiane. Paris, 1753. 2 vols , I, pp. 240-243.)*

Northeastern Algonquin

Micmac, Montagnais and Malecite

Origins: Nova Scotia/New Brunswick region. They also settled in locations in Quebec, Newfoundland, and Maine.

Montagnais, Micmac, and Malecite, all belonging to the great Algonquian family, and who occupied the region just mentioned. Although not always at peace with one another they undoubtedly had many customs in common, and these may have differed little from those of the neighboring tribes, all of which belonged to the same stock. And when recounting the ceremonies attending the death and burial of a member of one of these tribes he wrote : " The sick man having been appointed by the Autmoin to die . . . all the relations and neighbors assemble and, with the greatest possible solemnity, he delivers his funeral oration: he recites his heroic deeds, gives some directions to his family, recommends his friends: finally, says adieu. This is all there is of their wills. As to gifts, they make none at all; but, quite different from us, the survivors give some to the dying man.

"A feast is prepared, all gather, evidently in the presence of the dying man, and partake of the food, and having banqueted they begin to express their sympathy and sorrowful farewells, their hearts weep and bleed because their good friend is going to leave them and go away . . . they go on in this way until the dying man expires and then they utter horrible cries." These continue day and night and do not cease until the supply of food has been exhausted, the food having previously been provided by the dying man, and if there are no supplies they only bury the dead man, and

postpone the obsequies and ceremonies until another time and place, at the good pleasure of their stomachs. Meanwhile all the relatives and friends daub their faces with black, and very often paint themselves with other colors ... To them black is a sign of grief and mourning. They bury their dead in this manner: First they swathe the body and tie it up in skins; not lengthwise, but with the knees against the stomach and the head on the knees, as we are in our mother's womb. Afterwards they put it in the grave, which has been made very deep, not upon the back or lying down as we do, but sitting. A posture which they like very much, and which among them signifies reverence. For the children and the youths seat themselves thus in the presence of their fathers and of the old, whom they respect . . . When the body is placed, as it does not come up even with the ground on account of the depth of the grave, they arch the grave over with sticks, so that the earth will not fall back into it, and thus they cover up the tomb ... If it is some illustrious personage they build a Pyramid or monument of interlacing poles; as eager in that for glory as we are in our marble and porphyry. If it is a man, they place there as a sign and emblem, his bow, arrows, and shield; if a woman, spoons, or jewels, ornaments, etc. I have nearly forgotten the most beautiful part of all; it is that they bury with the dead man all that he owns, such as his bag, his arrows, his skins and all his other articles and baggage, even his dogs if they have not been eaten. Moreover, the survivors add to these a number of other such offerings, as tokens of friendship . . . These obsequies finished, they flee from the place, and, from that time on, they hate all memory of the dead. If it happens that they are obliged to speak of him sometimes, it is under another and a new name."
(Biard,(1) Relation of New France . . . 1616. In Jesuit Relations and Allied Documents, Vol. III. Cleveland, 1897 (1), pp. 127-131.)

Dogs were among the gifts presented to the dying man by his friends, and "they kill these dogs in order to send them on before him into the other world," and they were eaten at the feast prepared at the time of the death, " for they find them palatable."

This general description would probably have applied to the burial customs of the tribes occupying the greater part of the country east of the Hudson, the present New England States, and the closely flexed burials are easily explained and clearly described. The association of many objects with the remains is verified by the discoveries made by the Pilgrims when they landed on Cape Cod, early in November, 1620, and interesting indeed is their old narrative. They went ashore on the unknown coast to explore the woods and learn what they might contain. They advanced a short distance and encountered small mounds of earth which were found to cover pits or caches filled with corn. And then they found another : " It also was covered with boards, so as we mused what it should be, and resolved to dig it up, where we found, first a matt, and under that a Bow, and there another matt, and under that board about three quarters long, finely carved and painted, with three tynes, or broaches on the top, like a crown; also between the mats we found bowls.

Trays, dishes, and such like trinkets: at length we came to a fair new mat, and under that two bundles, the one bigger, the other less, we opened the greater and found in it a great quantity of fine and perfect red powder, and in it the bones and skull of a man. The skull had fine yellow hair still on it, and some of the flesh unconsumed, there was bound up with it a knife, a pack-needle, and two or three old iron things. It was bound up in a sailor's canvas cassack, and a pair of cloth breeches. . . . We opened the less bundle likewise, and found of the same powder in it, and the bones and head of a little child, about the legs, and other parts of it was bound strings, and bracelets of fine white beads ; there was also by it a little bow, about three quarters long, and some other odd knacks; we brought sundry of the prettiest things away with us, and covered the corpse up again." *(Mourt, A Relation or Journal of the beginning and proceedings of the English Plantation settled at Plinioth in New England. London, 1622. (1), p. 11.)*

This was probably just north of Pamet River, in Truro village, where at the present day rising ground, slightly more elevated than the surrounding country, continues to be known as Corn Hill. Near the western edge of this area it becomes more level and falls away abruptly on the shore of Cape Cod Bay, rising some 20 feet above high tide and exposing bare sand with little vegetation. During the summer of 1903 a dark line was visible on the face of the bank at an average depth of about 2 feet below the present surface and it could be traced for several hundred yards along the shore. This dark
stratum, several inches in thickness, proved to be an old sod line, and at three points where it was somewhat thicker than elsewhere fire beds were discovered and slight excavations revealed fragments of pottery, bits of charred bones, and ashes. This may have been the surface upon which stood the village of three centuries ago, and if so, the land upon which the Pilgrims trod has been covered by a mass of drifting sand, swept by the winds across the narrow cape.

Sailing from their safe anchorage near the end of the cape, the Pilgrims, on December 6, 1620, arrived in the vicinity of Wellfleet Bay, named by them Grampus Bay, by reason of discovering of eight or ten Saluages about a dead

Grampus, and near by we found a great burying place, one part whereof was encompassed with a large palazado, like a Church-yard, with long spires four or five yards long, set as close one by another as they could two or three foot in the ground, within it was full of graves, some bigger and some less, some were also paled about, & others had like an Indian house made over them, but not matted: those graves were more sumptuous than those at Corne-hill yet we digged none of them up . . . without the Palazado were graves also, but not so costly. (Op. cit., p. IT.) Not far away were several frames of wigwams, but the matt covers had been removed and the site had been temporarily abandoned.

The two burials encountered by the Pilgrims at Corn Hill were those of Indians and had evidently been made within a year. The "yellow hair " had been caused by the process of decay and would soon have disappeared. The objects of iron had been obtained from some Europeans who had touched upon the coast or whose vessel had been wrecked. Now, three centuries later, were these ancient burial places to be discovered it is doubtful whether any traces would remain in addition to the mass of "perfect red Powder," insoluble red oxide of iron. All human remains, mats, bows, and other objects of a perishable nature would have turned to dust and disappeared. But any ornaments or implements of stone which might have been deposited in the pit grave would remain. Within recent years many similar pits, with masses of the red oxide mingled with various objects of stone, have been encountered not far from the coast in Lincoln and Hancock Counties, Maine. But not a particle of bone, or even a tooth, has been discovered within the ancient pits to indicate the presence of human remains. Nevertheless they were probably once like the burials found by the Pilgrims at Corn Hill, but now all substance of a perishable nature has vanished. They were probably made by a kindred Algonquian tribe and may not be older than those occurring on Cape Cod. One of the most interesting groups of such pit graves was exposed at Bucksport, 18 miles below Bangor, on the left bank of the Penobscot; another was discovered on the west shore of Lake Alamoosook, both in Hancock County, Maine. (Willoughby, (1).

Wampanoag

Origins: southeastern Massachusetts and Rhode Island in the beginning of the 17th century, at the time of first contact with the English colonist

Similar deposits of the insoluble red oxide were associated with burials in an ancient cemetery discovered in 1913 in Warren, Bristol County, Rhode Island. This appears to have been a burying ground of the Wampanoag, within whose lands it was. When the site was destroyed some of the skeletons were exposed, together with a large number of objects of English, Dutch, and French origin, dating from the years between the first contact with the Europeans until the latter part of the seventeenth century. In some burials copper kettles were placed over the heads of the bodies. In such cases the copper salts acted as a preservative. One grave was of the greatest interest. It was that of a man well advanced in years, and associated with the remains were two ancient English swords, one or more gunlocks, a roll of military braid, and the traces of a feather headdress in a case. The suggestion has been made that these were the remains of the great Wampanoag chief, Massasoit, who met the Pilgrims at Plymouth in 1621, ever remained a friend of the colonists, and who died in 1662. One of his sons, Metacomet, became known as King Pliilip, famous in colonial history and leader in the war against the English settlements which terminated in the disastrous defeat of the Indians and the death of their leader, August 12, 1676.

Thus having three distinct references to the use of red oxide one on the coast of Maine in what should probably be accepted as graves, another in Rhode Island, and the third on Cape Cod—would make it appear that placing quantities of finely powdered red oxide of iron in graves with the human remains was a well-established custom of the Algonquian tribes found occupying the coast of New England when that rugged shore was settled by the English colonists. Similar burials will probably be discovered at some later day which will tend to substantiate this belief.

Plate 2

Closely flexed burials, examples of which are shown in plate 2, are characteristic of precolonial New England, but later, after coming under the influence and teachings of missionaries and others, the same tribes no longer used this form of burial, but placed the remains of the dead in an extended position, either wrapped in bark or deposited in roughly made wooden coffins. The latter form was

encountered during the partial exploration of the ancient Niantic cemetery, known as Fort Neck Burying Ground, in Charlestown, Washington County, Rhode Island, during the month of September, 1912. Another site, now designated "Indian Burying Hill," like wise in Charlestown, and now a State reservation, is known as the place of burial of the Niantic chiefs, among them Ninigret, by whom the Narraganset, who escaped destruction during King Philip's war, were later received.

According to Prof, H. H. Wilder, by whom the " Fort Neck Burying Ground" was examined, "the bodies had evidently been buried in winding-sheets only, as nothing was found indicating clothing." This would be consistent with the old custom of these Indians, as Roger Williams told of one "who winds up and buries the dead," and describing the burial customs said: " Mockkuttauce, One of the chiefest esteem, who winds up and buries the dead ; commonly some wise, grave, and well descended man hath that office. When they come to the grave, they lay the dead by the grave's mouth, and then all sit down and lament; that I have seen tears run down the cheeks of stoutest Captains, as well as little children in abundance; and after the dead is laid in Grave, and sometimes (in some parts) some goods cast in with them, they have then a second lamentation, and upon the grave is spread the Mat that the party died on, the Dish he eat in, and sometimes a fair coat of skin hung upon the next tree to the grave, which none will touch, but suffer it there to rot with the Dead : Yea I saw with mine own eyes that at my late coming forth of the country, the chief and most aged peaceable Father of the Country, Caunounicus, having buried his Sonne, he burned his own Palace, and all his goods in it (amongst them to a great value) in a solemne remembrance of his Sonne and in a kind of humble, Expiation to the Gods, who, (as they believe) had taken his sonne from him." *(Williams, A Key into the Language of America. London,]G48. Reprint in Collections Rhode Island Historical Society, Vol. T. I'rovidence 1827. (1), pp. 161-162.)*

Origin: Rhode Island

For this great Narraganset chief, Canonicus, to have destroyed his dwelling, with all its contents, at the time of the death and burial of his son was contrary to the usual customs of the Algonquian tribes, although such was the habit of several tribes of the South.

There is reason to suppose the burial customs of the many tribes who occupied New England did not differ to any great degree, and all may have had similar periods of mourning and enacted the same ceremonies to express their grief. Among the Housatonic or River Indians, later to be known as the Stockbridge Indians, the period of mourning was about one year. Thus it was described in the year 1736:

"The Keutikaw is a Dance which finishes the Mourning for the Dead and is celebrated about twelve Months after the Decease, when the guests invited make presents to the relations of the Deceased, to make up their Loss and to end their Mourning. The Manner of doing it is this:The Presents prepared are delivered to a Speaker appointed for the purpose; who, laying them upon the shoulders of some elderly person, makes a speech spewing the design of their present meeting, and the Presents prepared. Then he takes them and distributes them to the mourners adding some words of consolation, and desiring them to forget their sorrow, and accept of those presents to make up their loss. After this they eat together and make Merry." (*Hopkins, Historical Memoirs Relating to the Ilousntunnuk Indians. Boston, 1753.(1), p. 38.)*

This paragraph was taken from Sergeant's journal and bore the date January, 1736. It evidently recorded the customs of the Housatonic Indians at the time of the arrival of the missionary, and may have been the ancient custom of the Algonquian tribes of the region. Human remains have been discovered at various points in the valley of the Housatonic within the bounds of the lands once occupied by the tribe whose name the river perpetuates, and tradition locates one or more cemeteries west of the stream near the foot of the mountains, but no large group of burials is known to have ever been encountered.

Cairns, heaps of stones usually on some high and prominent point, are found throughout the southern mountains, but seldom have they been mentioned in the older settled parts of the north one, however, stood in the country of the Plousatonic Indians. As early as 1720 some English traders saw a large heap of stones on the " east side of Westenhook or Housatonic River, so called, on the southerly end of the mountain called Monument Mountain, between Stockbridge and Great Barrington." This circumstance gave rise to the name which has ever since been applied to the mountain, a prominent landmark in the valley. This ancient pile of stones may have marked the grave of some great man who lived and died before the coming of the colonists.

Many ancient graves have been discovered at different times and in widely separated parts of New England. Probably the most famed of the many burials thus encountered was the so-called " Skeleton in Armor," a closely flexed skeleton discovered in a sand bank at Fall River, Massachusetts, in 1831. Traces of several thicknesses of bark cloth were found about the remains and on the outside was a casing of cedar bark. Associated with the body were objects of brass, one being a plate of that material about 14 inches in length, and encircling the skeleton were traces of a belt to which had been attached many brass tubes each about 4 inches in length and one-quarter inch in diameter. The belt, made of metal obviously of European origin, was thought to be a piece of armor, which resulted in the name applied to the skeleton. The occurrence of brass with this burial is of interest as it is conclusive proof that flexed burials were prepared after the coming of the colonists. This example may date from about the middle of the seventeenth century.

Flexed skeletons are usually found in single graves, although two closely bound burials were discovered in one grave, on the left bank of the Connecticut River, at North Hadley, Massachusetts. This was on the site of an Indian village where, about the year 1675, the chief was named Quanquant, The Crow.

Cemeteries which may date from the earliest times are to be seen in the vicinity of Plymouth, and one of the largest in all New England is located in the town of Chilmark, on the island of Martha's Vineyard. Here 97 graves are marked by flat stones gathered from the surrounding surface and there are undoubtedly others which are not distinguishable. Several other burying places are known on the island, one being at Christiantown, the old Manitwatooiaii., or "God's Town," of 1668. It is well known that Marthas Vineyard was formerly the home of a large native population, by whom it was called Capawock.

Manhattan Island and Southward

An early description of the burial customs of the inhabitants of New Netherlands, probably based on some ceremonies witnessed on or near Manhattan Island, explains the manner and position in which the remains were deposited in the grave. "Whenever an Indian departs this life, all the residents of the place assemble at the funeral. To a distant stranger, who has not a friend or relative in the place, they pay the like respect. They are equally careful to commit the body to the earth, without neglecting any of the usual ceremonies, according to the standing of the deceased. In deadly diseases, they are faithful to sustain and take care of each other. Whenever a soul has departed, the nearest relatives extend the limbs and close the eyes of the dead ; after the body has been watched and wept over several days and nights, they bring it to the grave, wherein they do not lay it down, but place it in a sitting posture upon a stone or a block of wood, as if the body were sitting upon a stool ; then they place a pot, kettle, platter, spoon, with some provisions and money, near the body in the grave; this they say is necessary for the journey to the other world. Then they place as much wood around the body as will keep the earth from it. Above the grave they place a large pile of wood, stone or earth, and around and above the same they place palisades resembling a small dwelling." (Van der Donck,equally careful to commit the body to the earth, without neglecting any of the usual ceremonies, according to the standing of the deceased. In deadly diseases, they are faithful to sustain and take care of each other. Whenever a soul has departed, the nearest relatives extend the limbs and close the eyes of the dead ; after the body has been watched and wept over several days and nights, they bring it to the grave, wherein they do not lay it down, but place it in a sitting posture upon a stone or a block of wood, as if the body were sitting upon a stool ; then they place a pot, kettle, platter, spoon, with some provisions and money, near the body in the grave; this they say is necessary for the journey to the other world. Then they place as much wood around the body as will keep the earth from it. Above the grave they place a large pile of wood, stone or earth, and around and above the same they place palisades resembling a small dwelling." *(Van der Donck, Description of the New Netherlands. Reprint in Collections New York Historical Society. Second series, Vol. I. New York, 1841. (1), pp. 201-202.)*

This account may be equally applicable to the Algonquian tribes of the valley of the Hudson and the neighboring Iroquoian people who lived a short distance west of that stream. Evidently there is one slight error in the description, as the body was not placed in a horizontal position but arranged in a "sitting posture." It would have been useless to have extended the limbs as mentioned. Probably soon after death the body was flexed and wrapped, preparatory to being placed in the grave, and as will be shown later, this was likewise the custom among other tribes. It is interesting to recall how often the covering over the grave was likened to a small dwelling, and this tends to remind one of the customs of the ancient people of Egypt who, during the X, XI, and XII Dynasties (3600 to 3300 B. C.), placed pottery models of the dwellings of the living on the graves of the dead, "soul-houses" of various types and sizes, representing many forms of habitations and other structures. These were prepared as places for the soul to remain, to appease it and prevent it returning to the village. Could the dwelling-like covering over the graves of American aborigines have resulted from similar beliefs and desires?

A number of burials have been encountered at different times in the vicinity of Manhattan Island, on Staten Island, and near Pelham and other near-by places on the shore of the sound. A few years ago a Munsee cemetery was uncovered near Montague, New Jersey, where both flexed and extended burials were unearthed. This burial place evidently belonged to the transition period, the earlier graves being of the primitive form, the later containing various objects of European make. The Munsee, just mentioned, formed one of the three principal divisions of the Delaware, and it is within reason to suppose that when some of the burials discovered in the cemetery at Montague had been made ceremonies had been enacted similar to that described by Heckewelder. He wrote:

Delaware

A Delaware Indian,
with his Tomahawk Scalping knife &c.

Origins: New York state and eastern New Jersey, and western Long Island, New York.

"I was present in the year 1762, at the funeral of a woman of the highest rank and respectability, the wife of the valiant Delaware chief Shingask; . . . all the honors were paid to her at her interment that are usual on such occasions. ... At the moment that she died, her death was announced through the village by women especially appointed for that purpose, who went through the streets crying, *'She is no more! She is no more!'* The place on a sudden exhibited a scene of universal mourning; cries and lamentations were heard from all quarters." The following day the body was placed in a coffin which had been made by a carpenter employed by the Indian trader. The remains

81

had been " dressed and painted in the most superb Indian style. Her garments, all new, were set off with rows of silver broaches, one row joining the other. Over the sleeves of her new ruffled shirt were broad silver arm spangles from her shoulder down to her wrist, on which were bands, forming a kind of mittens, worked together of wampum, in the same manner as the belts which they use when they deliver speeches. Her long plaited hair was confined by broad bands of silver, one band joining the other, yet not of the same size, but tapering from the head downwards and running at the lower end to a point. On the neck were hanging five broad belts of wampum tied together at the ends, each of a size smaller than the other, the largest of which reached below her breast, the next largest reaching to a few inches of it, and so on, the uppermost one being the smallest. Her scarlet leggings were decorated with different colored ribbons sewed on,

the outer edges being finished off with small beads also of various colors. Her moccasins were ornamented with the most striking figures, wrought on the leather with colored porcupine quills, on the borders of which, round the ankles, were fastened a number of small round silver bells, of about the size of a musket ball. All these things together with the vermilion paint, judiciously laid on, so as to set her off in the highest style, decorated her person in such a manner, that perhaps nothing of the kind could exceed it." Later, " the spectators having retired, a number of articles were brought out of the house and placed in the coffin." These included articles of clothing, a dressed deerskin for the making of moccasins, needles, a pewter basin. " with a number of trinkets and other small articles which she was fond of while living." The coffin was then closed, the lid being held in place by three straps. Across it were then placed three poles, 5 or 6 feet in length, " also fastened with straps cut up from a tanned elk hide; and a small bag of vermilion paint, with some flannel to lay it on, was then thrust into the coffin through the hole cut out at the head of it. This hole, the Indians say, is for the spirit of the deceased to go in and out at pleasure, until it has found the place of its future residence." Six persons then grasped the ends of the three poles and carried the coffin to the grave. The six consisted of four men, at the front and back, and two women between. " Several women from a house about thirty yards off, now started off, carrying large kettles, dishes, spoons, and dried elk meat in baskets, and for the burial place, and the signal being given for us to move with the body, the women who acted as chief mourners made the air resound with their shrill cries. The order of the procession was as follows: first a leader or guide, from the spot where we were to the place of interment. Next followed the corpse, and close to it Shingask the husband of the deceased. He was followed by the principal war chiefs and counselors of the nation, after whom came men of all ranks and descriptions. Then followed the women and children, and lastly two stout men carrying loads of European manufactured goods upon their backs. The chief mourners on the women's side, not having joined in the ranks, took their own course to the right, at the distance of about fifteen or twenty yards from us, but always opposite to the corpse." Thus they moved along for a distance of about 200 yards to the open grave, and when it was reached the lid was removed from the coffin, and "the whole train formed themselves into a kind of semi lunar circle on the south side of the grave, and seated themselves on the ground, while the disconsolate Shingask retired by himself to a spot at some distance, where he was seen weeping, with his head bowed to the ground. The female mourners seated themselves promiscuously near to each other, among some low bushes that were at the distance of from twelve to fifteen yards east of the grave. In this situation we remained for the space of more than two hours; not a sound was heard from any quarter, though the numbers that attended were very great ; nor did any person move from his seat to view the body, which had been lightly covered over with a clean white sheet. All appeared to be in profound reflection and solemn mourning. ... At length, at about one o'clock in the afternoon, six men stepped forward to put the lid upon the coffin, and let down the body into the grave, when suddenly three of the women mourners rushed from their seats, and forcing themselves between these men and the corpse, loudly called to the deceased to ' arise and go with them and not forsake them. They even took hold of her arms and legs; at first it seemed as if they were caressing her, afterwards they appeared to pull with more violence, as if they intended to run away with the body, crying out all the while, ' Arise, arise ! Come with us !' ... As soon as these women had gone through their part of the ceremony, which took up about fifteen minutes, the six men whom they had interrupted and who had remained at the distance of about five feet from the corpse, again stepped forward and did their duty. They let down the coffin into the earth, and laid two thin poles of about four inches diameter, from which the bark had been taken off, length ways, and close together over the grave, after which they retired." The husband, Shingask, then came slowly forward and walked over the poles, and continued on to the prairie. Then a "painted post, on which were drawn various figures, emblematic of the deceased's situation in life and of her having been the wife of a valiant warrior, was brought by two men and delivered to a third, a man of note, who placed it in such a manner that it rested on the coffin at the head of the grave, and took great care that a certain part of the drawings should be exposed to the east, or rising of the sun; then while he held the post erect and properly situated, some women filled up the grave with hoes, and having placed dry leaves and pieces of bark over it, so that none of the fresh ground was visible, they retired, .and some men, with timbers fitted before hand for the purpose, enclosed the grave about breast-high, so as to secure it from the approach of the wild beasts."

After this food was prepared and passed about, then the presents were distributed, the many things which had been carried by the two men in the rear of the procession. Those who had rendered assistance were given the most valuable and highly prized pieces, but no one was omitted. Articles to the value of about $200 were thus given away. Men, women, and children alike were remembered. *(Heckewelder, An Account of the History, Planners, and Customs of the Indian Nations who once inhabited Pennsylvania and the Neighboring States. In Transactions American Philosophical Society, Vol. I. Philadelphia, 1819. (1), pp. 264-270.)* At dusk after the burial, a kettle of food was placed upon the grave, and this was renewed every evening for three weeks, after which time, so they thought, food was no longer required by the spirit.

When an Indian died away from his village, so Heckewelder wrote (op. cit., p. 270), "great care is taken that the grave be well fortified with posts and logs laid upon it, that the wolves may be prevented from getting at the corpse; when time and circumstances do not permit this, as, for instance, when the Indians are traveling, the body is enclosed in the bark of trees and thus laid in the grave. When a death takes place at their hunting camps, they make a kind of coffin as well as they can, or put a cover over the body, so that the earth may not sink on it, and then enclose the grave with a fence of poles." These scattered burials, made away from settlements, readily explain the occurrence of the isolated graves often found at the present time, and few if any objects of a lasting nature were deposited with the bodies.

Heckewelder did not give the exact location of the burial of the wife of the Delaware chief Skingask although he gave the date, 1762, and elsewhere in his narrative mentioned living at that time" at Tuscarawas on the Muskingum." To have reached Tuscarawas he would have traversed the great trail leading westward from western Pennsylvania, passing the mouth of Beaver River, a stream which flows from the north and enters the right bank of the Ohio 28| miles below Pittsburgh. On the map which accompanied Washington's Journal, printed in London in 1754, a Delaware village is indicated on the right bank of the Ohio just below the mouth of the Beaver. Two years later, on a small map in the *London Magazine for December, 1756*, this Delaware village bore the name Shingoes town, and so it continued on various maps until long after the Revolution, although the name was spelled in many ways. Undoubtedly Shingask of Heckewelder was the Shingoe whose town stood at the mouth of the Beaver, and here occurred the burial of the wife of the Delaware chief, probably when Heckewelder was on his way to Tuscarawas, some miles westward.

When Col. Bouquet traversed the same trail on his expedition against the native villages beyond the Ohio he crossed Beaver Creek. This was on Saturday, October 6, 1764, and there were then standing near the ford about seven houses, which were deserted and destroyed by the Indians, after their defeat at Bushy Run, when they forsook all their remaining settlements in this part of the country. The battle of Bushy Run took place during the two days, August 5 and 6, 1763, and consequently the village at the mouth of the Beaver, evidently Shingoes town, was abandoned the year after it was visited by Heckewelder, but the name continued on certain maps long after that time.

Some very interesting references to the burial customs of the people of the same region, more particularly the Delaware, are contained in a work by another missionary. It was said that the place of burial was some distance from the dwellings, and that the graves were usually prepared by old women, as the younger members of the tribes disliked such work. "Before they had hatchets and other tools,
they used to line the inside of the grave with the bark of trees, and when the corpse was let down, they placed some pieces of wood across, which were again covered with bark, and then the earth thrown in, to fill up the grave. But now they usually place three boards, not nailed together, into the grave, in such a manner that the corpse may lie between them. A fourth board being laid over it as a cover, the grave is filled up with earth. Now and then they procure a proper coffin. ... If they have a coffin, it is placed in the grave empty. Then the corpse is carried out, lying upon a linen cloth, full in view, that the finery and ornaments, with all the effects left by the deceased, may appear to advantage, and accompanied by as great a number of friends as can be collected. It is then let down into the coffin, covered with the cloth, and the lid being nailed down, the grave is filled up with earth. During the letting down of the corpse the women set up a dreadful howl, but it is deemed a shame in a man to weep. Yet in silence and unobserved, they cannot refrain from tears. At the head of the corpse, which always lies towards the east, a tall post is erected, pointing out who is buried there. If the deceased was the Chief of a tribe or nation, this post is only neatly carved, but not painted. But if he was a captain, it is painted red, and his head and glorious deeds are portrayed upon it. This is also done in honor of a great warrior, his warlike deeds being exhibited in red colors. The burial-post of a physician is hung with small tortoise shells or a calabash, which he used in his practice. After the burial the greater part of the goods left by the deceased are distributed among those who assisted in burying him, and are not related to him. . . . After the

ceremony is over, the mother, grandmother, and other near relations retire after sunset, and in the morning early, to weep over the grave. This they repeat daily for some time, but gradually less and less, till the mourning is over. Sometimes they place victuals upon the grave, that the deceased may not suffer hunger." And following this is an account of the mourning for the dead. (*Loskiel, History of the Mission of the United Brethren among the Indians in North America, 1794.(1), pt. 1, pp. 119-121.*)

In the preceding description of the manner in which graves were prepared by the Delaware about the last years of the eighteenth century there is something quite suggestive of the stone-lined graves. In
both instances pits were dug, to be lined in earlier days with thin, natural slabs of stone, and later, when boards were obtainable, they were used in the place of stones. Then when coffins were to be had they were looked upon as a ready-prepared grave lining, one which did not require any fitting together when placed inside the grave. And so the grave would be dug of a size to accommodate the wooden lining—the coffin—which had already been fastened together, and when the grave was thus lined the body would be placed within it. Such was the custom and such was the characteristic reasoning of the Indian.

The Nanticoke

Origins: Delaware and Maryland

The Nanticoke, who lived on the Eastern Shore of Maryland, were connected, linguistically, with the Delaware, and before the latter removed westward beyond the Alleghenies they were neighboring tribes. The Nanticoke were encountered by Capt. John Smith and his party of colonists from Jamestown in 1608, living on or near the river which continues to bear their tribal name. For many
years they were enemies of the colonists but remained in the region until about 1730, when the majority of the tribe began moving northward, stopping at the mouth of the Juniata, and elsewhere in the valley of the Susquehanna, at last arriving in southern New York on the eastern branch of the latter stream, where they rested under protection of the Iroquois, who then dominated that section. Tribal movements were often slow and deliberate, with stops of years on the way, and a generation elapsed between the starting of the Nanticoke from the Eastern Shore and their arrival among the Iroquois. Like many tribes, they removed the remains of the dead from their old home to their new settlements. This was witnessed by Heckewelder, who wrote (op. cit., pp. 75-76): "These Nanticokes had the singular custom of removing the bones of their deceased friends from the burial place to a place of deposit in the country they dwell in. In earlier times they were known to go from Wyoming and Chemenk, to fetch the bones of their dead from the Eastern Shore of Maryland, even when the bodies were in a putrid state, so that they had to take off the flesh and scrape the bones clean, before they could carry them along. I well remember having seem them between the years 1750 and 1760, loaded with such bones, which, being fresh, caused a disagreeable stench, as they passed through the town of Bethlehem."

One of the ancient Nanticoke sites, one probably occupied at the time of the discovery of the people by the Virginia colonists, stood on the left bank of Choptank River, some 2 miles below Cambridge, Dorchester County, on the Eastern Shore of Maryland. This village was occupied until the year 1722, or until the tribe began their movement northward. Since this site was abandoned, sand, blown and drifted by the winds, has covered the original surface to a depth of many feet. And during the same interval the exposed face of the cliff has receded, caused by the encroachment of the waters of the Choptank. Now, as the result of these two natural phenomena, the surface once occupied by the village of the Nantcoke appears on the face of the cliff as a dark line or stratum, from one-half to 1 foot in thickness, and extending for about one-third of a mile along the shore, thus proving the extent of the ancient settlement. At one point on the exposed face of the cliff a quantity of human bones were visible, and when examined this proved to be "a hard-set horizontal bed of human bones and skulls, many of them well preserved, about 1 to 2 feet thick, 10 feet long, 3 feet under the village site stratum," and further excavation showed this mass of bones to be " of irregular, circular shape, 25 feet in longest by 20 feet in shortest diameter and 1to 2 feet thick (thickest in the middle, and tapering at the sides)." A short distance inward and directly above the larger deposit was another mass of bones, this being about 7 feet long, 7 inches thick, and 2 feet wide. The two deposits were separated by about ½ feet of sand. "In the main or lower deposit some of the bones had and others had not, been subjected to fire. The bone layer might have been subdivided thus: First, the bottom (6 inches), Where the bones were in small fragments, blackened and bedded in masses of charcoal and ashes; second, the middle, next above (5 to 10 inches), where the skulls and bones, though somewhat charred, were intact; and third, the top (6 to 8 inches), where the bones, though mixed with bits of charcoal, showed no direct trace of fire. The conditions proved that many skeletons had been burned in the lower part of the main bed." The ones in the smaller deposit " were generally intact in tolerable preservation, and in spite of the bits of scattered charcoal found with them, showed no direct signs of charring." *(Mercer,) Exploration of an Indian Ossuary on the Choptank River, Dorchester County Maryland. In Publications University of Pennsylvania, Vol. VI. 1897 (1) pp. 93-94.)*

Ossuaries of this form are not characteristic of any Algonquian tribe, but at once suggest the customs of the Huron and other northern Iroquoian people. This large deposit of human remains may have resulted through some great emergency, at some time when it became necessary to dispose of many bodies which were placed in one common grave, rather than preparing a separate one for each.

Single graves have been exposed on the face of the cliff, evidently near the ossuaries, which tends to prove this particular spot to have been the cemetery adjoining the ancient village.

The county of Dorchester is bounded on the southeast by the Nanticoke River, and human remains have been discovered on the right bank of the stream just above the village of Vienna, and undoubtedly many other burial places have been encountered within this region, once comparatively thickly peopled, no records of which are preserved.

The Powhaton Confederacy

Origins: Virginia

It is to be regretted that more is not known concerning the burial customs of the Algonquian tribes of Virginia, those who constituted the Powhatan confederacy, people with whom the Jamestown colonists came in contact during the Spring of 1607. Several accounts are preserved, but unfortunately all are lacking in detail. Capt. Smith included burial customs under the general caption Of their Religion and in 1612 wrote:

"But their chief God they worship is the Devil, Him they call Oke and serve him more of fear than love. They say they have conference with him, and fashion themselves as near to his shape as they can imagine. In their Temples, they have his image evil favorably carved, and then painted and adorned with chains, copper, and beads; and covered with a skin, in such manner as the deformity may well suit with such a God. By him is commonly the sepulcher of their kings. Their bodies are first bowelled, then dried upon hurdles till they be very dry, and so about the most of their joints and neck they hang bracelets or chains of copper, pearl, and such like, as they use to wear: their inwards they stuff with copper beads and cover with a skin, hatchets, and such trash. Then lappe they them very carefully in white skins, and so rolls them in mats for their winding sheets. And in the Tombe, which is an arch made of mats, they lay them orderly. What remaineth of this kind of wealth their kings have, they set at their feet in baskets. These Temples and bodies are kept by their Priests In every Territory of a werowance is a Temple and a Priest or 2 or 3 more. Their principal Temple or place of superstition is at Vttamussack at Pamaunke, near unto which is a house Temple or place of Powhatans. Upon the top of certain red sandy hills in the woods, there are 3 great houses filled with images of their kings and Devils and Tombs of their Predecessors. Those houses are near 60 foot in length, built arbor wise, after their building. This place they count so holy as that none but the Priests and kings dare come into them: nor the Savages dare not go up the river in boats by it, but that they solemnly cast some piece of copper, white beads, or Pocones into the river, for fear their Oke should be offended and revenged of them." *(Smith,Capt. John. (1) A Map of Virginia, With a Description of the Country. Oxford, 1612, reprint Birmingham, 1884. (1), pp. 75-76.)*

Strachey's account of the burial customs does not differ greatly from the preceding; both writers referred to the same time and generation, and few of the natives then living had ever seen a white man until the coming of the Jamestown colonists in 1607.

A temple or tomb similar to those described by Smith was encountered by the English on the coast of North Carolina during the summer of 1585, at which time it was sketched by the artist John White, a member of the second expedition sent out by Sir Walter Raleigh. The original drawing, together with many others made at the same time, is preserved in the British Museum, London. A photograph of the original is now reproduced in plate 3, b:

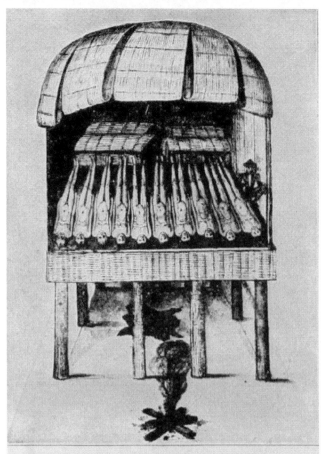

b. TOMB INSIDE THE "TEMPLE" AT SECOTAN, 1585

The legend on the sketch reads: "The Tomb of their Cherounes or chief personages their flesh clean taken of from the bones save the skin and hair of their heads, which flesh is dried and enfolded in matts laid at three feet their bones also being made dry are covered with" dear skins not altering their form or proportion. With their Kywash, which is an image of wood keeping the dead." This drawing was engraved and used by De Bry as plate 22 in Hariot's Narrative, published in 1591. But in the engraving the tomb, as drawn by White, is represented as placed within an enclosure, evidently the "temple," and this would conform with the legend near one of the buildings shown standing at the village of Secotan. In White's view of this ancient town the structure in the lower left corner bears this description : " The house where the Tomb of their werowans stand This is copied in plate 3, being a detail from the large sketch of Secotan. It is evident from the early drawing that the so-called "tomb" was an elevated platform erected within a structure of ordinary form, and the whole must have resembled rather closely the " temples " or " bone-houses " of certain Muskhogean tribes of the south, as will be shown later. But unfortunately nothing is told by the old writers of the final disposition of the human remains which were first placed in the " temples," as at Secotan. Later they may have been collected and deposited in graves, or they may have become scattered and lost, but this is doubtful.

The temple tombs, as already described, appear to have stood near, or rather belonged to, the larger, more permanent settlements, and so became the resting places of the more important dead of the community. However, it is quite evident the remains of the chief men were not placed in ordinary graves, even though a "temple" was not available. This is of great interest and is revealed in a deposition made by one Francis Tomes, relating to the Wyanoak or Weanoc, in the year 1661, after they had removed southward from the banks of the James. The deposition reads in part :"Then came in sight of the Wyanoak Indian Town which was on the South Side of Wyanoak River where they forded over to the town wherein stood an English built house, in which the King had been shot & an apple orchard. From thence they went about two or three miles to the Westward where in an elbow of a swamp stood a Fort near which in the swamp the murdered King was laid on a scaffold & covered with Skins & matts which I saw." *(Virginia Magazine,*

But a simpler form of burial existed among the native inhabitants of tidewater Virginia, and probably the great majority found their final resting places in graves prepared near the villages. Smith wrote (op. cit., p. 75) : " For their ordinary burials, they dig a deep hole in the earth with sharp stakes; and the corpses being lapped in skins and mats with their jewels, they lay them upon sticks in the ground, and so cover them with earth. The burial ended, the womennbeihg painted all their faces with black coal and oil, doe sit 24 hours in the houses mourning and lamenting by turns, with such yelling and howling as may express their great passions."Very few ancient burial places have been discovered within the region described by Smith, or probably it would be more correct to say few records of such discoveries, if made, have been preserved, therefore it is gratifying to find a single reference which tends to verify Smith's account of " their ordinary burials." This refers to discoveries made about the year 1835 on the right bank of the Chickahominy, in Charles City County, Virginia, on the land of Col. J. S. Stubblefield. It mentioned a large shell heap which extended for some 150 yards along the bank of the stream and had a width of from 30 to 40 yards, and continued by saying: "In this deposit of shells are found a number of human bones of all sizes, from the smallest infant to the full grown man, interred in pits of various size, and circular form; and in each pit are found intermingled, human bones of every size. Standing in one place I counted fifty of these hollows, from each of which had been taken the remains of human beings who inhabited this country before the present race of whites" *(Christian, Letter. In The Farmers' Register, Vol. Ill, No. 3. .Tuly. Peterburg, Va., 1835. (1), p. 150.)*

This site does not appear to have been known to Capt. Smith, as no town is shown by him as standing on the right bank of the river, in what would probably have been included in the present Charles City County. The burials discovered in 1835 may have been made before the days of the colony.

Werowance

Origin: Tidewater of Virgina

According to Pinkerton [Footnote: Collection of Voyages, 1812, vol. XIII, p 39.], the Werowanco preserved their dead as follows:

"… By him is commonly the sepulchre of their Kings. Their bodies are first bowelled, then dried upon hurdles till they be very dry, and so about the most of their joints and neck they hang bracelets, or chains of copper, pearl, and such like, as they used to wear. Their inwards they stuff with copper beads, hatchets, and such trash. Then lap they them very carefully in white skins, and so roll them in mats for their winding-sheets. And in the tomb, which is an arch made of mats, they lay them orderly. What remaineth of this kind of wealth their Kings have, they set at their feet in baskets. These temples and bodies are kept by their priests.

"For their ordinary burials, they dig a deep hole in the earth with sharp stakes, and the corpse being lapped in skins and mats with their jewels they lay them upon sticks in the ground, and so cover them with earth. The burial ended, the women being painted all their faces with black coal and oil do sit twenty-four hours in the houses mourning and lamenting by turns with such yelling and howling as may express their great passions….

"Upon the top of certain red sandy hills in the woods there are three great houses filled with images of their Kings and devils and tombs of their predecessors. Those houses are near sixty feet in length, built harbourwise after their building. This place they count so holy as that but the priests and Kings dare come into them; nor the savages dare not go up the river in boats by it, but they solemnly cast some piece of copper, white beads, or pocones into the river for fear their Okee should be offended and revenged of them.

"They think that their Werowances and priests which they also esteem, when they are dead do go beyond the mountains towards the setting of the sun, and ever remain there in form of their Okee, with their heads painted red with oil and pocones, finely trimmed with feathers, and shall have beads, hatchets, copper, and tobacco, doing nothing but dance and sing with all their predecessors. But the common people they suppose shall not live after death, but rot in their graves like dead dogs."

Algonquin West of the Alleghenies

Miami

Little Turtle. 1778.

Origins: Indiana, Illinois, and southern Michigan

Correspondence of Burial Customs
The tribe occupying this locality at the advent of the whites was the Miamis, having their principal seat of government at "Kekionga," now Fort Wayne, at the junction of the St. Mary's and St. Joseph's rivers, where they unite to form the Maumee (a corruption of the word Miami).
Three forms of burial have been noticed as belonging to the modern Indians in this locality.
1. The ordinary ground burial in a shallow grave, prepared to receive the body in a recumbent position. In these graves are usually found flint arrow and spear heads, occasionally stone axes and hatchets, pipes, shell and glass beads, some copper ornaments, and silver brooches and trinkets. The copper and silver ornaments are confined to comparatively late burials, since the advent of the whites. Sometimes guns, knives, and hatchet of civilized manufacture are found in these graves.
2. The surface burial in a hollow log. These have been found in heavy forests. Sometimes a tree has been split and the two halves hollowed out to receive the body, when it is either closed with with or confined to the ground by crossed stakes; or sometimes a hollow tree is used by closing the ends.
3. The surface burial, where the body was covered by a small pen of logs, laid up as we build a log cabin,

drawing in every course until they meet at the top in a single log. in this and neighboring counties, I find a great diversity. Home contain the remains of numerous skeletons, or fragmentary skeletons, which have among them many calcined bones. Others have been the burial place of but one individual, while others have held two or three. Those mounds which contain from one to five rarely show any signs of cremation, and usually have the accompanying arms, utensils, and ornaments, with one or two earthen vessels for food, etc., while those in which the' remains arc more numerous seldom have anything except broken   fragments of pottery and flints. Sometimes the burial is in a recumbent position, and sometimes a sitting posture. The indications of fire, in the form of ashes and charcoal, arc found in every mound I have seen opened, but it does not always indicate the practice of cremation.

4.   For further details of the aboriginal remains, 1 would refer to three articles published in the *Smithsonian Report for 1874*, entitled, *"Antiquities of Laporte County," "Antiquities of Allen and De Kalb Counties,"* and the *"Troglodytes of Breckenridge County, Ky." Also to a memoir of the Mound Builders which will appear in the Compte Rendu for 1877 of the Congress International des Americanistes, held at Luxembourg, Sept. 10-* R. S. Robertson.

W. A. Brice mentions a curious variety of surface burial not heretofore met with:

  And often had been seen, years ago, swinging from the bough of a tree, or in a hammock stretched between two trees, the infant of the Indian mother; or a few little log enclosures, where the bodies of adults sat upright, with all their former apparel wrapped about them, and their trinkets, tomahawks, &c., by their side, could be seen at any time for many years by the few pale-faces visiting or sojourning here. *Hist. of Ft. Wayne, 1868, p. 284.*

Pottawatomie

Potawatomi Chief Crane and Brave

Origin: southern Michigan and the upper peninsula of Michigan, in northern Indiana, northeastern Wisconsin,

  Judge H. Welchstates that "the Sauks, Foxes, and Pottawatomies buried by setting the body on the ground and building a pen around it of sticks or logs. I think the bodies lay heads to the east." And C.C. Baldwin, of Cleveland, Ohio, sends a more detailed account, as follows:

I was some time since in Seneca County and there met Judge Welch. In 1824 he went with his father-in-law, Judge Gibson, to Fort Wayne. On the way they passed the grave of an Ottawa or Pottawatomie chief. The body lay on the ground covered with notched poles. It had been there but a few days and the worms were crawling around the body. My special interest in the case was the accusation of witchcraft against a young squaw who was executed for killing him by her arts. *Tract No. 50, West. Reserve and North. Ohio Hist. Soc. (1879?), p. 107.*

Ojibwa

Origins: Michigan, Wisconsin, Minnesota, North Dakota, and Ontario.

The burial customs of some western Algonquian tribes were, in many respects, quite similar to those of the New England Indians. It will be recalled that soon after the Mayflower touched at Cape Cod a party of the Pilgrims went ashore and during their explorations discovered several groups of graves, some of which "had like an Indian house made over them, but not matted. They may when erected have been covered with mats. The similarity between this early reference and the description of certain Ojibway graves, two centuries and more later, is very interesting. Writing from the American Fur Company's trading establishment Fond du Lac, July 30, 1826," McKenney told of an Ojibway grave then standing at that post, near the extreme southwestern corner of Lake Superior. "The Indians' graves are first covered over with bark. Over the grave the same shelter is made, and of the same materials, as enter into the form and structure of a lodge. Poles are stuck into the ground, and bent over, and fastened at the top ; and these are covered with bark. Thus the grave is enclosed. An opening is left like that in the door of a lodge. Before this door (I am describing a grave that is here), a post is planted, and the dead having been a warrior, is painted red. Near this post, a pole is stuck in the ground, about ten feet long. From the top of this pole is suspended the ornaments of the deceased. From this, I see hanging a strand of beads, some strips of white fur, several trinkets, six bits of tobacco, that looked like quids, and a little frame of a circular form with net work, in the center of which (it being of thread) is fastened a scalp about three inches in diameter, the hair of which is of a dark brown color, and six inches long. In the top of the red post are three feathers." *(McKenney,) Sketches of a Tour to the Lakes. Baltimore, 1827(1), pp. 283-284.)*

Three days before, on July 27, McKenney entered m his journal: "We are yet about eighteen miles from the Fond du Lac. At this place. Burnt river is a place of divination, the seat of a Jongleux's incantations. It is a circle, made of eight poles, twelve feet high, and crossing at the top, which being covered in with mats, or bark, he enters, and foretells future events!"

a. OJIBWAY GRAVES AT MILLE LAC, MINNESOTA, 1900

The manner in which the bodies had been placed in the graves of the Fond du Lac cemetery was probably similar to that followed by other members of the tribe, as described of one well versed in the customs of the Ojibwa: "When an Ojibwa dies, his body is placed in a grave, generally in a sitting posture, facing the west. With the body are buried all the articles needed in life for a journey. If a man, his gun, blanket, kettle, fire steel, flint, and moccasins; if a woman, her moccasins, ax, portage collar, blanket and kettle." (Warren, Memoir. In Collections Minnesota Historical Society, Vol. V. St.

Paul, 1885. (1), pp. 72-73.) And following this is an account of the Ojibwa belief of happenings after death; how "the soul is supposed to stand immediately after the death of the body, on a deep beaten path, which leads westward." He first comes to strawberries, Which he gathers to eat on the way, and soon "reaches a deep, rapid stream of water, over which lies the much dreaded Ko-go-gaup-o-gun or rolling and sinking bridge." Thence, after traveling four days, and camping at night, "the soul arrives in the land of spirits," where all is joy and happiness.

The preceding is one of the most interesting records of the burial customs of a northern tribe extant and for that reason has been quoted at length. It was prepared by one who knew the Indian in his primitive state. The burials as they appeared at that time undoubtedly resembled others which stood in the same region a little more than half a century later, "the secluded Ojibway graves, on the banks of Red River," where were to be seen " Sioux scalps decorated with beads, bits of cloth, colored ribbons, and strips of leather suspended at the extremity of a long slender stick, near the head of the grave." (Hind, p. 120.) Two photographs, probably the first ever made in the Red River Valley, taken in the year 1858 by a member of the Hind expedition, are now reproduced in Plates 2 and 3. These show the covered graves surrounded by fences to serve as additional protection, and probably did not differ in appearance from the graves of the ancestors of the same people through many generations.

INDIAN GRAVES, COVERED WITH SPLIT STICKS

Photograph by Humphrey L. Hime, on the banks of Red River, 1858

INDIAN GRAVES, COVERED WITH BIRCH BARK

Photograph by Humphrey L. Hime, on the banks of Red River, 1858

SIOUX BURIAL MOUND, WITH RECENT OJIBWAY GRAVES

Mille Lac, Minn., May 29, 1900

Ojibwa Use Sioux Burial Mounds to Intrusively bury their Dead.

On the shores of Mille Lac and in the surrounding region, near the center of the present State of Minnesota, stood the numerous villages of the Dakota two centuries and more ago. It is quite evident, as will be shown in the following pages, that the Dakota were the builders of the many small burial mounds now discovered in the region, and it is of the greatest interest to know that the Ojibway, the later comers, acknowledge the mounds to have been erected by the earlier occupants of the land whom they, by force of arms, pushed southward and westward to and beyond the Mississippi. These mounds, the known burial places of the Siouan tribes, served the invaders as elevated sites for graves of their own dead. Thus we have the explanation of the origin of the so-called " intrusive burials," such as may be encountered in the majority of ancient mounds throughout the length and breadth of the Mississippi Valley.

During the spring of 1900 several of the larger ancient mounds at the Ojibway village of Sagawamick, on the south shore of Mille Lac, were covered with recent Ojibwaw graves. A typical example is shown in Plate 1, from a photograph made during the month of May of that year. The graves, as will be noticed, were surrounded by pickets to protect them from the innumerable dogs belonging to the village, and from wild animals as well. Great changes have taken place in the appearance of the country during the quarter of a century since the picture was made.

The Iroquois

Origin: Lake Ontario Region

The mortuary practices of the Five Nations Iroquois are inferred from sparse data that fits the pattern observed in the Seneca data. Unfortunately this view has many holes through it as there are major pieces of the Seneca pattern missing from the Mohawk, Oneida, Onondaga, and Cayuga sites. The mass of "negative evidence" for burials in these other nations indicates that different mortuary practices were followed and although this factor has been recognized it has not been explored. *Patterns of Iroquois Burial, Daniel H. Weiskotten 2000*

Iroquoian tribes occupied the greater part of the present State of New York, forming the League of the Iroquois, which often held the balance of power between the French and British colonies. Towns were numerous and frequently consisted of a strongly protected group of bark-covered houses, including the extended communal dwellings, some of which were 80 feet or more in length. The five nations of the league were the Mohawk, Cayuga, Oneida, Onondaga, and Seneca. The Susquehanna, met by a party of Virginia colonists in 1608 near the mouth of the stream which bears the tribal name, the Cherokee of the southern mountain country, and the Tuscarora and neighboring tribes, were members of this linguistic family. The Tuscarora moved northward early in the eighteenth century and in 1722 became the sixth nation of the league.

The Five Nations

Writing of the Iroquois or Five Nations, during the early years of the eighteenth century, at a time when they dominated the greater part of the present State of New York, it was said: "Their funeral Rites seem to be formed upon a notion of some kind of existence after death. They make a large round hole, in which the body can be placed upright, or upon its haunches, which after the body is placed in it, is covered with timber, to support the earth which they lay over, and thereby keep the body free from being pressed; they then raise the earth in a round hill over it. They always dress the corps in all its finery, and put wampum and other things into the grave with it; and the relations suffer not grass or any weed to grow on the Grave, and frequently visit it with lamentations."

The following account is out of the Iroquois homeland,but the burial type matches the description above. "A very singular case of aboriginal burial was brought to my notice recently by Mr. *William* Klingbeil, of Philadelphia. On the New Jersey bank of the Delaware River, a short distance below Gloucester City, the skeleton of a man was found buried in a standing position, in a high, red, sandy-clay bluff overlooking the stream. A few inches below the surface the neck bones were found, and below these the remainder of the skeleton, with the exception of the bones of the hands and feet. The skull being wanting, it could not be determined whether the remains were those of an Indian or of a white man, but in either case the sepulture was peculiarly aboriginal. A careful exhumation and critical examination by Mr. Klingbeil disclosed the fact that around the lower extremities of the body had been placed a number of large stones, which revealed traces of fire, in conjunction with charred wood, and the bones of the feet had undoubtedly been consumed. This fact makes it appear reasonably certain that the subject had been executed, probably as a prisoner of war. A pit had been dug, in which he was placed erect, and a fire kindled around him. Then he had been buried alive, or, at least, if he did not survive the fiery ordeal, his body was embedded in the earth, with the exception of his head, which was left protruding above the surface. As no trace of the cranium could be found, it seems probable that the head had either been burned or severed from the body and removed, or else left a prey to ravenous birds. The skeleton, which would have measured fully six feet in height, was undoubtedly that of a man." *Introduction to the Study of Mortuary Customs Among the North American Indians, 1880*

(Golden, The History of the Five Indian Nations of Canada. London, Second edition. (l),p. 16.)
The circular mound of earth over the grave was likewise mentioned a century earlier, having been seen at the Oneida village which stood east of the present Munnsville, Madison County, New York. Before we reached the castle we saw three graves, just like our graves in length and height; usually their graves are round. These graves were surrounded with palisades that they had split from trees, and they were closed up so nicely that it was a wonder to see. They were painted with red and white and black paint; but the chief's grave had an entrance, and at the top of that was a big wooden bird, and all around were painted dogs and deer and snakes, and other beasts." *(Van Curler, Journal of . . . 1634-1635 Annual Report American Historical Association for the year 1895. Washington, 1896. (1), p. 92.)*
Within recent years a cemetery has been discovered about 2 miles northeast of Munnsville, and just south of it has been located a site protected by a stockade. This may have been the position of the great Oneida town, but the nature of the burials is not known. Whether the two preceding accounts referred to graves of sufficient magnitude to be classed as mounds, or whether they alluded merely to a small mass of earth raised over an individual pit burial, is difficult to determine; nevertheless burial mounds do occur throughout the country of the Iroquois, but they are neither numerous nor large.
In Erie County, near the bank of Buffalo Creek, formerly stood a rather irregular embankment, semicircular in form, and touching the steep bank at both ends. The enclosed area was about 4 acres. This was one of the favorite sites of the Senecas, and within the enclosure was one of their largest cemeteries. Here is the grave of "the haughty and unbending Red Jacket, who died exulting that the Great Spirit had made him an Indian ! . . . Tradition fixes upon this spot as the scene of the final and most bloody conflict between the Iroquois and the ' Gah-kwas or Eries. . . . The old mission-house and church stand in close proximity to this mark.

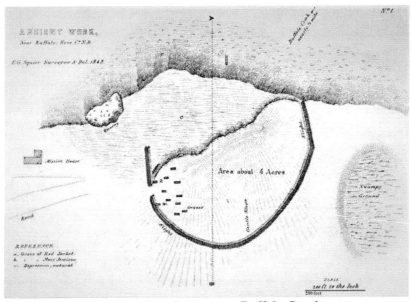

Earthwork and graves on Buffalo Creek

One of the most interesting works in this county is that here represented. It derives much of its interest from the associations connected with it. The site which it occupies was a favorite spot with the Senecas, and one of their largest cemeteries occurs within its walls. Here is buried an Indian chief whose name is inseparably interwoven with the history of the Five Nations. He was a man who possessed a rare combination of talents, which, developed under different circumstances, would have secured for him a high position among the greatest statesmen and proudest orators of the world. This is hardly a proper place to speak of his character; but his devoted patriotism, hi inflexible integrity, the unwavering firmness, calm and lofty dignity, and powerful eloquence with which he opposed the encroachments of the whites, notwithstanding that he knew all resistance was vain and hopeless—command an involuntary tribute to the memory of the last and noblest of the proud and politic Iroquois, the haughty and unbending Red Jacket, who died exulting that the Great Spirit had made him an Indian! Here, too, is buried Mary Jemison, "the white woman," who, taken a prisoner by the Indians when a child, conformed to their habits, became the wife of one of their chiefs, and remained with them until her death. The story of her life is one of the most eventful of those connected with our border history, filled as it is with thrilling adventures and startling incidents. *Aboriginal Monuments of the State of New York, 1849*

. . . Red Jacket's house stood above a third of a mile to the southward upon the same elevation; and the abandoned council-house is still standing, perhaps a mile distant, in the direction of Buffalo. A little distant beyond, in the same direction and near the public road, is a small mound, called Dah-do-sot artificial hill, by the Indians, who, it is said, were accustomed to regard it with much veneration, supposing that it covered the victims slain in some bloody conflict in the olden times It was originally between five and six feet in height by thirty-five or forty feet base, and composed of the adjacent loam. It was partially examined, and only a few bits of charcoal, some half-formed arrowheads, etc., were found. *(Squier, Aboriginal Monuments of the State of New York. In Smithsonian Contributions to Knowledge, Vol. II. Washington, 1851.(1), pp. 51-53.)*

Several other mounds may be mentioned, and these may be considered as being typical of all existing in the country of the Five Nations. Schoolcraft referred to a mound which stood about 1 mile distant, up the Tonawanda, in Genesee County. Another was some 2 miles south of the first. Both were discovered in the year 1810, and contained many human bones. Glass beads were recovered from the one which stood farther north. In the adjoining county of Monroe were two mounds, the larger being not more than 3 feet in height. They were on the "high, sandy grounds to the westward of Irondequoit Bay, where it connects with Lake Ontario."These are said to have been examined in 1811, at which time various objects of European origin were found, including a sword scabbard, bands of silver, belt buckles, and similar pieces.

Iroquois burial mound near Mount Morris, Livingston County, New York

The mounds already mentioned were within the territory of the Seneca, and those described in Genesee and Monroe Counties were erected within historic times.

The Oneida occupied the country northeast of Lake Ontario, and a site near the east end of Long Sault Island," in St. Lawrence County, may have been occupied by one of their villages. A mound south of this site was examined, and in it were discovered seven skeletons, and associated with the burials were various objects of native origin, including "a large pitcher-like vessel, four gouges, and some very coarse cloth, which looked like our hair cloth, only very coarse. Also seven strings of beads." *(Beauchamp, Aboriginal Occupation of New York, Bulletin New York State. Museum, No. 32, Vol. 7. 1900. (2).)* A mound on St. Regis Island, in Franklin County, which touches St. Lawrence on the west, was opened in 1818. It contained deposits of human remains, those nearer the upper surface being the best preserved. This would have been in the Mohawk country.

Mound burials are likewise to be encountered in the southern counties, one very interesting example having been discovered in Chenango, the region later occupied by the Tuscarora. This was in Green Township, near the mouth of Geneganstlet Creek. It was originally about 6 feet in height and 40 feet in diameter. "It was opened in 1829 and abundant human bones were found, and much deeper beneath them were others which had been burned. It was not an orderly burial, and the bones crumbled on being exposed. In one part were about 200 yellow and black jasper arrowheads, and 60 more in another place. Also a silver band or ring about 2 inches in diameter, wide but thin, and with what appeared to be the remains of a reed pipe within it. A number of stone gouges or chisels of different shapes, and a piece of mica cut in the form of a heart, the border much decayed and the laminae separated, were also discovered." *(Wilkinson, Annals of Binghamton. New York, 1840. (1).)*

The finding of a piece of mica in this burial at once suggests the mound may have been the work of the Tuscarora. The mica "cut in the form of a heart " was probably carried by them from Carolina when they went northward in the early years of the eighteenth century, and became the sixth nation of the league. A short distance beyond, in the adjoining county of Otsego, is an island in the Susquehanna near the mouth of Charlotte River, and a mound stands on the island which is known locally as the grave of the chief Kagatinga, probably a village chief not known in history. In the extreme northern part of the same county, near Richfield Springs, was a mound often visited by the Oneida, and said by them to have been the burial place of one of their chief men. This will tend to recall the visits made by parties of Indians to the burial mounds in Piedmont Virginia, a region once claimed and occupied by Siouan tribes.

From the few references just given it is quite evident the Iroquois followed a form of mound burial even after the coming of the French, and it is also clearly established that such burials were more
frequent in the western than in the eastern part of their country. Mounds similar to those mentioned have been encountered in every county west of a line running north and south through Oneida Lake, but are far less numerous to the eastward.

Ossuaries

Many ossuaries have been encountered in the western counties of the State of New York, which, however, may be attributed to the influence of the Huron. These great pits often contain vast quantities of skeletal remains, together with numbers of objects of native origin which had been deposited as offerings to the dead, and material obtained from the early traders is sometimes found associated with the later burials. The ossuaries appear to have been rectangular in form, to have occupied rather prominent positions, and to have been carefully prepared. Such a communal burial place was discovered in May, 1909, about 1 mile southwest of Gasport, Niagara County, but unfortunately no detailed record of its contents was preserved. A part of the excavation is shown in plate 10.

b. PARTIAL EXCAVATION OF OSSUARY, GASPORT, N. Y.

The Jesuit missionary, P. de Brebeuf, who assisted at one of the "feasts of the dead" at the village of Ossosane, before the dispersion of the Hurons, relates that the ceremony took place in the presence of 2,000 Indians, who offered 1,300 presents at the common tomb, in testimony of their grief. The people belonging to five large villages deposited the bones of their dead in a gigantic shroud, composed of forty-eight robes, each robe being made of ten beaver skins. After being carefully wrapped in this shroud, they were placed between moss and bark. A wall of stones was built around this vast ossuary to preserve it from profanation. Before covering the bones with earth a few grains of Indian corn were thrown by the women upon the sacred relics. According to the superstitious belief of the Hurons the souls of the dead remain near the bodies until the "feast of the dead"; after which ceremony they become free, and can at once depart for the land of spirits, which they believe to be situated in the regions of the setting sun. *Canadian Red River Exploring Expedition, 1860, ii, p. 164.*

1636 Huron Ceremony,

In contemplating the origin of the preceding burial it is of interest to read the description of a similar burial, as witnessed and recorded by the Jesuit Pere Le Jeune, in the year 1636. But the father had much to say about the manners and customs of the people among whom he labored—the Huron—whose villages were in the vicinity of Lake Simcoe. He told of the manner in which the family and friends gathered about the sick person while making various necessary plans and preparations in anticipation of the end, and continued : "As soon as the sick man has drawn his last breath, they place him in the position in which he is to be in the grave; they do not stretch him at length as we do, but place him in a crouching posture, almost the same that a child has in its mother's womb. Thus far, they restrain their tears. After having performed these duties the whole cabin begins to respond with cries, groans, and wails. . . . As soon as they cease, the Captain goes promptly through the cabins, making known that such and such a one is dead. On the arrival of friends, they begin anew to weep and complain. . . . Word of the death is also sent to the friends who live in the other villages; and, as each family has some one who takes care of its dead, these latter come as soon as possible to take charge of everything, and determine the day of the funeral. Usually they inter the Dead on the third day; as soon as it is light, the Captain gives orders that throughout the whole village a feast be made for the dead. "This being accomplished," the Captain publishes throughout the village that the body is about to be born to the cemetery. The whole village assembles in the cabin; and weeping is renewed; and those who have charge of the ceremonies get ready a litter on which the corpse is placed on a mat and enveloped in a beaver robe, and then four lift and carry it away ; the whole village follows in silence to the cemetery. A tomb is there, made of bark and supported on four stakes, eight to ten feet high. However, before the corpse is put into it, and before they arrange the bark, the

Captain makes known the presents that have been given by the friends. In this County, as well as elsewhere, the most agreeable consolations for the loss of friends are always accompanied by presents, such as kettles, axes, beaver robes, and porcelain collars. . . ." All these gifts were not deposited with the dead. Some were distributed among the relations of the deceased and others were given to those persons who assisted with the ceremonies. Others were offered as prizes in games played by the younger men."

"The graves are not permanent as their villages are stationary only during a few years, while the supplies of the forest last, the bodies only remain in the cemeteries until the Feast of the Dead, which usually takes place every twelve years." During the years between the death and the time of the final disposition of the remains the departed were often honored in many ways by the members of the family or by the entire village. And then came the great ceremony: "The Feast of the Dead is the most renowned ceremony among the Huron; they give it the name of feast because , , . when the bodies are taken from their cemeteries, each captain makes a feast for the souls in his village," and the feast was conducted with much form, "now usually there is only a single feast in each Nation; all the bodies are put into a common pit. I say, usually, for this year, which has happened to be the Feast of the Dead, the kettle has been divided; and five villages of the part where we are have acted by themselves, and have put their dead into a private pit. . . . Twelve years or thereabouts having elapsed, the old men and notables of the country assemble, to deliberate in a definite way on the time at which the feast shall be held to the satisfaction of the whole country and of the foreign nations that may be invited to it. The decision having been made, as all the bodies are to be transported to the village where is the common grave, each family sees to its dead, but with a care and affection that cannot be described: if they have dead relatives in any part of the country, they spare no trouble to go for them; they take them from the cemeteries, bear them on their shoulders, and cover them with the finest robes they have. In each village they choose a fair day, and proceed to the cemetery, where those called Aiheonde, who take care of the graves, draw the bodies from the tombs in the presence of the relatives, who renew their tears and feel afresh the grief they had the day of the funeral . . . after having opened the graves, they display before you all these corpses, on the spot, and they leave them thus exposed long enough for the spectators to learn at their leisure, and once for all, what they will be some day. The flesh of some is quite gone, and there is only parchment on their bones; in other cases, the bodies look as if they had been dried and smoked, and show scarcely any signs of putrefaction; and in still other cases they are still swarming with worms. When the friends have gazed upon the bodies to their satisfaction, they cover them with handsome beaver robes quite new: finally, after some time they strip them of their flesh, taking off skin and flesh which they throw into the fire along with the robes and mats in which the bodies were wrapped. As regards the bodies of those recently dead, they leave these in the state in which they are, and content themselves by simply covering them with new robes. . . . The bones having been well cleaned, they put them partly into bags, partly into fur robes, loaded them on their shoulders, and covered these packages with another beautiful hanging robe. As for the whole bodies, they put them on a species of litter, and carried them with all the others, each into his cabin, where each family made a feast to its dead." The bones of the dead were called by the Huron *Atisken,* "the souls."   For several days between the removal of the bodies from the tombs and the starting for the scene of the last rites, these many bundles of bones were either hung from the walls of the dwellings or lay upon the floor, and in one "Cabin there were fully a hundred souls hung to and fixed upon the poles, some of which smelled a little stronger than musk."At last the time arrived when all were gathered about

the great excavation in which the remains were to be deposited: Let me describe the arrangement of this place. It was about the size of the place Royale at Paris. There was in the middle of it a great pit, about ten feet deep and five brasses wide. All around it was a scaffold, a sort of staging very well made, nine to ten brasses in width, and from nine to ten feet high; above this staging there were a number of poles laid across, and well arranged, with cross poles to which these packages of souls were hung and bound. The whole bodies, as they were to be put in the bottom of the pit, had been the preceding day placed under the scaffold, stretched upon bark or mats fastened to stakes about the height of a man, on the borders of the pit. The whole company arrived with their corpses about an hour after midday, and divided themselves into different cantons, according to their families and villages, and laid on the ground their parcels of souls, almost as they do earthen pots at the village fairs. They unfolded also their parcels of robes, and all the presents they had brought, and hung them upon poles, which were from 5 to 600 toises in extent; so there were as many as twelve hundred presents which remained thus on exhibition two full hours, to give strangers time to see the wealth and magnificence of the country." Later in the day the pit was lined with new beaver robes, each of which was made of ten skins. The bottom and sides were thus covered, and the robes lay a foot or more over the edge. Forty-eight robes were required to form the lining, and others of a like nature were wrapped about the remains. The entire bodies were first placed in the bottom of the pit, and the bundles of bones were deposited above. "On all sides you could have seen them letting down half decayed bodies; and on all sides was heard a horrible din of confused voices of persons, who spoke and did not listen; ten or twelve were in the pit and were arranging the bodies all around it, one after another. They put in the very middle of the pit three large kettles, which could only be of use for souls; one had a hole through it, another had no handle, and the third was of scarcely more value."The entire bodies were placed in the pit the first day, and the bundles of loose bones were deposited on the morning of the second, after which the beaver robes were folded over the remains which reached nearly to the mouth of the pit. And then all was covered " with sand, poles, and wooden stakes, which they threw in without order," after which "some women brought to it some dishes of corn; and that day, and the following days, several Cabins of the Village provided nets quite full of it, which were thrown upon the pit." *(Le Jeiine, Relation. In Jesuit Relations and Allied Documents, Vol. X. Cleveland, 1897. (1), pp. 265-317.)*

Much detail not quoted at this time is to be found in this vivid narrative, and many of the beliefs and superstitions of the people are recorded. He told of the treatment of the body of a person accidentally drowned : "Last year, at the beginning of November [1635], a savage was drowned when returning from fishing; he was interred on the seventeenth, without any ceremonies. On the same day snow fell in such abundance that it hid the earth all the winter; and our savages did not fail to cast the blame on their not having cut up the dead person as usual. Such are the sacrifices they make to render Heaven favorable." (P. 165.)

And regarding the Huron belief in the future state the same father wrote (p. 143) : "As to what is the state of the soul after death, they hold that it separates in such a way from the body that it does not abandon it immediately. When they bear it to the grave, it walks in front, and remains in the cemetery until the Feast of the Dead ; by night, it walks through the village and enters the cabins, where it takes its part in the feasts, and eats what is left at evening in the kettle; whence it happens that many, on this account, do not willingly eat from it on the morrow; there are even some of them who will not go to the feasts made for the souls, believing that they would certainly die if they should even taste of the provisions prepared for the; others, however, are not so scrupulous, and eat their fill. At the Feast of the Dead, which takes place about every twelve years, the souls quit the cemeteries, and in the opinion of some are changed into turtledoves, which they pursue later in the woods, with bow and arrow, to broil and eat; nevertheless the most common belief is that after this ceremony . . . they go away in company, covered as they are with robes and collars which have been put into the grave for them, to a great village, which is toward the setting sun, except, however, the old people and the little children who have not as strong limbs as the others to make this voyage ; these remain in the country, where they have their own particular villages."

Several very interesting details are revealed in the account of this great burial which occurred nearly three centuries ago. The first is the reference to the entire bodies being placed in the bottom of the pit. This obviously alludes to entire skeletons as distinguished from the bundles of detached or dissociated bones. If this was a recognized custom of the makers of the ossuaries it would be expected, when examining a great burial of this sort, to find the positions and general arrangement of the remains differing in various parts of the ancient pit; to find several strata, with a greater variety of bones in one than in the other. The second point of interest mentioned in this early narrative is that in which reference is made to the richness of the material deposited in the pit with the remains, but the greater part was of a perishable nature and should this pit been countered at the present day its contents would probably resemble those of the ossuary discovered near Gasport in 1909.

Other great burial places, similar to that discovered near Gasport, have been encountered in the same county, 10 miles or more south of Lake Ontario, on the Tuscarora Reservation. On the northern border of the reservation stood an ancient enclosure, and "a little over half a mile west of the enclosure," and about 20 rods distant from the edge of the bluff upon which it stood," was a large bone pit. It was marked by a low conical elevation, not over a foot and a half high and 27 feet in diameter. Directly in the center was a slight depression in which lay a large flat stone with a number of similar stones under and around it. At the depth of 18 inches the bones seemed to have been disturbed. Among them was a Canadian penny. This, Mount Pleasant (the Tuscarora chief) thought, may have been dropped in there by a missionary who, thirty years before, had found on the reservation a skull with an arrowhead sticking in it; or by some Indian, for it is, or was, an Indian custom to do this where bones have been disturbed, by way of paying for the disturbance or for some article taken from the grave. The bones seemed to have belonged to both sexes and were thrown in without order; they were, however, in a good state of preservation. Three copper rings were found near finger bones. The roots of trees that had stood above the pit made digging quite difficult; yet sixty skulls were brought to the surface, and it is quite likely that the pit contained as many as a hundred skeletons. The longest diameter of the pit was 9 feet; its depth 5 feet. There were no indications on the skulls of death from bullet wounds. , Two similar elevations, one 18 or 20 feet, the other 10 rods, directly east of this pit, were opened sufficiently to show that they were burial places of a similar character. Like the first, these contained flat stones, lying irregularly near the top. Charcoal occurred in small pieces in all. Indian implements and ornaments, and several Revolutionary relics, were found in the adjoining field." *(Thomas, Report on the Mound Explorations of the Bureau of Ethnology. In Twelfth Annual Report, Bureau of Ethnology. Washington, 1894. (1), pp. 512-513.)*

Another ossuary, evidently quite similar to the one described by Pere Le Jeune, was discovered in 1824, some 6 miles west of Lockport, in Niagara County. "The top of the pit was covered with small slabs of Medina sandstone, and was 24 feet square by 4 1/2 in depth, the planes agreeing with the four cardinal points. It was filled with human bones of both sexes and all ages. ... In one skull, two flint arrow heads were found, and many had the appearance of having been fractured and cleft open, by a sudden blow. They were piled in regular layers, but with no regard to size or sex. Pieces of pottery were picked up in the pit, and had also been plowed up in the field adjacent. The finding of "some metal tools with a French stamp" prove the later burials to have been of comparatively recent origin. *(Schoolcraft, Notes on the Iroquois. New York, 1846. (1), pp. 217 218.)*

In the adjoining county of Erie, "upon a sandy, slightly elevated peninsula, which projects into a low tangled swamp, about 1 1/2 miles southwest of Clarence Hollow, stood a small, irregular enclosure. Human remains were discovered when plowing the neighboring heights. About 1 mile to the eastward of the enclosure, occupying a dry, sandy spot, was an extensive ossuary, estimated to have contained 400 skeletons, " heaped promiscuously together. They were of individuals of every age and sex. In the same field are found a great variety of Indian relics, also brass cap and belt plates, and other remains of European origin." Near this point was discovered, "a year or two since, a skeleton surrounded by a quantity of rude ornaments. It had been placed in a cleft of the rock, the mouth of which was covered by a large flint stone." *(Squier, Ancient Monuments of the Mississippi Valley. In Smithsonian Contributions to Knowledge, Vol. I. Washington, 1848. (l),p. 56.)*

Many other references to great communal burials, similar to those already described, could be quoted. All, however, seem to have been quite alike in appearance, the principal difference at the present time being in their size. When constructed some were undoubtedly more richly lined with robes of beaver skins and other furs than others, and the number and variety of objects deposited with the dead naturally varied. But as the greater proportion of the material placed in the pits with the remains was of a perishable nature all this has now disappeared, leaving only the fragmentary decomposed bones, which in turn will soon vanish, and little will remain to indicate the great communal burial places.

A note in Graham's Magazine, January, 1853, page 102, may refer to the discovery of an ossuary, similar to those already described, but if so it was not recognized as such. The note stated that " workmen on the line of the New York, Corning, and Buffalo Rail Road, on the east side of the Genesee River, and about fifteen rods from the water's edge, while cutting through a sand-bank, have exhumed many human skeletons, piled one above another, with every sign of a hasty military burial. . . . These discoveries strengthen a belief long entertained, that in 1687 the Marquis de Nouvelle fought his famous battle with the Senecas at or near the burial place mentioned, that on the banks of the Genesee, within the limits of Avon, Frank and Red Man closed in mortal death-struggle." This would have been across the river, and not far distant from Canawaugus, and may have been a burial place belonging to that village.

Later Huron Burial 1675

Having such a clear and vivid description of the early burial customs of the Huron, and the various ceremonies which were enacted by members of that tribe at the time of the death of one of their number, as recorded by Pere Le Jeune, in 1636, it is of interest to compare them with the later customs of the same people, after they had become influenced by the teachings of the missionaries. The later account relates to the people of la Mission de Notre-Dame de Lorette in the year 1675, at which time" about 300 souls, both Huron and Iroquois," were gathered about the Mission and heard the teachings of the Jesuits. And regarding the burial of their dead it was said: "Their custom is as follows: as soon as any one dies, the captain utters a lugubrious cry through the village to give notice of it. The relatives of the deceased have no need to trouble themselves about anything, beyond weeping for their dead; because every family takes care that the body is shrouded, the grave dug, and the corpse borne to it and buried, and that everything else connected with the burial is done,—a service that they reciprocally render to one another on similar occasions.

"When the hour for the funeral has come, the clergy usually go to the cabin to get the body of the deceased, which is dressed in his finest garments, and generally covered over with a fine red blanket, quite new. After that, nothing is done beyond what is customary for the French, until the grave is reached. Upon arriving there, the family of the deceased, who hitherto have only had to weep, display all their wealth, from which they give various presents. This is done through captain, who, after pronouncing a sort of funeral oration, which is usually rather short, offers the first present to the church,—generally a fine large porcelain collar,—in order that prayers may be said for the repose of the dead person's soul. Then he gives, out of all the dead man's effects, three or four presents to those who bury him ; then some to the most intimate friends of the deceased. The last of all these presents is that given to the relatives of the deceased, by those who bury him. Finally, the whole ceremony concludes by placing the body in the ground in the following manner. A wide grave is dug, 4 to 5 feet deep, capable of holding more than six bodies, but all lined with bark on the bottom and four sides. This forms a sort of cellar, in which they lay the body, and over which they place a large piece of bark in the shape of a tomb ; it is supported by sticks placed crosswise over the excavation, that this bark may not sink into the tomb, and that it may hold up the earth that is to be thrown on it ; the body thus lies therein as in a chamber without touching the earth at all. Finally, some days after the burial, when the tears of the relatives have been dried to some extent, they give a feast to give the deceased back to life, that is, to give his name to another, whom they urged to imitate the dead man's good actions while taking his name." *(Dablon, Etat Present des Missions en la Nouvelle-France, 1675. In Jesuit Relations and Allied Documents, Vol. LX. Cleveland, 1000. (1) , pp. 35-37.)*

A large grave as described in the preceding account would, in after years, when the supporting bark had become decayed and fallen, have been sunken and irregular. The remains would have become scattered within the excavated space, and all the lining would have disappeared. This may and undoubtedly does, explain the origin of many burials in the eastern part of the country, especially in New England.

"When tolling of the presents exchanged and given at the time of burial, Pere Dablon mentioned particularly that the first was made to the church, and this was "generally, a fine large porcelain collar," porcelain here referring to wampum. Such a specimen is now in the small museum connected with the Collegio di Propaganda Fide, at Rome, where it was deposited many years ago by some missionary when he returned from America. Unfortunately the history of the remarkable piece is not known, but is one of the most interesting examples of wampum preserved in any collection. It measures nearly 6 feet 6 inches in length and about 4 ½ inches in width, made up of 15 rows of beads, each row consisting of 646 beads, or 9,690 in all. The design suggests the attempt to represent on one side Christianity, on the other paganism. At the end of the first side is evidently shown the chapel of the mission, with one window and a cross above the doorway. Next are several characters which may identify the mission; and beyond these are two keys, crossed. In the middle are two figures, evidently a missionary on the right and an Indian on the left, holding between them a cross, the Christian symbol. This most unusual and interesting piece of native workmanship, although showing so clearly the influence of the teachings of the missionaries, should undoubtedly be considered as having served as a " present to the church" at the time of burial of some native convert, possibly two centuries or more ago. Arranged and fastened as it is suggests its use as a collar or stole, something more elaborate than an ordinary wampum " belt." T

Having described tins remarkable piece of wampum, the most interesting example of such work known to exist, it may be well to refer briefly to wampum in general.

The term wampum, derived from an Algonquian word, has often been applied to all shell beads, but the true wampum beads are of a cylindrical form, averaging about one-eighth inch in diameter and one-fourth inch in length. They are of two sorts, white and violet, the latter by many writers being termed black. The violet beads were made of a part of the *Venus mercenaria* while various shells were used in making the white variety. It is quite probable that such beads were made and used by the native tribes along the Atlantic coast before the coming of Europeans, although it is equally probable

that after acquiring metal tools, or bits of metal capable of being fashioned into drills, they were made in greater quantities and of a more regular form.

In the year 1656 there appeared in London a small printed catalogue of the collections belonging to John Tradescant. This was the first publication of such a nature in the English language. The title of this little volume is "Museum Tradescantianum: or a Collection of Rarities preserved at South Lambeth near London, by John Tradescant. London,

M.DC.LVI." On page 51 of the catalogue is mention of a "Black Indian girdle made of wampum peek best sort." This is probably the earliest reference to a piece of wampum in a European collection, and it proves that various qualities were recognized. This was made clear by an entry in the Catalogue and Description of the Natural and Artificial Rarities, belonging to the Royal Society, and preserved at Gresham College, London, 1681. A most valuable reference to and description of wampum appears on page 370, and is quoted in full:

" Several sorts of Indian Money, called wampam peage, 'Tis made of a shell, formed into small *Cylinders* about a `1/4 of an inch long, and 1/5 over, or somewhat more or less: and so being bored as beads and put upon *Strings*, pass among the Indians, in their usual commerce, as *Silver and Gold* amongst us. But being loose is not so current.

Seneca Ceremony 1731

Throughout the greater part of the region once occupied by the Five Nations are discovered their ancient cemeteries, often situated near the sites of their former villages. Some have been examined, and these usually reveal the human remains, now rapidly disappearing, lying in an extended position. Few accounts of the ceremonies which attended the death and burial of these people have been preserved, but one of the most interesting relates to the Seneca, as enacted during the month of June, 1731. True, the two persons who were buried at this Seneca village were not members of the tribe, but, nevertheless, the rites were those of the latter. The relation is preserved in the journal of a Frenchman who visited the Seneca at that time, accompanied by a small party of Algonquian Indians. During the visit one of the Algonquian women was killed by her husband and he in turn was executed by the Seneca. The double funeral which followed was described by the French traveler, who recorded many interesting details. He first referred to a structure where the bodies were kept for several days after death and there prepared for burial, and when he arrived at this cabin it was already crowded with men and women, "all seated or rather squatting on their knees, with the exception of four women, who, with disheveled locks, were lying face downward, at the feet of the dead woman."These were the chief mourners. The body of the woman was placed on an elevated stage. It was dressed in blue and white garments and a wampum belt was the only ornament. The face was painted, with vermilion on the lips. In her right hand was placed a garden implement," to denote that during her life she had been a good worker,"and in the left hand rested the end of a rope, the other end of which, floating in a large bark dish, indicated the sad fate which brought her life to an end."

This refers to her having been drowned. The body of her husband, who had been executed by the Seneca, was on the opposite side of the cabin, " but in a most humiliating posture, for he had been stretched at length on his blanket, face downward, with his hands joined over his head, as if to bear witness to the despair or the repentance which he would have felt for his crime, had he been alive."His body and face were painted with white and black, and he was partly covered with rags. Suspended from a pole placed for the purpose between his legs were "his gun, his hatchet, his knife, his pouch of tobacco, and all his belongings." The interior of the cabin was crowded, and as many more were grouped about outside, and now the "Mistress of Ceremonies . . . began to chant her doleful lamentations." She related how the two had met their deaths, and " scarcely had she made the first movement, weeping alone, when the four other women whom I have mentioned, arose and responded regularly to her cadence that is to say, they made their lamentations in turn and with the same intonation as the leader, whose every gesture they imitated.

. . . These women tore their hair, joined their hands toward heaven, and poured forth in a plaintive tone a torrent of words suitable to the person whose part they represented, according to the different degrees of relationship or connection, which this same person bore to the deceased man or woman ." This chanting continued for nearly half an hour, when "an Algonquian, who was no relation of the dead woman, imposed silence, rising, and instantly no more lamentations were heard. This Indian first made the Funeral Oration of this unfortunate woman, whose good qualities he set forth in particular, as I was told, to make it understood that she must be happy in the land of departed souls, and that her relatives should be consoled for her loss." The Algonquian speaker was immediately followed by an old man of the Iroquois, who "made a defense for the dead man, that is to say he undertook to account for his action in representing to the assembly that this unfortunate husband had doubtless been possessed with the evil Spirit on the day that he had drowned his wife, and that consequently this Indian not having
been master of himself at the time of this evil deed, he rather merited pity than the condemnation of the present assembly." He referred to the dead man as a great warrior and hunter, and deplored the act which made it necessary for the Tsonnontouanrue, to slay him. He then called attention to the position of the body. " Finally, in order the more to excite the compassion of the spectators, this Iroquois threw himself at the feet of the dead woman whose pardon he besought, in the name of her husband, and he protested that had it been in his power to restore her to life, she would certainly not be in her sad plight. Then to crown his discourse he addressed the father-in-law of the executed man and

asked if he was not satisfied with the repentance of his late son-in-law. At these last words, this good man replied ' Etho,' which means yes." The body of the man was then carried to the river, near the village, where it was thoroughly washed, all traces of paint being removed, then "four young men carried it back with great ceremony into the same cabin from which they had taken it. As soon as it was replaced it was repainted, but in beautiful and divers colors, after which it was neatly clothed, a gun was placed in his hand, a pipe in his mouth, and he was seated beside his wife." Thus the bodies remained during the night and until the following morning, and this interval "was spent in condolences among a number of Indians who came by turn to speak to the two corpses."

The burial occurred on the following day, June 17, 1731. That morning all were quiet in the village; they were seated or lying about, with heads on their knees and often wrapped in blankets, and each cabin was to hold a feast for the dead. The Frenchman again entered the cabin and there saw the bodies "each in a coffin made of a piece of white bark, without covering, so that the face and body were visible." Both were dressed as on the previous day. "Their knees were raised so as to support a cross four feet high, which had been placed with each body in such a way that, the coffin of the woman being opposite to that of her husband, the two crosses formed a sort of arch, under which all the Indians passed back and forth, prostrating themselves to the ground, and in turn offering prayers to the Great Spirit for the repose of the souls of these two dead people. About eleven o'clock the doleful lamentations began again and were heard on all sides. The chief mourners seemed only to serve as leaders to show the other women how they should groan or weep. The men said no word and one heard only the groanings and lamentations of the women. However, this pitiful music did not last long as the chief made a sign for them to stop, to make way for the Orators of the occasion to speak. At the end of their speech, which was sad and very short, one of the old people made presents of marten and beaver skins to the Algonquians, relations of the deceased, he also gave some marten skins to my *Abenaquis,* to the mourners, and to several other Indians among the company. At last they took the crosses off the bodies, after which four young Indians painted black, raising the husband's body, and four others painted white and red, taking the wife's body, carried them on their shoulders to the village cemetery, about 40 or 50 fathoms distant. The two young men who served as cross bearers preceded the funeral procession. Immediately after them came the Mistress of Ceremonies for the mourners, she was followed by her four female mourners around the two bodies, and lastly the men carrying their guns brought up the rear of the funeral procession. As soon as the two bodies had reached the cemetery they were placed at the side of the graves which had been prepared for them, and all their clothing and ornaments "were taken off.

b. CEMETERY AT A SENECA VILLAGE, 1731

The old engraving showing the procession after it had entered the cemetery is here reproduced as plate 11 b. The open graves are shown, all surrounded by a palisade, and beyond are the cabins. "Whilst this last office was being performed the men formed a large circle around them, said prayers in a loud voice, and sung three hymns; these hymns were really the same as ours, which the Jesuits had doubtless translated for them. After the Indians had finished these three canticles each one placed their hands on those of the two bodies, as if to say good bye. Then they cut a lock of hair from the tops of their heads which were given to the nearest relative, and they were lowered into the graves. It was then that the women vied with each other in making grimaces and shedding tears, and groaning in a horrible manner. It was now that they said indeed : Adieu my good friend, the great warrior, the splendid hunter. Adieu then Jeanne, the fine singer, the graceful dancer."The bodies were placed in separate graves, very deep. "The graves were filled in with straw and they were not filled up with earth. They were simply covered with strong pieces of bark placed in the form of a roof, surmounted by stones. Finally they placed at the head of the graves the same crosses which had been on the bodies. There were a number of others in the cemetery. When these crosses begin to decay the Indians are careful to renew them, as well as the palisade with which the burial ground is surrounded, for fear that dogs or wild beasts might come and dig up the dead." *(Le Beau,) Avantures du . . . Amsterdam, 1738. 2 vols. (1), pp. 300-315.)* The writer continues, saying that in earlier days the graves of these people were' "hollowed out round like pits."

This was the principal town of the Seneca, and the river which flowed near by, and to which the body of the man was carried to wash away the black and white with which it had, at first, been covered, was the Genesee. The valley of this stream, passing through the counties of Monroe and Livingston, was the home of the Seneca, and, as Squier wrote when describing the latter region, "It is unsurpassed in beauty and fertility by any territory of equal extent in the State, and abounds with mementos of its aboriginal possessors, who yielded it reluctantly into the hands of the invading whites. Here, too, once existed a considerable number of ancient earthworks, but the leveling plough has passed over most of them; and though their sites are still remembered by the early settlers, but few are sufficiently well preserved to admit of exact survey and measurement." *(Squier, (1), pp. 43-44.)*

But although the embankments which once surrounded the ancient villages are rapidly disappearing, and all traces of the palisades have vanished, nevertheless the cemeteries are to be discovered, and the same writer continued (p. 45) : "At various places in the county large cemeteries are found ; but most, if not all, of them may be with safety referred to the Senecas. Indeed, many articles of European origin accompany the skeletons. A cemetery of large size, and, from the character of the relics found in the graves, of high antiquity, is now in part covered by the village of Lima. Pipes, pottery, etc., are discovered here in great abundance; and it is worthy of remark, they are identical with those found within the ancient enclosures."

Possibly the cemetery in which the two Algonquians were buried during the month of June, 1731, was among those examined by Squier. It is of interest to add that on the left bank of the Genesee, nearly opposite Avon, stood the town of Canawaugus the birthplace of the great Chief Cornplanter, and on the site are found objects of both European and native origin. Just north of the preceding site, on the western edge of Scottsville, in Monroe County, is an old cemetery " in a gravel pit. The skeletons are drawn up, but no articles are found except a flat stone at the feet of each." *(Beauchamp, Aboriginal Occupation of New York, Bulletin New York State. Museum, No. 32, Vol. 7. 1900. (1).)* This seems to refer to flexed remains as distinguished from the extended bodies discovered in the more recent graves, and may have been those " hollowed out round like pits," mentioned by Le Beau as being the older form.

Seneca

"My people," he continued, "always buried their dead in the ground. The body was wrapped in skins, with a piece of bark laid above and beneath. Before burial the body of the dead was laid upon a piece of bark elevated a little from the ground. He was dressed in the best he had. The feet were encased in moccasins. Some chief of his clan was appointed to tell of his bravery in war, his skill in hunting, his loyalty to his clan and tribe. He publicly mourned the great loss to the tribe.

"Then," said he, dropping into the present tense, "relatives approach the body, addressing the departed with significant gestures. They thank and praise him for his kindness and virtues. They deplore his loss, while they know he has gone to the Happy Home beyond the Setting Sun. They charge him with mes sages to the friends who have preceded him to the Happy Home. After this the whole circle bursts out in a heart-rending wail, which continues a long time and then gradually dies away. The body is then carried to the dwelling place of each relative in turn, where the same ceremony is repeated. Then the upper piece of bark is laid over the body and it is placed in the ground, lying upon the back with the feet toward the west. In the grave are placed articles of ornament, clothing, cooking utensils, and food, also pipes, bows and arrows, and stone knives.

"After the burial a company of ten hired mourners come to the wigwam of the departed and have a season of wailing with the family. Then the wailers go to the grave, build a fire at the head, and spend the night watching the grave. Early in the morning they return to the house of the dead and commence wailing there, in which they are joined by the family. The family feed these wailing women and treat them with great attention. They rest and sleep during the day, and at night return to the grave to watch and wail again. This ceremony continues ten days.

"During these ten days the family and relatives take off all ornaments and clothe themselves in the poorest garments they can find, even to rags. If a garment looks worse on the wrong side, it is worn wrong side out. Even the silver brooches necessary to fasten the clothes are put on wrong side out. The faces are not washed nor the hair combed. The more filthy and disgusting they appear the more sincere the grief. A more abject-looking object than the mother and wife of a dead man during these ten days can hardly be imagined.

"At the end of the days of mourning comes the funeral feast, in which all the clan participate. It consists of the very best provisions that can be obtained. The possessions of the dead man are now distributed among his relatives, and each one of the hired mourners receives a present.

"At this feast a portion of each kind of food is set apart in a secret place for the use of the departed, who during these ten days has been constantly with them taking note of every expression of grief. At the close of the day of the feast he takes his final departure to the Happy Home beyond the Setting Sun.   "It was often the case, months and years after, that some friend was notified by a dream that the departed wished to have assurance that he was not forgotten. Then the friends held another feast, at which they recounted his virtues and reviewed their memories of him. At this feast the wailing and   disfigurement of the person were omitted and each was obliged to furnish a share of the provisions."

Mohawk

"The Mohawks of New York made a large round hole in which the body was placed upright or upon its haunches, after which it was covered with timber, to support the earth which they lay over, and thereby kept the body from being pressed. They then raised the earth in a round hill over it. They always dressed the corpse in all its finery, and put wampum and other things into the grave with it; and the relations suffered not grass nor any weed to grow upon the grave, and frequently visited it and made lamentation." *[Footnote: Hist. Indian Tribes of the United States, 1853, part 3, p 183.]*

The next of kin closes the eyes of the deceased. After being waked for a few days, they are thus interred. The body hath a stone under the head; it is placed in a sitting posture; they place beside it a pot, kettle, a platter, spoon, money, and provisions, to be made use of in the other world. They then stow wood all around, which they cover with planks; on the planks, which are covered with earth and stones, palisades are fastened in such a manner that the tomb resembles a little house, to which they pay divine reverence; wherefore they consider it a great profanation to violate such places. The men make no noise over the dead, but the women carry on uncommonly; they strike their breasts, tear their faces, call the name of the deceased day and night. The mothers make the loudest lamentations on the death of their very their sons They cut off their hair, which they burn on the the grave in the presence of all the relatives. Wives do the same on the death of their husbands, in addition to painting the face pitch black; and thus in a deer skin jerkin they mourn the dead a whole year, notwithstanding they sometimes lived unhappily together. *The Documentary History of New York 1850*

1724 engraving of the Wyandot-Huron Feast of the Dead

Origin: North shore of Lake Ontario

[Footnote: Canadian Red River Exploring Expedition, 1860, ii, p. 164.] mentions an account of a burial feast by De Brebeuf which occurred among the Hurons of New York:

"The Jesuit missionary, P. de Brebeuf, who assisted at one of the 'feasts of the dead' at the village of Ossosane, before the dispersion of the Hurons, relates that the ceremony took place in the presence of 2,000 Indians, who offered 1,200 presents at the common tomb, in testimony of their grief. The people belonging to five large villages deposited the bones of their dead in a gigantic shroud, composed of forty-eight robes, each robe being made of ten beaver skins. After being carefully wrapped in this shroud, they were placed between moss and bark. A wall of stones was built around this vast ossuary to preserve it from profanation. Before covering the bones with earth a few grains of Indian corn were thrown by the women upon the sacred relics. According to the superstitious belief of the Hurons the souls of the dead remain near the bodies until the 'feast of the dead'; after which ceremony they become free, and can at once depart for the land of spirits, which they believe to be situated in the regions of the setting sun."

Somewhat similar to this rude mode of sepulture is that described in the life of Moses Van Campen, which relates to the Indians formerly inhabiting Pennsylvania:

"Directly after the Indians proceeded to bury those who had fallen in battle, which they did by rolling an old log from its place and laying the body in the hollow thus made, and then heaping upon it a little earth"

As a somewhat curious, if not exceptional, interment, the following account, relating to the Indians of New York is furnished, by Mr. Franklin B. Hough, who has extracted it from an unpublished journal of the agents of a French company kept in 1794:

"Saw Indian graves on the plateau of Independence Rock. The Indians plant a stake on the right side of the head of the deceased and bury them in a bark canoe. Their children come every year to bring provisions to the place where their fathers are buried. One of the graves had fallen in and we observed in the soil some sticks for stretching skins, the remains of a canoe, &c., and the two straps for carrying it, and near the place where the head lay were the traces of a fire which they had kindled for the soul of the deceased to come and warm itself by and to partake of the food deposited near it.

"These were probably the Massasauga Indians, then inhabiting the north shore of Lake Ontario, but who were rather intruders here, the country being claimed by the Oneidas."

Hudson Bay

Cree

Origin: Canada, to the north and west of Lake Superior, in Ontario, Manitoba, Saskatchewan, Alberta and the Northwest Territories

Mackenzie wrote regarding the Cree, or Knisteneaux : " The funeral rites begin, like all other solemn ceremonials, with smoking, and are concluded by a feast. The body is dressed in the best habiliments possessed by the deceased, or his relations, and is then deposited in a grave, lined with branches; some domestic utensils are placed on it, and a kind of canopy erected over it. During this ceremony, great lamentations are made, and if the departed person is very much regretted the near relations cut off their hair, pierce the fleshy part of their thighs and arms with arrows, knives, &c. and blacken their faces with charcoal. If they have distinguished themselves in war, they are sometimes laid on a kind of scaffolding; and I have been informed that women, as in the East, have been known to sacrifice themselves to the manes of their husbands. The whole of the property belonging to the departed person is destroyed, and the relations take in exchange for the wearing apparel, any rags that will cover their nakedness. The feast bestowed on the occasion, which is, or at least used to be, repeated annually, is accompanied with eulogiums on the deceased, and without any acts of ferocity. On the tomb are carved or painted the symbols of his tribe, which are taken from the different animals of the country." (Mackenzie, pp. xcviii-xcix.) And the same writer when describing the many strange beliefs of the Cree wrote : "Among their various superstitions, they believe that the vapor which is seen to hover over moist and swampy places, is the spirit of some person lately dead. They also fancy another spirit which appears, in the shape of a man, upon the trees near the lodge of a person deceased, whose property has not been interred with them. He is represented as bearing a gun in his hand, and it is believed that he does not return to his rest, till the property that has been withheld from the grave has been sacrificed to it."

While at Fort Union, September 28, 1851, Friedrich Kurz witnessed another form of Cree mourning. He wrote in his journal at that time : " Today I saw a Cree squaw with the upper part of her body entirely uncovered; a sign, they of mourning for the loss of a child. She was walking and wore a buffalo robe. The Cree squaw's garb is like that of the Sauteuse woman, i. e. shoulders and arms bare, skirt held up by means of bands or straps." *Smithsonian Bureau of Ethnology, Bulletin 83 1927*

Southeast

Cherokee

Origins:North and South Carolina, Georgia, and Tennessee after migrating south from the Great Lakes region.

Far to the southward, occupying the beautiful hills and valleys of eastern Tennessee and the adjoining parts of Georgia and Carolina, lived that great detached Iroquoian tribe, the Cherokee. Here they lived when the country was traversed by the Spaniards in 1540, and here they continued for three centuries. But although so frequently mentioned by early writers, and so often visited by traders, very little
can be learned regarding their burial customs. Nevertheless it is evident they often placed the body on the exposed surface, on some high, prominent point, and then covered it with many stones gathered from the surface. Such stone mounds are quite numerous, not only on the hills once occupied by the Cherokee, but far northward. Many of the western towns of the Cherokee, often termed the Overhill Towns, were in the vicinity of Blount County, Tennessee. Many stone mounds were there on the hilltops, and these may justly be attributed to the Cherokee, but all may not have covered the remains of the dead." Leaving Chilliowee Valley and crossing the Allegheny range toward North Carolina, in a southeast course, having Little Tennessee River on my right, and occasionally in sight from the cliffs, my attention was called along the road, to stone heaps. . . . After an examination of the objects and a talk with Indians and the oldest inhabitants, I came to the conclusion that there were two kinds of these remains in this part of

Tennessee, which are sometimes confounded, viz, landmarks, or stone piles, thrown together by the Indians at certain points in their journeys, and those which marked a place of burial. At a pass called Indian Grave Gap, I noticed the pile which has given its name to the mountain gorge. The monument is composed simply of round stones raised three feet above the soil, and is six feet long and three wide. As the grave had been disturbed I could make no satisfactory examination of its contents. On the opposite side of the Gap, a stone heap of another description was observed, which had been thrown together in accordance with Cherokee superstition, that assigns some good fortune to the accumulation of those piles. They had the custom, in their journeys and war-like expeditions, at certain known points, before marked out, of casting down a stone and upon their return another. . . . Four miles from Indian Grave Gap, on the west side of my path, on a ridge destitute of vegetation, I observed twenty-five of these stone heaps which covered human remains. I examined a number of them, which were four or five feet high and eight in diameter, and shaped like a hay-cock. . . . In one I found pieces of rotten wood that had been deposited there, fragments of bones, and animal mold. The deposit had been made on the surface of the earth, covered with wood and bark, and crowned with a cone of round stones. From the center of one heap three small bells were extracted, having the letters   J R engraved on them. They much resemble sleigh bells. . . . The Cherokee custom of burying the dead under heaps of stone, it is well known, was practiced as late as 1730." *(Dunning, Account of Antiquities in Tennessee. In Annual Report Smithsonian Institution for the year 1870. Washington, (1), pp. 376-380.)*

This should probably be accepted as the characteristic custom of the early Cherokee before coming under the influence of the whites.

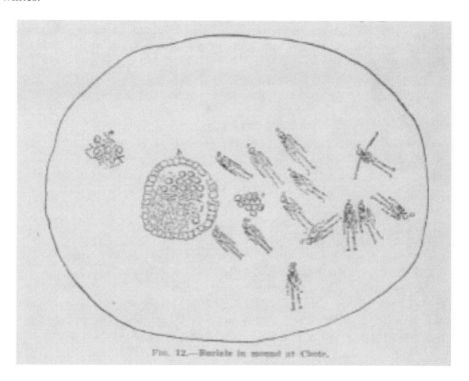

FIG. 12.—Burials in mound at Chote.

As already mentioned, the western towns of the Cherokee were in eastern Tennessee, and of these many were in the valley of the Little Tennessee. Here stood " Cote *the Metropolis,'*" "the scene of many important gatherings during the eighteenth century. The great town house stood on the summit of an artificial mound, undoubtedly one of those described by Thomas, and may have been the large mound on the south side of the river, in Monroe County, designated the McGee mound, No. 2." The diameters of the mound were 70 and 55 feet; its height when examined, 5 feet, which was probably much less than its original height. The excavation of the work revealed burials as indicated on the plan (fig. 12), Thirteen entire skeletons were found, and "at lay 12 skulls on the same level, three feet below the surface of the mound, touching each other, with no other bones in connection with or immediately about them. At 5, a little west of the center, and resting on the original surface, was a rough wall, about two feet high, built of slate stones; circular in form, enclosing a space about nine feet in diameter. The dirt inside being cleared away, twelve skulls and a large number of long and other bones were discovered. Eleven of the skulls were lying close together on one side, as shown in the figure, the other lying alone on the opposite side, but each entirely disconnected from the other parts of the skeleton to which it belonged. The other bones were much broken and mingled together in a promiscuous mass. West of the wall and near the west end of the mound were five more skulls lying together, and amid other bones, marked a in the figure. The bottom of the enclosure, which corresponded with the original surface of the ground, was covered for an inch or two with coals and ashes, on which the skulls and other bones rested. But neither coal nor ashes were found outside of the wall. All the skeletons and other remains outside of the wall lay a foot or more above the original surface of the ground." *(Thomas, Report on the Mound Explorations of the Bureau of Ethnology. In Twelfth Annual Report 1894.(1), pp. 378-879.)*

A few objects of stone and shell and some copper beads were associated with the various burials, but apparently nothing bf European origin was encountered. Other mounds of equal interest marking the positions of the same period were examined and described by the same writer.

The interior arrangement of the mound just mentioned, the mound upon which the great rotunda of Chote may have stood for many years, is quite suggestive of the traditional account of such a mound as related to Mooney by one of his most conservative informants. The circle of stones, with a mass of ashes and charcoal within the enclosure, seems to be explained by this tradition.

", Some say that the mounds were built by another people. Others say they were built by the ancestors of the old Ani Kituhwagi for townhouse foundations, so that the townhouses would be safe when freshets came. The townhouse was always built on the level bottom lands by the river in order that the people might have smooth ground for their dances and ball plays and might be able to go down to water during the dance. When they were ready to build the mound they began by laying a circle of stones on the surface of the ground. Next they made a fire in the center of the circle and put near it the body of some prominent chief or priest who had lately died—some say seven chief men from the different clans. . . . the mound was then built up with earth, which the women brought in baskets . . ." *(Mooney, Myths of the Cherokee. Bureau of Ethnology. Washington, 1900. (2), p. 395.)*

And so the tradition continues, relating the various ceremonies which attended the construction of the work. This was not the account of the building of any particular mound, but merely the description, in general, of the construction of an elevated site upon which the town house would later be reared. Of what great interest would be a detailed account of the various rites which were enacted at the time the fire was kindled within the circle of stones; at the time the bodies of the great men were placed on the surface, later to be covered by the mound of earth. The remains were probably wrapped and decorated with the richest possessions of the living, with ornaments and objects of a perishable nature, all of which, unfortunately, soon crumbled away and so disappeared, leaving only scant traces of what had once been covered by the earth, " which the women brought in baskets.'"

"Mr. F. W. Putnam gives an account of his explorations of the ancient mounds and burial places in the Cumberland Valley, Tennessee.

"The excavations had been carried on by himself, assisted by Mr. Edwin Curtis, for over two years, for the benefit of the Peabody Museum at Cambridge. During this time many mounds of various kinds had been thoroughly explored, and several thousand of the singular stone graves of the mound builders of Tennessee had been carefully opened.... Mr. Putnam's remarks were illustrated by drawings of several hundred objects obtained from the graves and mounds, particularly to show the great variety of articles of pottery and several large and many unique forms of implements of chipped flint. He also exhibited and explained in detail a map of a walled town of this old nation. This town was situated on the Lindsley estate, in a bend of Spring Creek.

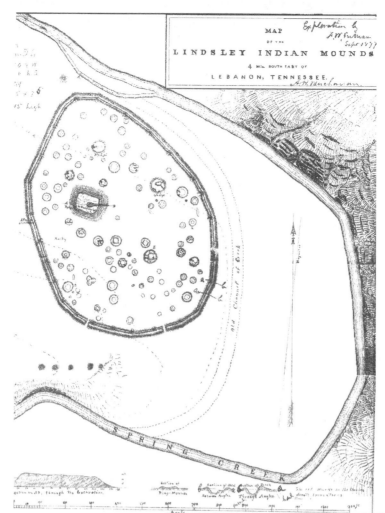

The mound and earthworks are now known as the The Sellar's Farm archaeological site from the Mississippian Period (AD 1000-1450)

The earth embankment, with its accompanying ditch, encircled an area of about 12 acres. Within this enclosure there was one large mound with a flat top, 15 feet high, 130 feet long, and 90 feet wide, which was found not to be a burial mound. Another mound near the large one, about 50 feet in diameter, and only a few feet high, contained 60 human skeletons, each in a carefully-made stone grave, the graves being arranged in two rows, forming the four sides of a square, and in three layers…. The most important discovery lie made within the enclosure was that of finding the remains of the houses of the people who lived in this old town. Of them about 70 were traced out and located on the map by Professor Buchanan, of Lebanon, who made the survey for Mr. Putnam. Under the floors of hard clay, which was in places much burnt, Mr. Putnam found the graves of children. As only the bodies of adults had been placed in the one mound devoted to burial, and as nearly every site of a house he explored had from one to four graves of children under the clay floor, he was convinced that it was a regular custom to bury the children in that way. He also found that the children had been undoubtedly treated with affection, as in their small graves were found many of the best pieces of pottery he obtained, and also quantities of shell-beads, several large pearls, and many other objects which were probably the playthings of the little ones while living." [Footnote: A detailed account of this exploration, with many illustrations, will be found in the *Eleventh Annual Report of the Peabody Museum, Cambridge, 1878.]*

This cist mode of burial is by no means uncommon in Tennessee, as they are frequently mentioned by writers on North American archaeology.

Allied somewhat to cremation is a peculiar mode of burial which is supposed to have taken place among the Cherokees or some other tribe of North Carolina, and which is thus described by J. W Foster. [Footnote: Pre-Historic Races, 1873, p. 149.]

Burial mound from the Sellar's Farm archaeological site

The next account is by Maj. J. W. Powell, the result of his observation in Tennessee. "These ancient cemeteries are exceedingly abundant throughout the State, often hundreds of graves may be found on a single hillside. In some places the graves are scattered and in others collected in mounds, each mound being composed of a large number of cist graves. It is evident that the mounds were not constructed at one time, but the whole collection of graves therein was made during long periods by the addition of a new grave from time to time. In the first burials found at the bottom and near the center of a mound a tendency to a concentric system, with the feet inward, is observed, and additions are made around and above these first concentric graves, as the mound increases in size the burials become more and more irregular:

"Some other peculiarities are of interest. A larger number of interments exhibit the fact that the bodies were placed there before the decay of the flesh, while in other cases collections of bones are buried. Sometimes these bones were placed in some order about the crania, and sometimes in irregular piles, as if the collection of bones had been emptied from a sack. With men, pipes, stone hammers, knives, arrowheads, &c., were usually found; with women, pottery, rude beads, shells, &c.; with children, toys of pottery, beads, curious pebbles, &c.

"Sometimes, in the subsequent burials, the side slab of a previous burial was used as a portion of the second cist. All of the cists were covered with slabs."

Dr. Jones has given an exceedingly interesting account of the stone graves of Tennessee, in his volume published by the Smithsonian Institution, to which valuable work *[Footnote: Antiquities of Tennessee, Cont. to Knowledge, Smith. Inst., 1876, No. 259, 4 deg., pp. 1, 8, 37, 52, 55, 82.]* the reader is referred for a more detailed account of this mode of burial.

Cherokee?

"Up to 1819 the Cherokees held possession of this region, when, in pursuance of a treaty, they vacated a portion of the lands lying in the valley of the Little Tennessee River. In 1821 Mr. McDowell commenced farming. During the first season's operations the plowshare, in passing over a certain portion of a field, produced a hollow rumbling sound, and in exploring for the cause the first object met with was a shallow layer of charcoal, beneath which was a slab of burnt clay about 7 feet in length and 4 feet broad, which, in the attempt to remove, broke into several fragments. Nothing beneath this slab was found, but on examining its under side, to his great surprise there was the mould of a naked human figure. Three of these burned clay sepulchers were thus raised and examined during the first year of his occupancy, since which time none have been found until recently…. During the past season (1872) the plow brought up another fragment of one of these mods, revealing the impress of a plump human arm.

"Col. C. W. Jenkes, the superintendent of the Corundum mines, which have recently been opened in that vicinity, advises me thus:

"'We have Indians all about us, with traditions extending back for 500 years. In this time they have buried their dead under huge piles of stones. We have at one point the remains of 600 warriors under one pile, but a grave has just been opened of the following construction: A pit was dug, into which the corpse was placed, face upward; then over it was molded a covering of mortar, fitting the form and features. On this was built a hot fire, which formed an entire shield of pottery for the corpse. The breaking up of one such tomb gives a perfect cast of the form of the occupant.'

"Colonel Jenkes, fully impressed with the value of these archaeological discoveries, detailed a man to superintend the exhumation, who proceeded to remove the earth from the mould, which he reached through a layer of charcoal, and then with a trowel excavated beneath it. The clay was not thoroughly baked, and no impression of the corpse was left, except of the forehead and that portion of the limbs between the ankles and the knees, and even these portions of the mould crumbled. The body had been placed east and west, the head toward the east. 'I had hoped,' continues Mr. McDowell, 'that the cast in the clay would be as perfect as one I found 51 years ago, a fragment of which I presented to Colonel Jenkes, with the impression of a part of the arm on one side and on the other of the fingers, that had pressed down the soft clay upon the body interred beneath.' The mound-builders of the Ohio Valley, as has been shown, often placed a layer of clay over the dead, but not in immediate contact, upon which they built fires; and the evidence that cremation was often resorted to in their disposition are too abundant."

This statement is corroborated by Mr. Wilcox: [Footnote: Proc. Acad. Nat. Soc. Phila., Nov 1874, p 168.]

"Mr. Wilcox also stated that when recently in North Carolina his attention was called to an unusual method of burial by an ancient race of Indians in that vicinity. In numerous instances burial places were discovered where the bodies had been placed with the face up and covered with a coating of plastic clay about an inch thick. A pile of wood was then placed on top and fired, which consumed the body and baked the clay, which retained the impression of the body. This was then lightly covered with earth."

It is thought no doubt can attach to the statements given, but the cases are remarkable as being the only instances of the kind met with in the extensive range of reading preparatory to a study of the subject of burial, although it must be observed that Bruhier states that the ancient Ethiopians covered the corpses of their dead with plaster (probably mud), but they did not burn these curious coffins.

Timucuan Tribes

Origin: North Florida

Long before the Seminole reached central Florida the peninsula had been the home of other native tribes who have left many mounds and other works to indicate the positions of their villages. The northern half of the peninsula, from the Ocilla River on the north to the vicinity of Tampa Bay on the south, and thence across to about Cape Canaveral on the Atlantic coast, was. when first visited by the Spaniards, the home of tribes belonging to the Timucuan family, of whom very little is known. They were encountered near the site of the present city of St. Augustine by Ponce de Leon

115

in 1513, on the west coast by Narvaez in 1528, and in the same region by De Soto 11 years later. The southern half of the peninsula, especially along the Gulf coast, was also occupied by many villages, but even less is known of the inhabitants, nor is it definitely known to what linguistic family they belonged, although they may have been Muskhogean.

Much of interest regarding the burial customs of the ancient people who occupied this region at the time of the coming of Europeans has been learned as a result of the careful examination of many mounds, both on the east and west coast. Moore has examined many mounds on the west coast between Tampa Bay and the mouth of the Ocilla, and has discovered innumerable burials contained in them. Various forms are represented, with a large proportion closely flexed, and in other instances only skulls without any other bones in contact. But of all the works examined in this region the most interesting stood near Tarpon Springs, near the Gulf shore, in the far northwestern corner of Hillsboro County. This is the county in which Tampa is located. The mound was thoroughly explored and " the remains of more than six hundred skeletons " were encountered. "These, with notable exception—probably those of chiefs and head men—had been dismembered previously to interment, but were distributed in distinct groups that I regarded as communal or totemic and phratral, and of exceeding interest ; for they seemed to indicate that the burial mound had been regarded by its builders as a tribal settlement, a sort of 'Little City of their Dead,' and that if so, it might be looked on as still, in a measure, representing the distribution and relation of the clans and phratries in an actual village or tribal settlement of these people when living. Moreover, in the minor disposition of the skeletons that had not been scattered, but had been buried in parks, or else entire and extended, in sherd-lined graves or wooden cists within and around each of those groups, it seemed possible to still trace somewhat of the relative ranks of individuals in these groups, and not a few of the social customs and religious beliefs of the ancient builders. This possibility was still further borne out by the fact that with the skeletal remains were associated, in different ways, many superb examples of pottery and sacrificial potsherds, and numerous stone, shell and bone utensils, weapons, and ornaments." *(Gushing, Preliminary Report on the Explorations of Ancient Key-Dweller Remains on the Gulf of Florida. In Proceedings American Philosophical Society, Vol. XXXV. Philadelphia, (1), pp. 24—26.)*

642. Indian Mound, Salt Lake, Fla.

Burial mound in Salt Lake, Florida, north of Tampa

This interesting and plausible conclusion reached by Gushing regarding the placing of the dead belonging to the different totemic groups in distinct graves, or rather in distinct parts of the great burial mound, tends to recall Adair's description of the " bonehouses " of the Choctaw. He said "each house contained the bones of one tribe, separately."This must have referred to the clans and phratries, and if such a distinction was made when the bodies were first placed in the "bone-honses," it is more than probable the same rule was followed when they were finally removed from them, then carried, and with certain ceremony placed on the surface and covered with earth. This may be the explanation of many groups of bundled burials encountered in mounds in the South, and again this would tend to prove some connection between the builders of the mound in question and the Muskhogean tribe, the Choctaw. The mound just mentioned, although larger than the majority, may be considered typical of the region.

The mounds on the east coast, or more correctly in the eastern portion of the peninsula, were somewhat different from those to the westward, and probably the burial customs were likewise different. Drawings made by the French artist Jacobo Le Moyne, who visited the east coast in the year 1564, were reproduced by De Bry in the second part of his famous collection of voyages, printed in 1591. One of the engravings, representing a burial ceremony in one of the Timucuan villages, is reproduced in plate 13, h. The description of the plate as given in the old work reads : "When a chief in that province dies, he is buried with great solemnities, his drinking-cup is placed on the grave, and many arrows are planted in the earth about the mound itself. His subjects mourn for him three whole days and nights, without taking any food. All the other chiefs, his friends, mourn in like manner; and both men and women, in testimony of their love for him, cut off more than half their hair. Besides this, for six months afterwards certain chosen women three times every day, at dawn, noon, and twilight, mourn for the deceased king with a great howling. And all his household stuff is put into his house, which is set on fire, and the whole burned up together. In like manner, when their priests die, they are buried in their own houses; which are then set on fire, and burned up with their furniture." *(Le Moyne, (1) Brevis Narratio. Part II of de Bry, 1591. Reprint Boston, 1875. (1).)*

h. BURIAL CEREMONY IN FLORIDA, 1564. FROM LE MOYNE

It will be noticed that in the drawing the house, evidently that of the deceased, is shown wrapped in flames, thus conforming with the description. The custom of destroying the houses in which death had occurred was also followed by the Natchez, the Taensa, and probably others. The Creeks are known to have abandoned their habitations after the death of one of the occupants, and may under some conditions have burned the structure; in other instances they continued to occupy the house after having interred the remains beneath the floor.

The village drawn by the French artist in 1564 probably stood in the present Duval County, Florida, a region in which many very interesting burial mounds have been discovered and examined. Many of the mounds appear to have been erected over an area previously excavated, a detail lacking in the old drawing, which, however, should not be accepted as being very accurate. But the scene depicted may be the very beginning of the erection of such a structure. This may show the nucleus of such a work, prepared soon after the death of a great man whose tomb was later to be reared. But in regard to this most interesting question nothing can now be stated with any degree of certainty.

Moore has given a very graphic description of the construction of a mound examined by him which stood in Duval County, Florida, not far from the banks of the St. Johns. Its diameters were 63 feet and 58 feet, and its height, then greatly reduced by cultivation, was only 2 feet 2 inches. He wrote : "It was evident that the mound had been constructed in the following manner. First, a fire was built on the surface, possibly to destroy the underbrush. Next, a pit of the area of the intended mound was dug to a depth of about 3 feet. In a central portion of this pit was made a deposit of human remains with certain artifacts. . . . Then the pit was filled with the sand previously thrown out, through which was plentifully mingled charcoal from the surface fire. During the process of filling, various relics but no human remains, were deposited, and covered by the sand. When the pit was filled to the general level, a great fire was made over its entire area as was evidenced by a well marked stratum of sand discolored by fire and containing particles of charcoal, extending entirely through the mound at the level of the surrounding territory. Upon this the mound proper was constructed and various bunched burials and art relics introduced.

Various bunched burials and art relics introduced. " In all human remains were encountered eleven times, once at the base of the pit, the remainder in the body of the mound. The burials were of the bunched variety, but small portions remaining." *(Moore,Certain Aboriginal Mounds of the Georgia Coast In (Journal Academy of Natural Sciences, XI. Philadelphia, 1897.6), pp. 27-29.)*

Objects of shell, stone, pottery, and copper were recovered from the mound, which was entirely destroyed. Traces of great fires are characterstic of many mounds along the St. Johns, but whether they were supposed to have served some practical purpose, or were ceremonial, can not be told.

The mounds of this part of Florida often present some very interesting features. One of evidently quite recent origin was discovered about one-half mile north of Bayard Point, which is on the left bank of the St. Johns nearly opposite Picolata, in Clay County. Its height was about 4 feet 9 inches, diameter 4.5 feet. It was formed of unstratified whitish sand, with occasional pockets of charcoal. Associated with the several burials were objects of European origin. " Somewhat south of the center of the mound was a male skeleton at length, placed with the head northwest. At one side of the remains was a flint-lock gun, in reverse position with muzzle toward the feet. And nearby were traces of a bone handled awl, and probably a powder horn partly decorated with brass-headed nails, also a flint and steel, undoubtedly used in striking fire. Scattered in the mound, but not in direct contact with the human remains, were some fragments of pottery." Moore also found where other mounds had served the later inhabitants as burial places, intrusive burials often having many objects of foreign origin in contact. Some of these may be attributed to the Seminole of the past 150 years.

Midway across the peninsula, in the present Lake County, and within the Timucuan territory, have been encountered many mounds, shell deposits, and other signs of the occupancy of the country by a comparatively large native population. Some of the works were quite remarkable. One mound which stood about 200 yards from the right bank of Blue Creek was practically destroyed : "Its height was 5 feet 6 inches, its circumference 165 feet. . . . About one foot beneath the surface of the mound, which was otherwise composed of white sand of the surrounding territory, ran a layer of pinkish sand, having a maximum thickness of eighteen inches. . . . Chemical analysis showed the coloring matter to be pulverized hematite." Burials were encountered only beneath the unbroken stratum of pink sand. " They were mainly on or below the base and were all disconnected bones, crania greatly preponderating."

About 2 miles distant from the preceding was another mound of equal interest, and likewise presenting several curious features. Examining this, "thirty crania were met with. ... At times bundles of long bones were found without the skull, while in other portions of the mound fragments of isolated crania were encountered. At times great bunches of long bones were found with two or three crania in association. . . . Most skeletons lay near or upon the base."

No extended, complete skeletons were encountered in this mound, but it is evident that here, as elsewhere, the later burials were made more after the customs of the whites. It is likewise of interest to know positively that mounds were reared after the coming of Europeans. Such a work was examined and described by Moore. It stood about 1 mile northwest of Fort Mason, just north of Lake Yale. When examined it was 50 feet in diameter but only 2 feet in height, having been reduced by cultivation. " Unlike other mounds demolished by us on the Oklawaha, the method of burial in this mound was in anatomical order, in various forms of flexion. In all fifteen skeletons were encountered."Objects of iron, silver, and copper were associated with them, being of European origin; and in addition to these pieces of foreign work three skeletons had each one polished stone celt near by. Stone arrowheads were also found in the mound, the whole of which had been erected after contact with Europeans, The mound probably belongs to the transition period, before native implements and weapons had been entirely superseded by others of European make, but while they were still retained and used. And although this mound was not far from the site of a late village of the

Seminole, it would seem that it belonged to a somewhat earlier period, as it is doubtful if these late comers would have had, and evidently used, implements of stone. (The preceding references to mounds in Lake County, are quoted from Moore, (6).)

It is difficult, if not impossible, to distinguish between the different burials now found in central Florida. Many are unquestionably quite ancient, dating from some generations before the coming of the Spaniards ; others are comparatively recent. The older forms may be Timucuan or even of the people who may have traversed this section when going farther southward; possibly some very old Muskhogean tribe. But no human remains yet found in Florida, or elsewhere east of the Mississippi, can justly be attributed to a people more ancient than the native American tribes, as now known and recognized.

"**The Ormond Mound, a Native American burial mound on the west bank of the Halifax River, Ormond Beach, Volusia County, Florida. The archaeologists concluded that the mound was constructed by Timucuan Indians, also identified as the St. Johns people.**" **Picture and text from Wikipedia.**

Another interesting detail was noted by Moore in a mound on the bank of the St. Johns, in St. Johns County, about 3 miles north of Picolata. The mound was about 6 feet 6 inches in height and 64 feet in diameter. On the original surface, covering the center of the base of the mound, " was a flooring of split plank in the last stages of decay, about 13 feet square. Its thickness was 2 inches." This was red cedar. Within the work were discovered 34 separate bundles of bones, but no entire skeletons. This discovery was made in 1894. For the sake of comparison, to show the similarity of customs in widely separated parts of the country, but by people in no way connected with one another, a reference may be made to a discovery made in a mound far north in Ohio. The mound referred to stood "upon the broad and beautiful terrace on which Chillicothe stands, about 1 mile to the north of that town," in Ross County. It was about 15 feet in height and 70 feet in diameter. The work was excavated, but nothing was encountered until the human skeleton, at the base of the mound, was reached. " The course of preparation for the burial seemed to have been as follows: The surface of the ground was first carefully leveled and packed, over an area perhaps ten or fifteen feet square. This area was then covered with sheets of bark, on which, in the center, the body of the dead was deposited, with a few articles of stone at its side, and a few small ornaments near the head. It was then covered over with another layer of bark, and the mound heaped above." *(Squier and Davis, (1), p. 164.)*

The latter burial also closely resembled those discovered in a mound on Creighton Island, Mcintosh County, Georgia, although there the deposits of bark or wood were only of sufficient size to cover a single skeleton. But a great many burials within mounds may originally have been so protected by slabs of wood, or sheets of bark, all traces of which have long ago decayed and disappeared.

Muskhogean

The southern pine lands, from the Mississippi to the Atlantic and from the lowlands of the Gulf coast to the southern Alleghenies, was the home of Muskhogean tribes. The Choctaw, Natchez, and Chickasaw lived in the West. Numerous smaller tribes, later recognized as forming the Creek confederacy, occupied the valleys of the Coosa Tallapoosa, and Chattalioochee, The Yamasi and others were nearer the coast on the east. The Seminole of Florida were immigrants from the Lower Creek towns on the Chattahoochee and did not enter the peninsula until about the middle of the eighteenth century. Their number was increased from time to time by others from the same towns. Certain members of this linguistic group erected great circular town houses, frequently a strong framework of wood covered with clay, in which to conduct their various ceremonies. These were the largest and most imposing structures reared by any of the eastern tribes. Similar buildings were erected by the neighboring Cherokee. The majority of these village houses appear to have stood on mounds raised for the purpose. The habitations of these people were, in many instances, frames of either circular or quadrangular form, covered with thatch, or clay applied in a plastic state and allowed to dry and harden.

The Seminole

Origin: Florida

The Seminole, the immigrants from the Creek towns who settled in Florida during the eighteenth century, were little influenced by the whites until very recent years. Living as they did in the midst of the great swamps of the southern part of the peninsula, with no roads penetrating the tangle of semitropical vegetation, and with even the location of their settlements unknown to the occupants of other parts of Florida, they were never visited, and seldom seen except when they chose to make journeys to the traders near the coast. Consequently the burial customs of the people, as witnessed 40 years ago, were probably little different from those practiced during the past generations. The account written at that time referred particularly to the death and burial of a child:

FIG. 14.—Carrying the dead, among the Seminole.

"The preparation for burial began as soon as death had taken place. The body was clad in a new shirt, a new handkerchief being tied about the neck and another around the head. A spot of red paint was placed on the right cheek and one of black upon the left. The body was laid face upwards. In the left hand, together with a bit of burnt wood, a small bow about twelve inches in length was placed, the hand lying naturally over the middle of the body. Across the bow, held by the right hand, was laid an arrow, slightly drawn. During these preparations, the women loudly lamented, with hair disheveled. At the same time some men had selected a place for the burial and made the grave in this manner: Two palmetto logs of proper size were split. The four pieces were firmly placed on edge, in the shape of an oblong box, lengthwise east and west. In this box a floor was laid, and over this a blanket was spread. Two men, at next sunrise, carried the body from the camp to the place of burial, the body being suspended at feet, thighs, back, and neck from a long pole. The relatives followed. In the grave, which is called ' To-hop-ki '—a word used by the Seminole for ' stockade,' or ' fort,' also, the body was then laid the feet to the east. A blanket was then carefully wrapped around the body. Over this palmetto leaves were placed and the grave was tightly closed by a covering of logs. Above the box a roof was then built. Sticks in the form of an X, were driven into the earth across the overlying logs; these were connected by a pole, and this structure was covered thickly with palmetto leaves. [Pl. 13, a.] " The bearers of the body then made a large fire at each end of the ' To-hop-ki,' With this the ceremony at the grave ended and all

Plate 14

returned to the camp. During that day and for three days thereafter the relatives remained at home and refrained from work. The fires at the grave were renewed at sunset by those who had made them, and after nightfall torches were waved in the air, that ' the bad birds of the night' might not get at the Indian lying in his grave. The renewal of the fires and waving of the torches were repeated three days. The fourth day the fires were allowed to die out. Throughout the camp ' medicine ' had been sprinkled at sunset for three days. On the fourth day it was said that the Indian ' had gone.' From that time the mourning ceased and the members of the family returned to their usual occupations.

" The interpretation of the ceremonies just mentioned, as given me. is this: The Indian was laid in the grave to remain there, it was believed, only until the fourth day. The fires at head and feet, as well as the waving of the torches, were to guard him from the approach of ' evil birds ' who would harm him. His feet were placed toward the east, that when he arose to go to the skies he might go straight to the sky path, which commenced at the place of the sun's rising; that were he laid with the feet in any other direction he would not know when he rose what path to take and he would be lost in the darkness. He had with him his bow and arrow, that he might procure food on his way. The piece of burnt wood in his hand was to protect him from the ' bad birds ' while he was on his skyward journey. These 'evil birds ' are called Ta-lak-i-clak-o. The last rite paid to the Seminole dead is at the end of four moons. At that time the relatives go to the To-hop-ki and cut from around it the overgrowing grass. A widow lives with disheveled hair for the first twelve moons of her widowhood." *(MacCauley, The Seminole Indians of Florida. In Fifth Annual Report Bureau of Ethnology. Washington, 1887. (1), pp. 520 -522.)*

Another form of Seminole burial has been mentioned, but it could not have been followed to any great extent. " The Seminoles of Florida are said to have buried in hollow trees, the bodies being placed in an upright position, occasionally the dead being crammed into a hollow log lying on the ground." *(Yarrow, A Further Contribution to the Study of the Mortuary Customs of the North American Indians. In First Annual Report Bureau of Ethnology. Washington, 1881. (1) , p. 138.)* The writer failed to give his authority for the statement.

Choctaw

Origin: Mississippi, Alabama, Louisiana, and Florida.

Thus the greater part of the southern country was claimed and occupied by tribes belonging to the Muskhogean group, Who were first encountered by the Spanish explorers of the early sixteenth century, and who continued to occupy the region until removed during the first half of the nineteenth century. For three centuries they are known to have remained within the same limited area. On the west were the Choctaw, whose villages extended over a large part of the present State of Mississippi and eastward into Alabama. And to this tribe should undoubtedly be attributed the many burial mounds now encountered within the bounds of their ancient territory, but the remains as now found embedded in a mass of sand and earth forming the mound represent only one, the last, phase of the ceremonies which attended the death and burial of the Choctaw. These as witnessed and described by Bartram were quite distinct.

"As soon as a person is dead, they erect a scaffold eighteen or twenty feet high, in a grove adjacent to the town, where they lay the corpse lightly covered with a mantle; here it is suffered to remain, visited and protected by the friends and relations, until the flesh becomes putrid, so as easily to part from the bones; then undertakers, who made it their business, carefully strip the flesh from the bones, wash and cleanse them, and when dry and purified by the air, having provided a curiously wrought chest or coffin, fabricated of bones and splints, they place all the bones therein; it is then deposited in the bone house, a building erected for that purpose in every town. And when this house is full, a general solemn funeral takes place; the nearest kindred or friends of the deceased, on a day appointed, repair to the bone house, take up the respective coffins, and follow one another in order of seniority, the nearest relations and connections attending their respective corpse, and the multitude following after them, all as one family, with united voice of alternate Allelujah and lamentation, slowly proceed to the place of general interment, where they place the coffins in order, forming a pyramid; and lastly, cover all over with earth, which raises a conical hill or mount. Then they return to town in order of solemn procession, concluding the day with a festival, which is called the feast of the dead." *(Bartram, Travels through North and South Carolina, Georgia, East and West Florida. London, 1792. (1), pp. 514-515.)*

The several writers who left records of the Choctaw ceremonies varied somewhat in their accounts of the treatment of the dead, but differed only in details, not in any main questions. And to quote from Capt. Romans: "As soon as the deceased is departed, a stage is erected *(as in the annexed plate is represented) [pl. 12], and the corpse is laid on it and covered with a bear skin ; if he be a man of note, it is decorated, and the poles painted red with vermillion and bears oil; if a child, it is put upon stakes set across ; at this stage the relations come and weep, asking many questions of the corpse, such as, why he left them? did not his wife serve him well? was he not contented with his children? had he not corn enough? did not his land produce sufficient of everything? was he afraid of his enemies? &c. and this accompanied by loud howlings; the women will be there constantly and sometimes with the corrupted air and heat of the sun faint so as to oblige the by standers to carry them home; the men also come and mourn in the same manner, but in the night or at other unseasonable times, when they are least likely to be discovered. The stage is fenced round with poles, it remains thus a certain time but

not a fixed space, this is sometimes extended to three or four months, but seldom more than half that time. A certain set of venerable old gentlemen who wear very long nails as a distinguishing badge on the thumb, fore and middle finger of each hand, constantly travel through the nation (when I was there I was told there were but five of this respectable order) that one of them may acquaint those concerned, of the expiration of this period, which is according to their own fancy; the day being come, the friends and relations assemble near the stage, a fire is made, and the respectable operator, after the body is taken down, with his nails tears the remaining flesh off the bones, and throws it with the entrails into the fire, where it is consumed; then he scrapes the bones and burns the scrapings likewise; the head

being painted red with vermillion is with the rest of the bones put into a neatly made chest (which for a Chief is also made red) and deposited in the loft of a hut built for that purpose, and called bone house ; each town has one of these ; after remaining here one year or thereabouts, if he be a man of any note, they take the chest down, and in an assembly of relations and friends they weep once more over him, refresh the color of the head, paint the box red, and then deposit him to lasting oblivion." *(Romans, A Concise Natural History of East and West Florida. New York. 1775.(1), pp. 89-90.)*

Plate 12

Fortunately another description gives more details of the form of the so-called " bone houses " and the manner in which they were entered. According to Adair, the body was placed on a high scaffold stockaded round, at the distance of twelve yards from his house opposite to the door." At the beginning of the fourth moon after burial a feast was prepared, the bone picker removed all adhering flesh from the bones, which were then placed in a small chest and carried to the bone-house, which stands in a solitary place, apart from the town. . . . Those bone-houses are scaffolds raised on durable pitch pine forked posts, in the form of a house covered a-top, but open at both ends. I saw three of them in one of their towns, pretty near each other, the place seemed to be unfrequented; each house contained the bones of one tribe, separately. ... I observed a ladder fixed in the ground, opposite to the middle of the broad side of each of those dormitories of the dead. . . . On the top was the carved image of a dove, with its wings stretched out, and its head inclining downward." *(Adair, The History of tlie American Indians. London, (1), pp. 183-184.)*

The time for holding the great ceremony for the dead is mentioned in another account, written, however, during the same generation as the preceding. This was prepared by a French officer, the others having been the observations of Englishmen.

"'When a Choctaw dies, his corpse is exposed upon a bier, made on purpose, of cypress bark, and placed on four posts fifteen feet high. When the worms have consumed all the flesh, the whole family assembles; some one dismembers the skeleton, and plucks off all muscles, nerves and tendons that still remain, they bury them and deposit the bones in a chest, after coloring the head with vermillion. The relations weep during this ceremony, which is followed by a feast, with which those friends are treated who come to pay their compliments of condolence; after that, the remains of their late relation are brought to the common burying ground, and put in the place where his ancestor's bones were deposited.   In the first days of November they celebrate a great feast, which they call the Feast of the Dead, or of the souls; all the families then go to the burying-ground, and with tears in their eyes visit the chests which contain the relics of relations, and when they return, they give a great treat, which finishes the feast." *(Bossu, (1) Travels through that part of North America formerly called Louisiana. London, 1771. 2 vols. (1),* I, pp. 298-299.) One narrative remains to be quoted, a manuscript treating of Louisiana soon after the coming of the French, and although the name of the author is not known and it does not bear a date, it was without doubt prepared by some French officer about the year 1730. Referring to the burial customs of the Choctaw, he wrote:

"As soon as he is dead his relatives erect a kind of cabin, the shape of a coffin, directly opposite his door six feet from the ground on six stakes, surrounded by a mud wall, and covered with bark in which they enclose this body all dressed, and which they cover with 11 blanket. They place food and drink beside him, give a change of shoes, his gun, powder, and balls. . . . The body rests in this five or six months until they think that it is rotted, which makes a terrible stench in the house. After some time all the relatives assemble ceremoniously and the *femme de valleur* of the village who has for her function to strip off the flesh from the bones of the dead, comes to take off the flesh from this body, cleans the bones well, and places them in a very clean cane hamper, which they enclose in linen or cloth. They throw the flesh into a field, and this same flesh stripper, without washing her hands, comes to serve food to the assembly. This woman is very much honored in the village. After the repast they go singing and howling to carry the bones into the charnel house of the canton which is a cabin with only one covering in which these hampers are placed in a row on poles. The same ceremony is performed over chiefs except that instead of putting the bones in hampers they are placed in chests ... in the charnel-house of the chiefs." *(Relation de La Louisianne.)*

According to this unknown writer it was the belief of the Choctaw that in after life all performed the same acts and had the same requirements as in this; therefore the dead were provided with food, weapons, articles of clothing, and other necessaries.

Summarizing the several accounts presented on the preceding pages, it is possible to form a very clear conception of the burial customs of the Choctaw, which evidently varied somewhat in different parts of their country and at different times. Then again, the observers may not have been overly careful in recording details, but in the main all agree.

Soon after death a scaffold was erected near the habitation of the deceased or in a near-by grove. Resting upon the scaffold was " a kind of cabin, the shape of a coffin," which undoubtedly varied greatly in form, and in early days these appear to have been made of wattlework coated with mud and covered over with bark. The body would be placed within this box-like enclosure after first being wrapped in bearskins, a blanket, or some other material of a suitable nature. Food was deposited with the body, and likewise many objects esteemed by the living. With children a lighter frame would serve—crossed poles, as mentioned by Romans and likewise indicated in his drawing.

Thus the body would remain several months and until the flesh became greatly decayed. Then certain persons, usually men, although women at times held the office, would remove all particles of flesh from the bones, using only their fingers in performing this work. The flesh so removed, and all particles scraped from the bones, would be burned, buried in the ground, or merely scattered. Next the bones would be washed and dried ; some were then painted with vermilion mixed with bear's oil; then all would be placed in baskets or chests and carried and deposited in the "bone house," Every town had one such structure, which evidently stood at the outskirts of the village. Adair mentioned having seen three of them in one of their towns, pretty near each other . . . each house contained the bones of one tribe "—i. e., clan. And this proves the recognition of clan distinction or rights, even after death. These "bone houses" seem to have resembled the houses of the living, being roofed but open at both ends. They were raised above the ground on stout posts and were reached by ladders. Some were surmounted by carved figures, one being that of "a dove, with its wings stretched out, and its head inclined downward." In some instances in olden times the remains of the chief men appear to have been placed in a separate house set apart for that particular purpose.

When the remains of many had thus accumulated in the "bone houses" the friends and relatives of the dead would gather and "a general solemn funeral"would take place. On the day appointed the chests and baskets containing the bones would be removed from the "bone houses" and the friends and relatives would carry them in procession, " with united voice of alternate Allelujah and lamentation," to a chosen spot, where they were placed one upon another in the form of a pyramid, and when thus arranged all would be covered by a mass of earth, so making a conical mound, many of which now stand scattered over the region once occupied by this numerous tribe. But now the chests and baskets in which the bones were deposited have disappeared, together with all else of a perishable nature, and the bones themselves are fast crumbling to dust.

The strange Choctaw custom gradually passed, and just a century ago, in January, 1820, it was said: " Their ancient mode of exposing the dead upon scaffolds, and afterwards separating the flesh from the bones, is falling into disuse, though still practiced ... by the six towns of the Choctaws on the Pascagoula." *(Nuttall, A Journal of Travels into the Arkansa Territory, during the year 1819. Philadelphia, 1821. (1), p. 235.)* This refers to the Oklahannali, or " Sixtowns," the name of the most important subdivision of the tribe, who occupied the region mentioned.

Undoubtedly many mounds now standing in parts of Mississippi and Alabama owe their origin to the burial custom of the Choctaw, but, unfortunately, few have been examined with sufficient care to reveal their true form. One, however, was of the greatest interest, and the discovery of glass beads and sheet metal in contact with many of the burials proved the mound to have been erected after the coming of Europeans to the lower Mississippi Valley. This mound stood on the bank of the Mississippi, at Oak Bend Landing, in Warren County, Mississippi. It had been greatly modified and a house had been built upon it, so it had been reduced to 3 feet in height, with diameters of 50 and 60 feet. When examined, 28 burials were encountered, " mostly belonging to the bunched variety, but a few burials of adults extended on the back, and the skeletons of several children also were present in the mound, . . . Some of the bunched burials were extensive, one having no fewer than thirty skulls (many in fragments) and a great quantity of other bones. . . The skulls of the bunched burials, as a rule, were heaped together at one side of the burial. . . . Forty-six vessels of earthenware, mostly in small fragments, were recovered from this mound." *(Moore, Some Aboriginal Sites on Mississippi River. In .Journal Academy of Natural Sciences, Vol. XIV. Philadelphia, 1911. (2), pp. 378-381.)*

The great masses or deposits of human remains encountered in this mound is at once suggestive of the final disposition of the Choctaw dead, after the bodies had been removed from their earlier resting places, the flesh stripped from the bones, and the latter enclosed in baskets, finally to be arranged in heaps and covered with earth, thus forming a mound, to be added to from time to time. It is highly probable that in the older mounds all traces of the remains have disappeared, leaving no evidence of the original nature or form of the structure.

But other mounds within this region, revealing many human remains in such positions as to prove the bodies to have been buried without the removal of the flesh, may also be of Choctaw origin, but erected under far different conditions. It is interesting to learn causes which led to the erection of several of these great tombs. Two, covering the dead of two tribes, stood about 2 miles south of West Point, Clay County, Mississippi. " The Choctaws and Chickasaws had occasional conflicts, particularly after the whites appeared in the country. The former were allies of the French. The latter were under English control, and the rivalry of these kept the two hundred tribes on bad terms. They had a great battle about two miles south of West Point. There may yet be seen two mounds, about one hundred yards apart. After the fight they came to terms, and erected these mounds over their dead, and to the neighboring stream they gave the name Oka-tibbe-ha, or Fighting Water." *(Claiborne,Mississippi as a Province, Territory and Stale. Vol. I, all printed. Jackson, 1880. (1), pp. 484-485.)*

In the southwestern part of Alabama, the heart of the old Choctaw country, are numerous mounds, many of which when examined revealed more clearly than did those already mentioned the peculiarities of the Choctaw burial customs. Among these were two which stood not far from the left bank of the Tombigbee, near Jackson, Clarke County, Alabama. The more northerly of these was about 43 feet in diameter and 2 feet in height. "Human remains were found in eleven places, consisting of lone skulls, small bunches, and fragments of bone, all in the last stage of decay." *(Moore, Certain Aboriginal Remains of the Black Warrior River, etc. I)i Journal Academy of Natural Sciences, Vol. XIII. Philadelphia, 1905. (3), pp. 258-259.)* A number of small stone implements were associated with some of the burials, and a single object of copper was found near where a skeleton may have rested, all traces of which had disappeared.

Nanih Waiya burial mound is a Choctaw Indian name meaning "leaning hill." Located near Philadelphia, Mississippi

A mound only a short distance northward from the preceding, examined and described at the same time (op. cit., pp. 260-262), proved even more interesting. It was somewhat larger, being 48 feet in diameter and 5 feet in height. In it "human remains were met with in forty-five places, the deepest being 3 feet from the surface. All bones were in the last stage of decay and crumbling to bits." Of the burials, 23 were described as "isolated skulls," others were skulls with various bones, or bones without the skulls. Objects of stone and copper and vessels of earthenware were encountered during the exploration of the burial place. It is quite evident the smaller, more fragile bones had disappeared through decay.

A small group of Choctaw lived, until a few years ago, near Bayou Lacomb, St. Tammany Parish, Louisiana, on the north shore of Lake Pontchartrain. They were few in number, and the oldest person among them was probably little more than 50 years of age, and unfortunately they were unable to describe the old tribal burial customs. But although they knew little of the manner in which the bodies of their ancestors were treated, they were able to recall the manner in which the living mourned for the dead. According to the best informed, the period of mourning varied as did the age of the deceased. An older person, as the mother or father, was thus honored for six months or even a year, but for a child or young person the period did not exceed three months. During this time the women cut their hair and often gathered near the grave and " cried."When it was desired to cease mourning, the person stuck into the ground, so as to form a triangle, three pieces of wood, several feet in height. The three sticks were drawn together at the top and tied with a piece of bright colored cloth or some other material. These sticks, so tied and decorated, stood near the entrance of the habitation and indicated that the occupants desired to cease mourning. The three days following the mourners cried or wailed three times each day—at sunrise, at noon, and at sunset. And while thus expressing their grief they would be wrapped in blankets which covered their heads, and they sat or knelt upon the ground. During these three days their friends gathered and soon began dancing and feasting. At the expiration of the three days all ceased weeping and joined in the festivities, which continued another day. It is quite interesting to compare certain details of this brief description with the graphic drawing made by Capt. Romans, in which the manner of mourning as followed by the women is so clearly shown, sitting near the grave, wrapped in blankets which covered their heads.

According to the beliefs of the same Choctaw, " persons dying by violent deaths involving loss of blood, even a few drops, do not pass to the home of Aba (heaven), regardless of the character of their earthly lives, or their rank in the tribe. At night spirits are wont to travel along the trails and roads used by living men, and thus avoid meeting the bad spirit, Nanapolo, whose wanderings are confined to the dark and unfrequented paths of the forest. The spirits of men like the country traversed and occupied by living men, and that is why *Shilup* the ghost, is often seen moving among the trees or following persons after sunset. The spirits of all persons not meeting violent deaths, with the exception of those only who murder or attempt to murder their fellow Choctaw, go to the home of Aba. There it is always spring, with sunshine and flowers ; there are birds and fruit and game in abundance. There the Choctaw ever sing and dance, and trouble is not known. All who enter this paradise become equally virtuous without regard to their state while on earth. The unhappy spirits who fail to reach the home of Aba remain on earth in the vicinity of the places where they have died. But Nanapolo, the bad spirit, is never able to gain possession of the spirit of a Choctaw." *(Bushnell, The Choctaw of Bayou Lacomb, St. Tammany Parish, Louisiana. Bulletin 48, Bureau of American Ethnology. Washington, 1909. (5), pp. 27-29.)*

Bartram [Footnote: Bartram's Travel, 1791, p. 516.] gives a somewhat different account from Roman of burial among the Choctaws of Carolina:

"The Choctaws pay their last duties and respect to the deceased in a very different manner. As soon as a person is dead, they erect a scaffold 18 or 20 feet high in a grove adjacent to the town, where they lay the corps, lightly covered with a mantle; here it is suffered to remain, visited and protected by the friends and relations, until the flesh becomes putrid, so as easily to part from the bones; then undertakers, who make it their business, carefully strip the flesh from the bones, wash and cleanse them, and when dry and purified by the air, having provided a curiously-wrought chest or coffin, fabricated of bones and splints, they place all the bones therein, which is deposited in the bone-house, a building erected for that purpose in every town; and when this house is full a general solemn funeral takes place; when the nearest kindred or friends of the deceased, on a day appointed, repair to the bone-house, take up the respective coffins, and, following one another in order of seniority, the nearest relations and connections attending their respective corps, and the multitude following after them, all as one family, with united voice of alternate allelujah and lamentation, slowly proceeding on to the place of general interment, when they place the coffins in order, forming a pyramid; [Footnote: Some ingenious men whom I have conversed with have given it as their opinion that all those pyramidal artificial hills, usually called Indian mounds, were raised on this occasion, and are generally sepulchres. However, I am of different opinion.] and, lastly, cover all over with earth, which raises a conical hill or mount; when they return to town in order of solemn procession, concluding the day with a festival, which is called the feast of the dead."

Benson [Footnote: Life among the Choctaws, 1860, p. 294.] gives the following account of their funeral ceremonies, embracing the disposition of the body, mourning feast and dance:

"Their funeral is styled by them 'the last cry.'

"When the husband dies the friends assemble, prepare the grave, and place the corpse in it, but do not fill it up. The gun, bow and arrows, hatchet and knife are deposited in the grave. Poles are planted at the head and the foot, upon which flags are placed; the grave is then enclosed by pickets driven in the ground. The funeral ceremonies now begin, the widow being the chief mourner. At night and morning she will go to the grave and pour forth the most piteous cries and wailings. It is not important that any other member of the family should take any very active part in the 'cry,' though they do participate to some extent.

"The widow wholly neglects her toilet, while she daily goes to the grave during one entire moon from the date when the death occurred. On the evening of the last day of the moon the friends all assemble at the cabin of the disconsolate widow, bringing provisions for a sumptuous feast, which consists of corn and jerked beef boiled together in a kettle. While the supper is preparing, the bereaved wife goes to the grave, and pours out, with unusual vehemence, her bitter wailings and lamentations. When the food is thoroughly cooked the kettle is taken from the fire and placed in the center of the cabin, and the friends gather around it, passing the buffalo-horn spoon from hand to hand and from mouth to mouth till all have been bountifully supplied. While supper is being served, two of the oldest men of the company quietly withdraw and go to the grave and fill it up, taking down the flags. All then join in a dance, which not infrequently is continued till morning; the widow does not fail to unite in the dance, and to contribute her part to the festivities of the occasion. This is the 'last cry,' the days of mourning are ended, and the widow is now ready to form another matrimonial alliance. The ceremonies are precisely the same when a man has lost his wife, and they are only slightly varied when any other member of the family has died. (Slaves were buried without ceremonies.)"

special structures called by writers "bone-houses." Roman [Footnote: Hist. of Florida, 1775, p. 89.] relates the following concerning the Choctaws:

"The following treatment of the dead is very strange … As soon as the deceased is departed, a stage is erected (as in the annexed plate is represented) and the corpse is laid on it and covered with a bear skin; if he be a man of note, it is decorated, and the poles painted red with vermillion and bear's oil; if a child, it is put upon stakes set across; at this stage the relations come and weep, asking many questions of the corpse, such as, why he left them? did not his wife serve him well? was he not contented with his children? had he not corn enough? did not his land produce sufficient of everything? was he afraid of his enemies? etc. and this accompanied by loud howlings; the women will be there constantly, and sometimes with the corrupted air and heat of the sun faint so as to oblige the bystanders to carry them home; the men will also come and mourn in the same manner, but in the night or at other unseasonable times, when they are least likely to be discovered.

"The stage is fenced round with poles; it remains thus a certain time but not a fixed space; this is sometimes extended to three or four months, but seldom more than half that time. A certain set of venerable old Gentlemen who wear very long nails as a distinguishing badge on the thumb, fore and middle finger of each hand, constantly travel through the nation (when i was there, i was told there were but five of this respectable order) that one of them may acquaint those concerned, of the expiration of this period, which is according to their own fancy; the day being come, the friends and relations assemble near the stage, a fire is made, and the respectable operator, after the body is taken down, with his nails tears the remaining flesh off the bones, and throws it with the entrails into the fire, where it is consumed; then he scrapes the bones and burns the scrapings likewise; the head being painted red with vermillion is with the rest of the bones put into a neatly made chest (which for a Chief is also made red) and deposited in the loft of a hut built for that purpose, and called bone house; each town has one of these; after remaining here one year or thereabouts, if he be a man of any note, they take the chest down, and in an assembly of relations and friends they weep once more over him, refresh the color of the head, paint the box, and then deposit him to lasting oblivion.

"An enemy nor one who commits suicide is buried under the earth as one to be directly forgotten and unworthy the above ceremonial obsequies and mourning."

The Natchez

Origin:Mississippi and Louisiana

When referring to the burial customs of the Natchez, that most interesting of the many tribes of the lower Mississippi Valley, the early writers by whom the tribe was visited seldom alluded to the rites which attended the final disposition of the remains of the less important members of the nation, but devoted themselves to describing the varied and sanguinary ceremonies enacted at the time of the death and burial of a Sun. Swanton has already brought together the various accounts and descriptions of these most unusual acts, and consequently they need not be repeated at the present time. *(Swanton, Indian Tribes of the Lower Mississippi Valley and Adjacent Coast of the Gulf of Mexico. Bulletin 43, Bureau of American Ethnology. Washington, 1911. (1), pp. 138-157.)* Nevertheless the first two will be quoted to serve as means of comparing the remarkable ceremonies followed by members of this tribe with the manners and customs of their neighbors. Of the two accounts given below, Swanton said:

"The first was given to Gravier by the French youth whom Iberville left in 1700 to learn the Natchez language, and the second details the obsequies of a grand chieftainess of which the author Penicaut claims to have been a witness in 1704."

" The Frenchman whom M. Iberville left there to learn the language told me that on the death of the last chief they put to death two women, three men, and three children. They strangled them with a bowstring, and this cruel ceremony was performed with great pomp, these wretched victims deeming themselves greatly honored to accompany their chief by a violent death. There were only seven for the great chief who died some months before. His wife, better advised than the others, did not wish to follow him, and began to weep when they wished to oblige her to accompany her husband. Mr. de Montigni, who has left this country to go to Siam, being informed of what they were accustomed to do, made them promise not to put anyone to death. As a pledge of their word they gave him a little female slave, whom they are resolved to put to death but for his prohibition; but to keep their cursed custom without it being perceived, the woman chief, whom they call Ouachil Tamail, Sun women (who is always the sister and not the wife of the great chief), persuaded him to retire to a distant village so as not to have his head split with the noise they would make in a ceremony where all were to take part. Mr. de Montigni, not suspecting anything, believed her and withdrew, but in his absence they put to death those whom they believed to be necessary to go to cook and wait on the chief in the other world." *(Gravier, Journal of the Voyage of* . . . in 1700. Tn Jesuit Relations and Allied Documents, Vol. LXV. Cleveland, 1900. (1), pp. 140-143.)

The second account given by Swanton, that claimed to have been witnessed by Penicaut in 1704. follows: "It happened in our time that the grand chieftainess Noble being dead, we saw the burial ceremony, which is indeed the most horrible tragedy that one can witness. It made myself and all my comrades tremble with horror. She [i. e. the great female Sun] was a chieftainess noble in her own right. Her husband, who was not at all noble, was immediately strangled by the first boy she had had by him, to accompany his wife into the great village, where they believe that they go. After such a fine beginning they put outside of the cabin of the great chief all that was there. As is customary they made a kind of triumphal car in the cabin, where they placed the dead woman and her strangled husband. A moment later, they brought 12 little dead infants, who had been strangled, and whom they placed around the dead woman. It was their fathers and mothers who brought them there, by order of the eldest of the dead chieftainess's children, and who then, as grand chief, commands to have die to honor the funeral rites of his mother as many persons as he wishes. They had 14 scaffolds prepared in the public square, which they ornamented with branches of trees and with cloth covered with pictures. On each scaffold a man placed himself who was going to accompany the defunct to the other world. They stood on these scaffolds surrounded by their nearest relatives; they are sometimes warned more than ten years before their death. It is an honor for their relatives. Ordinarily they have offered to die during the life of the defunct, for the good will which they bear him, and they themselves have tied the cord with which they are strangled. They are dressed in their finest clothing, with a large shell in the right hand, and the nearest relative—for example, if it is the father of a family who dies, his oldest son—walks behind him bearing the cord under his arm and a war club in his right hand. He makes a frightful cry which they call the death cry. Then all these unfortunate victims every quarter of an hour descend from their scaffolds and unite in the middle of the square, where they dance together before the temple and before the house of the dead female chief, when they remount their scaffolds to resume their places. They are very much respected that day, and each one has five servants. Their faces are all reddened with vermilion. For my part I have thought that it was in order not to let the fear that they might have of their approaching death be apparent. "

At the end of four days they begin the ceremony of ' the march of the bodies.' " The fathers and the mothers who had brought their dead children took them and held them in their hands; the oldest of these children did not appear to be more than three years old. They placed them to right and left of the entrance to the cabin of the dead female chief. The 14 victims destined to be strangled repaired there in the same order; the chiefs and the relatives of the dead woman appeared there all in mourning—that is to say, with their hair cut. They then made such frightful cries that we thought the devils were come out of the hells to come and howl in this place. The unfortunate persons destined to death danced and the relatives of the dead woman sang. When the march of this fine convoy was begun by two and two, the dead woman was brought out of her cabin on the shoulders of four savages as on a stretcher. As soon as she had been taken out, they set fire to the cabin (it is the usual custom with the Nobles). The fathers, who carried their dead children in their hands, marched in front, four paces distant from each other, and after marching 10 steps they let them fall to the ground. Those who bore the dead woman passed over and went around these children three times. The fathers then gathered them up and reassumed their places in the ranks, and at every 10 paces they recommenced this frightful ceremony, until they reached the temple, so that these children were in pieces when this fine convoy arrived. While they interred the female Noble in the temple the victims were stripped before the door, and, after they had been made to sit on the ground, a savage seated himself on the knees of each of them while another behind held his arms. They then passed a cord around his neck and put the skin of a deer over his head; they made each of these poor unfortunates swallow three pills of tobacco, and gave him a draught of water to drink, in order that the pills should dissolve in his stomach, which made him lose consciousness; then the relatives of the deceased ranged themselves at their sides, to right and left, and each, as he sang, drew an end of a cord, which was passed around the neck with a running knot, until they were dead, after which they buried them. If a chief dies and still has his nurse, she must die with him. This nation still follows this execrable custom, in spite of all that has been done to turn them from it. Our missionaries have

never been able to succeed in that ; all that they were able to do was to succeed some
times in baptizing these poor little infants before their fathers strangled them. Besides, this nation is too much infatuated with its religion, which flatters the evil inclinations of their corrupt nature, for anyone ever to have made any progress in conversion and to have established Christianity there." *(Margry, Decouvertes et etalilissements des Francais dans Touest et dans le sud de I'Amerique Septentrionale (1614-1754). memoires et documents originaux. Paris, 1875-1880. vols. (1), V, p,p. 452-455.)*

This barbaric ceremony was unknown among any other eastern tribe, and while so much pomp attended the burial of a Noble, the less important were conducted to their last resting places with simple rites. And mourning among the Natchez, so Charlevoix wrote, consisted of "cutting off their hair, and in not painting their faces, and in absenting themselves from public assemblies," but, so he continued," I do not know how long it lasts. I know not, either, Whether they celebrate the grand festival of the dead. ... It seems as if in this nation, where everybody is in some sort the slave of those who command, all the honors of the dead are for those who do so, especially for the great chief and the woman chief."

The Temple of the Natchez, which in many respects resembled the temple-tomb of the Algonquian tribes of Virginia and Carolina, was described by all the early historians of lower Mississippi Valley.

"There are only four cabins in [the village] in which is the temple. It is very spacious and covered with cane mats, which they renew every year with great ceremonies, which it would be prolix to insert here. They begin by a four days' fast with emetics till blood comes. There is no window, no chimney, in this temple, and it is only by the light of the fire that you can see a little, and then the door, which is very low and narrow, must be open. I imagine that the obscurity of the place inspires them with respect. The old man who is the keeper keeps the fire up and takes great care not to let it go out. It is in the center of the temple in front of a sort of mausoleum after the Indian fashion. There are three about 8 or 9 feet long, 6 feet broad, and 9 or 10 feet high. They are supported by four large posts covered with cane mats in quite neat columns and surmounted by a platform of plaited canes. This would be rather graceful were it not all blackened with smoke and covered with soot. There is a large mat which serves as a curtain to cover a large table, covered with five or six cane mats on which stands a large basket that it is unlawful to open, as the spirit of each nation of those quarters reposes there, they say, with that of the Natchez. . . . There are others in the other two mausoleums, where the bones of their chiefs are, they say, which they revere as divinities. All that I saw somewhat rare was a piece of rock crystal, which I found in a little basket. I saw a number of little earthen pots, platters, and cups, and little cane baskets, all well made. This is to serve up food to the spirits of the deceased chiefs, and the temple keeper finds his profit in it." *(Gravier,) Journal of the Voyage of . . . in 1700. Jesuit Relations and Allied Documents, Vol. LXV. Cleveland, 1900. (1), pp. 138-141.)*

Du Pratz a generation later gave a more detailed description and told how the temple stood on "a mound of earth brought thither which rises about 8 feet above the natural level of the ground on the bank of a little river." Thus an artificial mound of earth had been reared to serve as a site for the temple. Du Pratz's drawing of the temple is reproduced in figure 13. *(Du Pratz, See Le Page du Pratz. (1), III, pp. 15-20.)*

Natchez Temple

The burial customs of the northern and southern tribes differed in many ways, but the habit of removing the bones of the dead from an old settlement to a new site, so vividly described by Heckewelder as being followed by the " Nanticoke during the first half of the eighteenth century, finds
a parallel in the far south. To quote from Pere Charlevoix, who wrote under date of January 26, 1722, there stood, on the eastern bank of the Mississippi, immediately below the English reach, a short distance below New Orleans, " not

long since, a village of the Chouachas the ruins of which, I have visited. Nothing remains entire but the cabin of the chief, which bears a great resemblance to one of our peasants houses in France, with this difference only, that it has no windows. It is built of the branches of trees, the voids of which are filled up with the leaves of the trees called lataniers [palmetto], and its roof is of the same materials." The "village is at present on the other side of the river, half a league lower, and the Indians have transported thither even the bones of their dead." *(Charlevoix, Journal of a Voyage to North America. London, 1761. 2 vols. (1), II, p. 292.)*

Jones [Footnote: Antiquities of the Southern Indiana, 1873, p. 105.] quotes one of the older writers, as follows, regarding the *Natchez* tribe:

"Among the Natchez the dead were either inhumed or placed in tombs. These tombs were located within or very near their temples. They rested upon four forked sticks fixed fast in the ground, and were raised some three feet above the earth. About eight feet long and a foot and a half wide, they were prepared for the reception of a single corpse. After the body was placed upon it, a basket-work of twigs was woven around and covered with mud, an opening being left at the head, through which food was presented to the deceased. When the flesh had all rotted away, the bones were taken out, placed in a box made of canes, and then deposited in the temple. The common dead were mourned and lamented for a period of three days. Those who fell in battle were honored with a more protracted and grievous lamentation."

Burial of the Stung Serpent

Among the Natchez the death of any of their Suns, as I have before observed, is a most fatal event; for it is sure to be attended with the destruction of a great number of people of both sexes. Early in the spring 1725, the Stung Serpent, who was the brother of the Great Sun, and my intimate friend, was seized with a mortal distemper, which filled the whole nation of the Natchez with the greatest consternation and terror; for the two brothers had mutually engaged to follow each other to the land of spirits; and if the Great Sun should kill himself for the sake of his brother, very many people would likewise be put to death. When the Stung Serpent was despaired of, the chief of the guardians of the temple came to me in the greatest confusion, and acquainting me with the mutual engagements of the two brothers, begged of me to interest myself in preserving the Great Sun, and consequently, a great part of the nation. He made the same request to the commander of the fort. Accordingly we were no sooner informed of the death of the Stung Serpent, than the commander, some of the principal French men, and I, went in a body to the hut of the Great Sun. We found him in despair; but, after some time, he seemed to be influenced by the arguments I used to dissuade him from putting himself to death. The death of the Stung Serpent was published by the firing of two muskets, which were answered by the other villages, and immediately cries and lamentations were heard on all sides. The Great Sun, in the mean time, remained inconsolable, and sat bent forwards, with his eyes towards the ground. In the evening, while we were still in his hut, he made a sign to his favorite wife; who in consequence of that threw a pailful of water on the fire, and extinguished it. This was a signal for extinguishing all the fires of the nation, and filled every one with terrible alarms, as it denoted that the Great Sun was still resolved to put himself to death. I gently chided him for altering his former resolution, but he assured me he had not, and desired us to go and sleep securely. We accordingly left him, pretending to rely on the assurance he had given us; but we took up our lodging in the hut of his chief servants, and stationed a soldier at the door of his hut, whom we ordered to give us notice of whatever happened. There was no need to fear our being betrayed by the wife of the Great Sun, or any others about him; for none of them had the least inclination to die, if they could help it. On the contrary, they all expressed the greatest thankfulness and gratitude to us for our endeavors to avert the threatened calamity from their nation.

Before we went to our lodgings we entered the hut of the deceased, and found him on his bed of state, dressed in his finest cloths, his face painted with vermilion, shod as if for a journey, with his feather-crown on his head. To his bed were fastened his arms, which consisted of a double-barreled gun, a pistol, a bow, a quiver full of arrows, and a tomahawk. Round his bed were placed all the calumets of peace he had received during his life, and on a pole, planted in the ground near it, hung a chain of forty-six rings of cane painted red, to express the number of enemies he had slain. All his domestics were round him, and they presented victuals to him at the usual hours, as if he were alive. The company in his hut were composed of his favorite wife, of a second wife, which he kept in another village, and visited when his favorite was with child; of his chancellor, his physician, his chief domestic, his pipe-bearer, and some old women, who were all to be strangled at his interment. To these victims a noble woman voluntarily joined herself, resolving, from her friendship to the Stung Serpent, to go and live with him in the country of spirits. I regretted her on many accounts, but particularly as she was intimately acquainted with the virtues of simples, had by her skill saved many of our people's lives, and given me many useful instructions. After we had satisfied our curiosity in the hut of the deceased, we retired to our hut, where we spent the night. But at day-break we were suddenly awaked, and told that it was with difficulty the Great Sun was kept from killing himself. We hastened to his hut, and upon entering it I remarked dismay and terror painted upon the countenances of all who were present. The Great Sun held his gun by the butt-end, and seemed enraged that the other Suns had seized upon it, to prevent him from executing his purpose. I addressed myself to him, and after opening the pan of the lock, to let the priming fall out, I chided him gently for his not acting according to his former resolution. He pretended at first not to see me; but, after some time, he let go his hold of the musket, and shook hands with me without speaking a word. I then went towards his wife, who all this while had appeared in the utmost agony and terror, and I asked her if she was ill. She answered me, "Yes, very ill," and added, "if you leave us, my husband is a dead man, and all the Natchez will die; stay then, for he opens his ears only to your words, which have the sharpness and strength of arrows. You are his true friend, and do not laugh when you speak, like most of the Frenchmen." The Great Sun at length consented to order his fire to be again lighted, which was the signal for lighting the other fires of the nation, and dispelled all their apprehensions.

Soon after the natives begun the dance of death, and prepared for the funeral of the Stung Serpent. Orders were given to put none to death on that occasion, but those who were in the hut of the deceased. A child however had been strangled already by its father and mother, which ransomed their lives upon the death of the Great Sun, and raised them from the rank of Stinkards to that of Nobles. Those who were appointed to die were conducted twice a day, and placed in two rows before the temple, where they acted over the scene of their death, each accompanied by eight of their own relations who were to be their executioners, and by that office exempted themselves from dying upon the death of any of the Suns, and likewise raised themselves to the dignity of men of rank.

Burial of the Stung Serpent

Meanwhile thirty warriors brought in a prisoner, who had formerly been married to a female Sun; but, upon her death, instead of submitting to die with her, had fled to New Orleans, and offered to become the hunter and slave of our commander in chief. The commander accepting his offer, and granting him his protection, he often visited his countrymen, who, out of complaisance to the commander, never offered to apprehend him: but that officer being now returned to France, and the runaway appearing in the neighborhood, he was now apprehended, and numbered among the other victims. Finding himself thus unexpectedly trapped, he began to cry bitterly; but three old women, who were his relations, offering to die in his stead, he was not only again exempted from death, but raised to the dignity of a man of rank. Upon this he after wards became insolent, and profiting by what he had seen and learned at New Orleans, he easily, on many occasions, made his fellow-countrymen his dupes.

On the day of the interment, the wife of the deceased made a very moving speech to the French who were present, recommending her children, to whom she also addressed her self, to their friendship, and advising perpetual union

133

between the two nations. Soon after the master of the ceremonies appeared in a red-feathered crown, which half encircled his head, having a red staff in his hand in the form of a cross, at the end of which hung a garland of black feathers. All the upper part of his body was painted red, excepting his arms, and from his girdle to his knees hung a fringe of feathers, the rows of which were alternately white and red. When he came before the hut of the deceased, he saluted him with a great hoo, and then began the cry of death, in which he was followed by the whole people. Immediately after the Stung Serpent was brought out on his bed of state, and was placed on a litter, which six of the guardians of the temple bore on their shoulders. The procession then began, the master of the ceremonies walking first, and after him the oldest warrior, holding in one hand the pole with the rings of canes, and in the other the pipe of war, a mark of the dignity of the deceased. Next followed the corpse, after which came those who were to die at the interment. The whole procession went three times round the hut of the deceased, and then those who carried the corpse proceeded in a circular kind of march, every turn intersecting the former, until they came to the temple. At every turn the dead child was thrown by its parents before the bearers of the corpse, that they might walk over it; and when the corpse was placed in the temple the victims were immediately strangled. The Stung Serpent and his two wives were buried in the same grave within the temple ; the other victims were interred in different parts, and after the ceremony they burnt, according to custom, the hut of the deceased. *The History of Louisiana: Or of the Western Parts of Virginia and Carolina: Containing a Description of the Countries that Lie on Both Sides of the River Mississippi: with an Account of the Settlements, Inhabitants, Soil, Climate, and Products Le Page du Pratz January 1, 1774*

The Chickasaw

Origin: Mississippi, Alabama, Tennessee, Kentucky and Missouri

The Chickasaw lived in the hilly country north of the Choctaw, and although of the same stock they were ever enemies. Many of their customs differed and instead of the elaborate burial ceremonies of the Choctaw, "They bury their dead almost the moment the breath is out of the body, in the very spot under the couch on which the deceased died, and the nearest relations mourn over it with woeful lamentations; the. women are very vociferous in it, but the men do it in silence, taking great care not to be seen any more than heard at this business; the mourning continues about a year, which they know by counting the moons, they are every morning and evening, and at first throughout the day at different times, employed in the exercise of this last duty." *(Romans, A Concise Natural History of East and West Florida. New York. 1775. (1), p. 71.)*

More details of the ceremony were recorded by Adair, who was well acquainted with the manners and customs of the Chickasaw, having traded among them for many years. According to his narrative : "When any of their people die at "home, they wash and anoint the corpse, and soon bring it out of doors . . . after a short eulogium, and space of mourning, they carry him three times around the house in which he is to he interred, stopping half a minute each time." The excavation was described as being clean inside, and after the body had been deposited within it was covered with logs, then several layers of cypress bark, and made level with the floor of the house. Beds were often made above the graves. *(Adair, (1) The History of the American Indians. London, (l),p. 181.)* .

It is of great interest to be able to trace this unusual custom of interring the dead beneath the floor of the house back to prehistoric times, and that within the region occupied by the same tribe. In Wilson County, Tennessee, was discovered the site of an ancient village. Surrounded by an enclosure were several mounds and about 100 earth circles with diameters varying from 10 to 50 feet. Each such ring represented the ruined site of a separate house of a form known to have been erected by certain tribes in the lower Mississippi Valley. Nineteen of the so-called hut rings were examined and bits of pottery, stone implements, some broken and others entire, and other traces of Indian occupancy were discovered. " On removing the hardened and burnt earth forming the floors of the houses, and at a depth of from 1 to 3 feet, small stone graves were found in 11 of the 19 circles that were carefully examined. These graves were in every case those of children, and were from 1 ft. to 4 ft. in length. These children's graves were found at one side of the center of the house, and. generally, it was noticed, that a fire had been built over the spot." *(Putnam,) Archaeological Explorations in Tennessee. In Eleventh Annual Report Peabody Museum. Cambridge. Mass., 1878. (1), pp. 339-360.)* Whether all the burials encountered on this site were really those of children may be questioned, but nevertheless the custom of burying beneath the floors of he houses conforms with the known habit of the Chickasaw, as already told. Undoubtedly many other similar discoveries may be made at some future time.

Adair also described the customs of the Chickasaw when any of their number died away from home. " When any of them die at a distance, if the company be not driven and pursued by an enemy, they place the corpse on a scaffold, covered with notched logs to secure it from being torn by wild beasts", or fowls of prey; when they imagine the flesh is consumed, and the bones are thoroughly dried, they return to the place, bring them home, and inter them in a very solemn manner. . . . The Indians use the same ceremonies to the bones of their dead, as if they were covered with their former skin, flesh, and ligaments. It is but a few days since I saw some return with the bones of nine of their people, who had been two months before killed by the enemy. They were tied in white deer skins, separately; and when carried by the door of one of the houses of their family, they were laid down opposite to it, till the female relations convened, with flowing hair, and wept over them about half an hour. Then they carried them home to their friendly magazines of mortality, wept over them again, and then buried them with the usual solemnities; putting their valuable effects, and as I am informed, other convenient things in along with them." (Adair, (1), pp. 180-181.)

When the Spanish expedition led by De Soto crossed the southern country during the years 1539-1541, the Chickasaw were evidently living in the vicinity of the present Union and Pontotoc Counties, in the northern part of the State of Mississippi, a region they continued to occupy for many generations. Traces of an enclosure surrounding a group of mounds is standing in the southern part of Union County, and may not be very ancient, as objects of European origin have been recovered from several of the mounds. Small pits were discovered beneath certain mounds of the group, as in "Mound 8 . . . Six feet north of the center, in the original soil, was a hole 18 inches across and 11 inches deep, the sides burnt hard as brick, filled with charcoal and dirt. Seven feet northeast of the center was a similar but smaller hole. The gray layer' at the bottom was undisturbed over both these spots, showing that the mound was built after this part of the field had been occupied." *(Thomas, Report on the Mound Explorations of the Bureau of Ethnology. In Twelfth Annual, Washington,1894.(1), pp. 276-277.)*

This makes it quite evident the mounds were erected on an old village site. A trench was cut through a section of another mound of the group, that designated as No. 1, and was carried " down to underlying red clay which was so hard as to be difficult to loosen with a pick. In this clay two holes had been dug 6 feet apart, one north of the other. Each was a foot across and 3 feet deep, rounded at the
bottom, and filled with a shiny gray ooze. In the one to the south was found a piece of small bone, in the northern one nothing but the soft mud or slime. Fourteen feet from the center were two similar holes, one 11 inches across and 3 feet deep, the other 3 feet south of it of the same depth and 18 inches across. . . . No traces of bones were found in these." (Op. cit., p. 271.)

As these mounds were erected on the site of a more ancient settlement, it is possible the pits were graves made by the early Chickasaw beneath the floors of their dwellings, and during the many years that have intervened since the habitations were occupied the bones have disappeared, with only a fragment of a skull remaining.

The Chakchiuma, related linguistically to the Chickasaw and Choctaw, lived on the upper Yazoo River, and lower down the stream, near its junction with the Mississippi, were the villages of the Tunican group, including the Koroa, Yazoo, and the Tunica proper. The burial customs of the people then living in the valley of the Yazoo were undoubtedly quite similar, although the inhabitants of the scattered towns belonged to different stocks. And when referring to "the Yazoux and the Chacchoumas" (i. e., the Yazoo and Chakchiuma), Dumont wrote: "When their chief is dead they go into the woods to bury him, just as in the case of an ordinary man, some on one side, some on the other, the relatives of ,the deceased accompanyng the convoy and bearing in their hands a pine stick lighted like a torch. When the body is in the trench all those taking part throw their lighted torches into it in the same way, after which it is covered with earth. That is what the entire ceremony is confined to. It is true that it continues more than six months longer for the relations of the dead and for his friends, who during all that time go almost every night to utter howls over the grave, and on account of the difference in their cries and voices form a regular charivari. These ceremonies, as I have said, are common to the chiefs and people. The only difference which marks the first is that at their head is planted a post on which is cut with the point of a knife the figures they have worn painted on their body during life." (Dumont, (1), The Chakchiuma, related linguistically to the Chickasaw and Choctaw, lived on the upper Yazoo River, and lower down the stream, near its junction with the Mississippi, were the villages of the Tunican group, including the Koroa, Yazoo, and the Tunica proper. The burial customs of the people then living in the valley of the Yazoo were undoubtedly quite similar, although the inhabitants of the scattered towns belonged to different stocks. And when referring to "the Y'azoux and the Chacchoumas" (i. e., the Yazoo and Chakchiuma), Dumont wrote: "When their chief is dead they go into the woods to bury him, just as in the case of an ordinary man, some on one side, some on the other, the relatives of ,the deceased accompanying the convoy and bearing in their hands a pine stick lighted like a torch. When the body is in the trench all those taking part throw their lighted torches into it in the same way, after which it is covered with earth. That is what the entire ceremony is confined to. It is true that it continues more than six months longer for the relations of the dead and for his friends, who during all that time go almost every night to utter howls over the grave, and on account of the difference in their cries and voices form a regular Richard. These ceremonies, as I have said, are common to the chiefs and people. The only difference which marks the first is that at their head is planted a post on which is cut with the point of a knife the figures they have worn painted on their body during life." (DuPont, (1)See Betel-Dumont G. M. , I, pp. 246-247.)

The Tunics, although forming a distinct linguistic family from the Muskogee tribes with whom they were so closely associated, and practically surrounded, were few in number, but they may, at some earlier time, have been a more numerous and powerful people. To quote Wanton: "Although affected by Christian beliefs, the mortuary ceremonies observed by the Tunics until recent times were
evidently directly descended from older customs.

"The only specific reference by an early writer to the mortuary customs of this tribe is by La Source, who says: 'They inter their dead, and the relations come to weep with those of the house, and in the evening they weep over the grave of the departed and make a fire there and pass their hands over it, crying out and weeping.' *(Shea, Early Voyages Up and Down the Mississippi. Albany, 1801. (1), p. 81.)*

"Accounts of the modern ceremonies were obtained from different sources by Doctor Hatchet and the writer, and the following is an attempt to weave them together:

"The body of a dead person was kept for one day and then interred, many persons making speeches on the occasion. The corpse was laid with its head toward the east, which the Tunics chief told the writer was simply 'their way of burying,' the reason having evidently been forgotten. For four successive nights thereafter a fire was lighted at the head, as Hatchet's informant explained, to keep away the bad spirits who sat in that direction for the same period. During that time the people watched the grave and fasted, and on the morning of the day after the fourth, just before daybreak, all, both old and young, went to plunge four times in water. By that time the soul was satisfied and had ' gone up.' Then all reassembled in the house from which the burial had taken place and breakfasted together, eating white dumplings and the fresh meat of large geese. Then the principal speaker delivered an address, after which he made all put on mourning, he himself and the other near relations wearing it for six months and the father and mother of the deceased for one year. A mourning garb is thought not to have been known before the people 'learned how to pray;' i. e. before Christianity was introduced, which seems probable. During their days of mourning people did not eat or drink until noon.

" Cemeteries were placed on hills in the open country, and because spirits were believed to dwell around them the protection of each cemetery was entrusted to one man. Each new year the guardian said to all those who had ripe corn: 'Ripe corn must be thrown on the cemetery! Ripe beans must be thrown on the cemetery!' Then all went to work to collect their corn and beans and place them there. This took three or sometimes four days, and at the same time, evidently in later years, they cut the cemetery grass. These last statements are according to Hatchet's informant. The Tunics chief only stated that a second fast, called the ' corn fast, took place for the benefit of the dead at the time when little corn had just become good to eat. The ears were roasted close to the fire and then placed in a saucer at the head of the grave. Before this time a 'sign,' which in later times was probably a cross, had been made by a particular person who always performed this office and placed at the grave. The offering of corn was also made for four days. On the last of these the people fasted until noon and assembled at the house of the cemetery guardian. Then they plunged into water four times, also for the dead, and after a speech from the guardian, he gave them all a dinner by way of payment. In later times this ended the fast, but anciently the dinner was followed by a dance." *(Wanton, An Early Account of the Choctaw Indians. Memoirs of the American Anthropological Association. Vol. V, No. 2, 1918. (1), pp. 324—326.)*

Other Muskogee tribes may now be mentioned.

Creek

Origin: Georgia, Alabama, Florida, and North Carolina

The Creeks had customs resembling those of the Chickasaw, and, in some instances, deposited the remains of their dead beneath the floors of their habitations. To quote from Bertram

"The Muskellunges bury their deceased in the earth. They dig a four-square deep pit under the cabin or couch which the deceased lay on, in his house, lining the grave with Cypress bark, where they place the corpse in a sitting posture, as if it were alive; depositing with him his gun, tomahawk, pipe, and such other matters as he had the greatest value for in his life time." *(Bertram, Travels through North and South Carolina, Georgia, East and West Florida. London, 1792. (l),pp. 513-514.)* And when Romans referred to the same people, he said: "The dead are buried in a sitting posture, and they are furnished with a musket, powder and ball, a hatchet, pipe, some tobacco, a club, a bow and arrows, a looking glass, some vermillion and other trinkets, in order to come well provided in the land of spirits." *(Romans, A Concise Natural History of East and West Florida. New York. 1775(1),pp. 98-99.)*

Another traveler a few years later, in 1791, left a brief account of the customs of the Creeks, and said in part : "Upon the Decease of an Adult of either Sex, the Friends and Relations of the Decedent religiously collect whatever he or she held most dear in life, and inter them close by and sometimes in their owner's grave. This pious tribute to their dead includes horses, cows, hogs, and dogs, as well as things inanimate." *(Pope, A tour through the Southern and "Western*

Territories of the United States. Richmond, 1792, reprint New York, 1888. (1), p. 58.) And the same writer mentioned the Creek's belief in ghosts, which tends to recall the somewhat similar belief prevalent among the Choctaw. He told how "The Creeks in approaching the frontiers of Georgia always encamp on the right hand side of the road or path, assigning the left, as ominous, to the Ghosts of their departed heroes who have either unfortunately lost their scalps, or remain unburied. The Ghost of any Hero in either predicament, is refused admittance into the mansions of bliss, and sentenced to take up its invisible and darksom abode, in the dreary caverns of the wilderness; until the indignity shall be retaliated on the enemy, by some of his surviving Friends." (Pp. 63-64.)

About the time of the preparation of the preceding account an even more interesting record was made by an officer in the army, Maj. C. Swan, who visited the Creek nation during the autumn of 1790, and returned to Philadelphia March 13, 1791. After referring to various customs of the people with whom he had been he said: "When one of a family dies, the relations bury the corpse about four feet deep, in a round hole dug directly under the cabin or rock whereon he died. The corpse is placed in the hole in a sitting posture, with a blanket wrapped about it, and the legs bent under it and tied together. If a warrior, he is painted, and his pipe, ornaments, and warlike appendages are deposited with him. The grave is then covered with canes tied to a hoop round the top of the hole, and then a firm layer of clay, sufficient to support the weight of a man. The relations howl loudly and mourn publicly for four days. If the deceased has been a man of eminent character, the family immediately remove from the house in which he is buried, and erect a new one, with a belief that where the bones of their dead are deposited, the place is always attended by goblins and chimeras dire.'They believe there is a state of future existence, and that according to the tenor of their lives they shall hereafter be rewarded with the privilege of hunting in the realms of the Master of Breath, or of becoming Seminolies [i. e. wanderers] in the regions of the old sorcerer. But as it is very difficult for them to draw any parallel between virtue and vice, they are most of them flattered with the expectation of hereafter becoming great war-leaders, or swift hunters in the beloved country of the great Hesakadum Esse." (Schoolcraft, (2), V, p.270.)

Several mounds of the greatest interest have been discovered in the territory which was formerly the home of Muskhogean tribes, and from their nature it is evident they were constructed long after the coming of the Spaniards. One stood about one-quarter mile from the left bank of Alabama River, 6 miles below the city of Montgomery, in Montgomery County, Alabama. This was in the midst of the Creek towns. The mound was 9 feet in height, with a diameter of 67 feet. Objects of iron, of glass, and other materials, all derived from the whites, were encountered throughout the work, from the summit to the base, which proves the entire work to have been erected after the advent of Europeans. And, in addition to these objects of foreign make, were associated others of stone, shell, and earthenware of aboriginal workmanship. This was one of the most remarkable of the many mounds examined by Moore throughout the South. Two others far south of the preceding, also discovered by Moore, may be mentioned. Of these the first was situated about 200 yards north of Alligator Harbor and 1 mile from its lower end, in Franklin County, Florida. When examined, 79 burials were discovered, among them the flexed; the bunched, which sometimes included several skulls together; and bones scattered. All the burials were in the southeastern half of the mound, and in the same section were encountered 62 pottery vessels and various objects of stone and shell. The lack of European objects in this mound makes it appear to be quite ancient, but in the adjoining county of Calhoun, on the northern bank of Chipola cut-off, stood a mound which had undoubtedly been reared at a much later time, as glass beads and pieces of brass, found at the base of the work, indicate the entire tumulus to have been reared since the first part of the sixteenth century. Forty-two burials were encountered scattered throughout the mound, and these included flexed skeletons, bundles of bones, and separate skulls, the latter not in contact with other bones. Now, it is more than probable that both mounds just mentioned were erected by the same people one before, the other after, contact with the whites. The forms of burials in both were similar, characteristic of the region, and resembling those revealed in mounds farther south on the peninsula. The mounds in Franklin and Calhoun Counties were probably erected by a Muskhogean tribe, whose identity has not been determined, who may have had customs resembling those of the Choctaw. The bundles of bones had probably been gathered from the "bonehouses" after all flesh had disappeared, then wrapped or put in baskets, and so deposited and covered with a mass of earth, thus forming the mound. In some instances the bones were put in large earthenware vessels which, by reason of their imperishable nature, are now found containing the remains, but there is no reason to attribute any special meaning to these so-called urn burials. This merely proves that large vessels were sometimes used to hold the remains when prepared for the last disposition, rather than baskets, bags, skins, or some such material, which soon decayed and disappeared, allowing the bones to become as now found—matted and massed in the earth, broken and compressed by the weight of the superstratum. And it is highly probable that as these burial mounds are now found they may represent not more than one-half of their original height. The baskets in which the bones had been buried crumbled away, the remains sunk and became more compact, and gradually the entire accumulation of bones and earth, baskets, mats, and vessels became a comparatively solid but confused mass. All materials of a perishable nature soon disappeared, allowing some of the firmer bones to remain, together with vessels of earthenware and objects of stone, now to be discovered embedded in the sand or clay with which they were originally covered.

The islands lying off the coast of Georgia appear to have been the home of a Muskhogean tribe, the Guale, at the time this part of the country was first visited by the Spaniards during the early part of the sixteenth century. And the many burial mounds standing on the islands and near-by mainland may have been erected by these people. Many of the mounds have been examined and have revealed several forms, or rather methods, of disposing of the dead. One such burial place, a mound of exceptional interest, was near the bank of the Sapelo River, about 2 miles from Sutherland Bluff, in the present Mcintosh County, Georgia. When examined it was about 6 feet in height and 46 feet in diameter. "It   was composed of rich, loamy, brown sand with many local layers of oyster shells. The usual charcoal and fireplaces were present. A black layer from three inches to one foot in thickness, made up of sand mingled with charcoal in minute particles, ran through the mound at about the level of the surrounding territory."Human remains were discovered at 30 points, and "in no one mound investigated by us has there been so well exemplified the various forms of aboriginal disposition of the dead—the burial in anatomical order; the burial of portions of the skeletons ; the interment of great masses of human bones; the pyre;the loose deposit of incinerated remains ; the burial of cinerary urns." *(Moore,Certain Aboriginal Mounds of the Georgia Coast In the Academy of Natural Sciences, Philadelphia, I897. (1), p. 45.)*

Probably few mounds yet found have revealed such a great variety of forms of burial as did this low, spreading work on the bank of the Sapelo. tribe followed at the same time many method disposing of their dead. A short distance northward from the preceding, on Ossabaw Island, in Bryan County, Georgia, was a similar low, spreading mound. And when excavated it likewise proved to be of great interest. "In no part of the mound, outside of the calcined remains, among which were parts of adult skeletons seemingly belonging to males, were skeletal remains of adult males—the skeletons being exclusively those of women, adolescents, children, and infants—and that in one portion of the mound burial vases exclusively contained skeletons of infants, unaffected by fire, while in other portions cinerary urns were present filled with fragments of calcined human skeletons. Again we see pockets of calcined human remains and skeletal remains of women and children unaffected by fire and not included in vessels of earthenware." (Moore, (1), p. 89.)

The most remarkable feature of this discovery was the lack of male skeletons in the body of the mound; in other words, the exclusion of males from this particular tomb. This fact tends to verify to some extent a statement made by Oviedo, who observed the burial customs of the inhabitants of this coast early in the sixteenth century. He mentioned the custom then followed by the people of placing the remains of the children and young persons apart from, the others, and continued by saying the principal men of the tribe were buried in a distinct group. He failed to mention the disposition of the remains of the women, but they may have been placed with those of the children and younger members of the tribe. *(Oviedo, Historia general y natural de las Indias. Madrid, 1851. (1), III, p. 630.)* Thus the discovery and careful examination of this low mound on Ossabaw Island has tended to verify an observation made some four centuries ago.

It is possible within this same region to trace another custom from historic back into prehistoric times, and whenever this may be done it tends to make more clear the customs of the inhabitants of ancient America at the time of the coming of Europeans.

About the year 1730 a small group of Creeks, together with a few Yamasee, all belonging to the same linguistic family, settled on the south or right bank of the Savannah, at a place now known as Yamacraw Bluff, within the limits of the present city of Savannah. Their chief was the famous Tomochichi, who, together with others, later accompanied Gov. Oglethrope to England. While there, during the year 1734, a member of the party died, and "previous to interment in the church-yard of St. John's, Westminster, the body was sewn up in a blanket and bound between two boards." *(Jones, C. C, Explorations of the Aboriginal Remains of Tennessee. In Smithsonian Contributions to Knowledge, Vol. XXII. Washington, 1878. (1), pp. 185-187.)* It was placed in a grave together with many ornaments and other objects. Moore drew attention to the occurrence when describing burials encountered by him in a mound on Creighton Island, Mcintosh County, Georgia, only a short distance south of Savannah, and consequently not far from the former village on Yamacraw Bluff. He remarked on the discovery of traces of wood associated with the skeletal remains, and said in part: "In seven cases years of decayed wood or bark, occasionally showing marks of fire, lay above human remains, and in two cases, above and below." (Moore, (1), p. 30.) There is little doubt of these mound burials having been similar, in all essential details, to that of the Indian who died in London in 1734. And although it

139

is not possible to determine the exact age of the mound on Creighton Island, nevertheless it is reasonable to attribute it to a period after the coming of the Spaniards to the coast of Florida. It is interesting to know that a small mound which stood in Chatham County, Georgia, not far from the preceding, when examined revealed a human skeleton resting upon the original surface, and associated with it was a sword of European origin.

Caddoan and Other Plains Indians

Arikara

Origin: North and South Dakota

The Arikara, once closely united with the Pawnee, from whom they separated generations ago, occupied villages of earth-covered lodges, the ruins of which were recognized by the earliest explorers who ascended the Missouri. Evidently the tribe did not remain long at any one site. In the year 1837 a great epidemic of smallpox swept through the upper valley of the Missouri. The Mandan, whose great villages stood near Fort Clark, suffered greatly and few members of the tribe survived, and those who escaped the dreaded disease abandoned the site and removed to dwell nearer the Hidasta About this time the Arikara moved and took possession of the deserted village of the Mandan, and there remained until midsummer of 1862, when they again moved up the Missouri to the vicinity of Fort Berthold.

Culbertson arrived at Fort Clark June 12, 1850. At that time the Arikara village—the old Mandan site—was prosperous and flourishing. He visited the village, and when returning, so he wrote in his journal : " On passing to the fort, I observed a great number of hillocks, scattered over the prairie, and these, I was told, are graves, this people having abandoned the old method of scaffolding their dead." *(Culbertson,Journal of an Expedition to the Mauvaises Terres and the Upper Missouri in 1850. In Fifth Annual Report of the Smithsonian Institution. Washington. 1851. p. 117.)*

During the summer of 1859 Carl Wimar, the artist, whose home was in St. Louis, visited the upper Missouri for the purpose of sketching the Indian in his native environment. Although he had made many excursions among the Indians of the then far West, this proved one of his most interesting journeys. On June 25 of that year he was at Fort Clark, near which post stood the old village of the Mandan, but which at that time was occupied by the Arikara. A sketch made at that time now proves of the greatest interest and value. It shows two graves of the Arikara, evidently the same as were mentioned three years later by Morgan. writing of his visit to the Arikara village at Fort Clark in 1862, Morgan said in part:

"The Arickarees buried their dead in the ground, and in a sitting posture, judging from the form and size of the mounds. Just back of the village upon the open prairie, was a long row of these mounds quite near together. There were several hundred of them forming a segment of a great circle apparently a mile in length. They were about three feet high, seven feet long, and five feet wide at the level of the ground. Other mounds were grouped together. The most conspicuous mound was that of an Arickaree chief killed by the Sioux a few years before. It was somewhat larger than the others, with a smaller mound, probably that of a relative intersecting it. Around the two, the sod had been removed for the space of five feet, thus forming an area fifteen or more feet in diameter, with a floor of bare earth, the mounds being in the centre. On the top of the mound over the chief's grave, were two bull buffalo skulls, side and side, their horns wound with strips of red flannel and the forehead of one spotted with vermilion. The outer border of the cleared area was decorated with seventeen buffalo skulls, occupying about two-thirds of the circuit, and enclosing the grave of the chief. With what religious motive these skulls were used in their burial customs was not ascertained." *(Morgan, The Stone and Bone Implements of the Arickarees. In Twenty-first Annual Report of the Regents of the University of the State of New York, Albany, 1871. pp. 44-45.)* The description by Morgan applies perfectly to the sketch made by Wimar three years before, which is reproduced in Plate 37. The two mounds, the surrounding cleared area, and the encircling row of buffalo skulls are clearly shown. Two skulls remained on the top of the larger grave in 1862 but it is evident the single skull which had been placed on the smaller mound had fallen away and had not been replaced, Wimar indicated the bits of red cloth attached to the horns of the three skulls resting upon the graves, as mentioned by Morgan.

Plate 37

W. Stirling, during the month of June, 1923, examined four ancient village sites, all of which were within "the 12-mile strip between Grand River and Elk Creek, South Dakota," on the banks of the Missouri. Three of these, on the west bank of the Missouri,were identified as Arikara; one being the historic upper village of the Arikara visited by Lewis and Clark in 1804 and later by Brackenridge and Bradbury in 1811. "The remaining two sites were probably occupied during the preceding century. In the cemeteries belonging to the three villages the bodies had been buried in excavated graves, and it is highly probable that small, low mounds had formerly stood over them, but all traces of such elevations have disappeared. Much interesting material was recovered from the sites, including objects which may have been secured from Europeans two centuries or more ago. *(Stirling, Archaeological Investigations in South Dakota. In Explorations and Field-Work of the Smithsonian Institution in 1923. Smith. Misc. Colls., vol. 76, No. 10. Washington, 1924. p. 66.)* The entire region should be carefully examined while the sites may still be identified.

The discovery of a large variety of objects, some of European and others of native origin, in graves known to have been made by the Arikara, suggests an observation made by Maximilian in 1833. He wrote in part : " The Arikkaras affirm that God said to them that they were made of earth, and must return to earth ; on which account they bury their dead in the ground. Various things are sometimes cast into the grave of eminent men ; the corpse is dressed in the best clothes, the face painted red, and sometimes a good horse is killed on the grave. If the deceased has left a son, he receives his father's medicine apparatus; if not, it is buried with him in the grave." *(Maximilian,Travels in the Interior of North America. London, 1843. p. 411.)*

Pawnee

Origin: Nebraska, Kansas

The Pawnee, whose large villages of earth-covered lodges stood in eastern Nebraska, west of the Missouri, buried their dead in excavated graves. According to Francis La Flesche the bodies were placed in the graves in a sitting position, which would conform with the known customs of other tribes of the Missouri Valley. Small, low" mounds of earth evidently surmounted the graves, which were probably similar in every respect to those of the kindred Arikara. The groups of small mounds, the cemeteries belonging to the several villages, were evidently situated on high ground some distance from the lodges. Ir the summer of 1833 the Pawnee towns were visited by an official party, accompanied by J. T. Irving and others. Irving's narrative is most interesting. The night spent at the Republican Pawnee village, he walked "along the high bluff, looking down upon the Platte, which was dimly seen, reflecting the stars that twinkled upon its restless waters . . . We strolled along the bank for half a mile ... At length, however, we turned for the purpose of retracing our steps, when our attention was attracted by a low, mournful cry, from the midst of a number of small mounds, at a short distance, the burial ground of the village. We approached the spot so cautiously, as not to disturb the person who was stationed there. Upon the top of one of the graves, a large mound covered with grass, was lying an Indian girl . . . Believing that she was some female belonging to the tribe, singing a dirge over the grave of some departed friend, we listened attentively to her song. At one moment, it would rise in the air with a plaintive sound, as if she was dwelling with mournful tenderness upon the virtues of the deceased." (*Irving, J. T., A Tour on the Prairies. New York, 1856. II, pp. 102-105.*) The graves were undoubtedly similar in appearance to those shown in the very remarkable old photograph which is now reproduced in Plate 36.

The low mounds of earth in the photograph resemble heaps of sod rather than mounds of earth. And they were probably constructed of sod, otherwise they could not have been so steep and would not have been so rough and irregular. Certainly a most interesting and valuable picture, made half a century ago, and according to La Flesche made near the great Pawnee village then standing on the banks of the Platte. These small mounds of earth and sod were probably similar to the graves sketched by Wimar at the Arikara village some years before. The latter are shown in Plate 37.

Plate 37

Caches in which various articles and supplies were preserved were constructed by the Pawnee in or near their lodges, and it is of interest to find a reference to the caches having served as burial places for the dead killed at the time of an attack on the village by a band of Sioux warriors. The fight occurred in June, 1845, at which time:"the Pawnees were so badly frightened they threw their dead into corn caches and heads of ravines, covered them lightly, picked up some of their traps and left some in their lodges, crossed the river and went about three miles that night." *(Allis, Forty Years among the Indians and on the Eastern borders of Nebraska. In Transactions and Reports of the*

Nebraska State Historical Society. Vol. II. Lincoln, 1887. p. 155.) Human remains have been encountered in caches in the Ohio Valley and elsewhere, and probably all such burials were made when the living were hard pressed, or when it would have been extremely difficult if not impossible to have excavated graves in the usual manner.

Dunbar, while among the Pawnee, witnessed the manner of treating a man who had been frightfully burned in a prairie fire. "The wives of the sick man showed their affection by preparing food for him, and urging him to eat . , . They were also very attentive to give him drink, whenever he wanted, and to change his position when he desired it. Twice each day this dying man was carried out into the open air, as soon as it was light in the morning, and twilight in the evening." And the narrative continues : "Early the next morning, two of their physicians called to see the sick man. In the first place, they sat down and smoked, which was done with many ceremonies. "The various ceremonies were described in detail. The visits of the two were repeated twice each day, and just before the death of the sufferer they were hastily called, when " They came and with redoubled fury repeated their savage, foolish, and fiendish actions." Then" as soon as the man was dead,his wives, children, and relatives broke out in the most doleful lamentations. His wives were particularly vociferous in their grief, venting their sorrow at
the highest pitch of the voices, wringing their hands, beating their breasts, disheveling their hair, letting it hang down over their faces, covering themselves entirely with their robes, together with many other expressions of savage grief. As soon as it was light, the dead man was taken out and buried. His wives and friends followed, loudly howling, and weeping to the grave lamenting their loss. When they came into the lodge, they covered themselves entirely with their robes, and set mourning in silence." (Dunbar, Journal of. In Collections of the Kansas State Historical Society, 1915-1918, Vol. XIV. Topeka, 1918. pp. 600-002.) The entry in the journal from which the preceding notes were quoted was dated October 25, 1834, two days before the village started on their winter hunt. They advanced over the prairie, often being a line 4 miles or more in length, when " the women, boys, and girls led each of them a horse, and walk in the trail before them." The buffalo were discovered and many were killed. A camp was established where they were to remain some days preparing meat, and while there, during the latter part of November, the missionary wrote in his journal : " One cold morning as I was returning from my walk, I saw several women, bearing the lifeless remains of a little child, that had died the preceding night, to its burial. They carried it a short distance, then placed it on the ground, stopped and wept awhile, then took it up and went forward, all the Awhile howling sadly. The father, a young man, followed at a little distance, apparently, in an agony of grief. Though it was very cold, the ground being covered with snow and ice, he wore no clothing, save the indispensable garment. In this condition, he remained weeping at the grave, probably two hours, perhaps more. I should have thought, he would have frozen to death in this time, but his mind seemed to be so much absorbed in his grief, that he did not appear, at all, to regard the cold." (Op. cit., p.605.)

The Pawnee mourned for their dead, as did other tribes, but they had one quite unusual custom, as was witnessed by the English traveler Murray late in the year 1835. During the summer and autumn he had been with the Pawnee in one of the camps, not at their permanent earth lodge village, and later attempted to return to Fort Leavenworth, but soon after leaving the Pawnee he met with an accident and was thus compelled to retrace his way to the native encampment. He passed the site of the Pawnee camp of the preceding night and there encountered " Two small circular lodges, the apertures to which were closed, and from which proceeded the low wailing chant of Indian mourning." He then continued : " This I observed to be a common custom among the Pawnees. After the rest of the village had been for several hours on the march, a mourning family would remain behind and sing this melancholy kind of dirge. I should think that it must be a very dangerous mode of lamentation while in these remote excursions ; because, if any hostile war-party was hovering on the Pawnee trail, they would inevitably fall victims to the pursuers. But this risk may be the very reason for its being esteemed so great a tribute to the dead; or, possibly, they may trust to the distant out-posts of well-mounted warriors, with which the Pawnees always secure their rear and flanks. The duration of mourning among this tribe seems very unfixed; the widow always mourns a year for her husband ; but I have sometimes seen squaws moaning and chanting in the evening at a little distance from camp ; and, on inquiry, have learnt that they were mourning for a relative, who had been some years dead." *(Murray, Travels in North*

America during the years 1834, 1835, and 1836, including a summer residence with the Pawnee Tribe. Vols. i-ii. London, 1839.I,p. 439.)

Men are said to have expressed their grief by other means. It was their custom to " cut their hair close, except a tuft on the top, which they suffer to remain, and which they plait as a valued ornament, the removal of which is disgraceful. In seasons of mourning, however, they make the sacrifice, to express their grief." *(Morse, A report to the Secretary of War of the United States on Indian Affairs. New Haven, 1822. p. 239.)*

Southwest

Navajo

Origin: Arizona, New Mexico, Utah and California

"The Navajo custom is to leave the body where it dies, closing up the house or hogan or covering the body with stones or brush. In case the body is removed, it is taken to a cleft in the rocks and thrown in, and stones piled over. The person touching or carrying the body, first takes off all his clothes and afterwards washes his body with water before putting them on or mingling with the living. When a body is removed from a house or hogan, the hogan is burned down, and the place in every case abandoned, as the belief is that the devil comes to the place of death and remains where a dead body is. Wild animals frequently (indeed, generally) get the bodies, and it is a very easy matter to pick up skulls and bones around old camping grounds, or where the dead are laid. In case it is not desirable to abandon a place, the sick person is left out in some lone spot protected by brush, where they are either abandoned to their fate or food brought to them until they die. This is done only when all hope is gone. I have found bodies thus left so well enclosed with brush that wild animals were unable to get at them; and one so left to die was revived by a cup of coffee from our house and is still living and well."

Lieut. George E. Ford, Third United States Cavalry, in a personal communication to the writer, corroborates the account given by Dr. Menard, as follows:

This tribe, numbering about 8,000 souls, occupy a reservation in the extreme northwestern corner of New Mexico and Northeastern Arizona. The funeral ceremonies of the Navajos are of the most simple character. They ascribe the death of an individual to the direct action of *Chinde*, or the devil, and believe that he remains in the vicinity of the dead. For this reason, as soon as a member of the tribe dies a shallow grave is dug within the hogan or dwelling by one of the near male relatives, and into this the corpse is unceremoniously tumbled by the relatives, who have previously protected themselves from the evil influence by smearing their naked bodies with tar from the piñon tree. After the body has thus been disposed of, the hogan (composed of logs and branches of trees covered with earth) is pulled down over it and the place deserted. Should the deceased have no near relatives or was of no importance in the tribe, the formality of digging a grave is dispensed with, the hogan being simply leveled over the body. This carelessness does not appear to arise from want of natural affection for the dead, but fear of the evil influence of *Chinde* upon the surviving relatives causes them to avoid doing anything that might gain for them his ill-will. A Navajo would freeze sooner than make a fire of the logs of a fallen hogan, even though from all appearances it may have been years in that condition. There are no mourning observances other than smearing the forehead and under the eyes with tar, which is allowed to remain until worn off, and then not renewed. The deceased is apparently forgotten, as his name is never spoken by the survivors for fear of giving offense to *Chinde*.

Apache

Origin: Arizona, New Mexico, and Texas

The Coyotero Apaches, according to Dr. W. J. Hoffman, [Footnote: U.S. Geol. Surv. of Terr. for 1876, p. 473] in disposing of their dead, seem to be actuated by the desire to spare themselves any needless trouble, and prepare the defunct and the grave in this manner.

"The Coyoteros, upon the death of a member of the tribe, partially wrap up the corpse and deposit it into the cavity left by the removal of a small rock or the stump of a tree. After the body has been crammed into the smallest possible space the rock or stump is again rolled into its former position, when a number of stones are placed around the base to keep out the coyotes. The nearest of kin usually mourn for the period of one month, during that time giving utterance at intervals to the most dismal lamentations, which are apparently sincere. During the day this obligation is frequently neglected or forgotten, but when the mourner is reminded of his duty he renews his howling with evident interest. This custom of mourning for the period of thirty days corresponds to that formerly observed by the Natchez."

Pima

Origin: Arizona

Capt. F. E. Grossman, [Footnote: Rep. Smithson. Inst., 1871, p. 414] USA, furnishes the following account of burial among the Pimas of Arizona:

"The Pimas tie the bodies of their dead with ropes, passing the latter around the neck and under the knees and then drawing them tight until the body is doubled up and forced into a sitting position. They dig the grave from four to five feet deep and perfectly round (about two feet in diameter), then hollow out to one side of the bottom of this grave a sort of vault large enough to contain the body. Here the body is deposited, the grave is filled up level with the ground, and poles, trees, or pieces of timber placed upon the grave to protect the remains from the coyotes (a species of wolf). Burials usually take place at night, without much ceremony. The mourners chant during the burial, but signs of grief are rare. The bodies of their dead are buried, if possible, immediately after death has taken place, and the graves are generally prepared before the patients die. Sometimes sick persons (for whom the graves had already been dug) recovered; in such cases the graves are left open until the persons for whom they were intended die. Open graves of this kind can be seen in several of their burial-grounds. Places of burial are selected some distance from the village, and, if possible, in a grove of mesquite bushes. Immediately after the remains have been buried, the house and personal effects of the deceased are burned, and his horses and cattle killed, the meat being cooked as a repast for the mourners. The nearest relatives of the deceased, as a sign of their sorrow, remain in the village for weeks and sometimes months; the men cut off about six inches of their long hair, while the women cut their hair quite short"

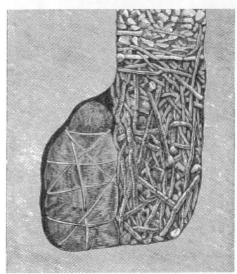

The custom of destroying all the property of the husband when he dies impoverishes the widow and children and prevents increase of stock. The women of the tribe, well aware that they will be poor should their husbands die, and that then they will have to provide for their children by their own exertions, do not care to have many children, and infanticide, both before and after birth, prevails to a great extent. This is not considered a crime, and old women of the tribe practice it. A widow may marry again after a year's mourning for her first husband; but having children no man will take her for a wife and thus burden himself with her children. Widows generally cultivate a small piece of ground, and friends and relatives (men) plow the ground for them.

Fig. 2, drawn from Captain Grossman's description by my friend Dr. W. J. Hoffman, will convey a good idea of this mode of burial.

Kiowa

Origin: New Mexico, Oklahoma, and Texas

Kiowa Indian Death Ritual

"Mr. James Mooney has been studying the Kiowa Indians, in Oklahoma, for about six years. This is one of the most primitive 'tribes in the West. Their tepees, built of poles, are of a conical form. In the summer they live under arbors. They bury their dead in caves, and have a custom that when a person dies all his property is immediately accumulated and burned. All his horses, dogs and animals are killed. All his relatives change their names. Their mythology is quite as elaborate as that of the Zunis. All the objects of creation and the nature powers are deified by them. They have a tradition that their ancestry were released from an underground cave by a person called the " sun-boy." Hypnotism prevails among them. They also practice the ghost dance. They believe that the next world resembles the present world, and good and bad dwell together. The rites of initiation resemble that of the Mandans. The boy usually goes to the mountains, where he fasts and prays for a medicine and a guardian spirit. He spends several days and nights without sleep, finally becomes unconscious, and sees visions, and receives the instructions. On returning to his tepee, he begins to carry out the instructions, and makes for himself an image of the person seen in the trance, and wears this as a charm about his person." *American Antiquarian and Oriental Journal Vol. 18 1886*

Wichita

Origin: Northern Texas

The Wichitas call themselves *Kitty-ka-tats*, or those of the tattooed eyelids.

When a Wichita dies the town-crier goes up and down through the village and announces the fact. Preparations are immediately made for the burial, and the body is taken without delay to the grave prepared for its reception. If the grave is some distance from the village, the body is carried thither on the back of a pony, being first wrapped in blankets and then laid prone, across the saddle, one person walking on either side to support it. The grave is dug from three to four feet deep and of sufficient length for the extended body. First blankets and buffalo-robes are laid in the bottom of the grave, then the body, being taken from the horse and unwrapped, is dressed in its best apparel and with ornaments is placed upon a couch of blankets and robes, with the head towards the west and the feet to the east; the valuables belonging to the deceased are placed with the body in the grave. With the man are deposited his bows and arrows or gun, and with the woman her cooking utensils and other implements of her toil. Over the body sticks are placed six or eight inches deep and grass over these, so that when the earth is filled in, it need not come in contact with the body or its trappings. After the grave is filled with earth, a pen of poles is built around it, or as is frequently the case, stakes are driven so that they cross each other from either side about midway over the grave, thus forming a complete protection from the invasion of wild animals. After all this is done, the grass or other debris is carefully scraped from about the grave for several feet, so that the ground is left smooth and clean. It is seldom the case that the relatives accompany 103the remains to the grave, but they more often employ others to bury the body for them, usually women. Mourning is similar in this tribe, as in others, and it consists in cutting off the hair, fasting, &c. Horses are also killed at the grave. *Annual Report of the Bureau of Ethnology 1881*

The Wichita was among the first of the plains tribes encountered by Europeans, the Quivira of the Spanish narratives of the Coronado expedition. During the year 1541 they were occupying villages located in the eastern part of the present State of Kansas, on the edge of the vast prairies over which then roamed innumerable herds of buffalo. They constructed a curious form of habitation, a conical thatched structure, well suited to the region. They at once suggest a modified form of the earth lodge of the Pawnee, both being of circular base, the walls sloping downward from an opening at the center of the top. The Wichita and Pawnee are related linguistically, and possibly generations ago were even more closely allied. The two types of habitations may have had a common origin. Both tribes buried their dead in prepared graves. A brief account of the rites and customs of the Wichita was prepared by Dr. Fordyce Grinnell before the, .year 1879. This now proves of much interest. It is told how, "When a Wichita dies the town crier goes up and down through the village and announces the fact. Preparations are immediately made for the burial, and the body is taken without delay to the grave prepared for its reception. If the grave is some distance from the village, the body is carried thither on the back of a pony, being first wrapped in blankets and then laid prone across the saddle, one person walking on either side to support it. The grave is dug from three to four feet deep and of sufficient length for the extended body. First blankets and buffalo-robes are laid in the bottom of the grave, then the body, being taken from the horse and unwrapped, is dressed in its best apparel and with ornaments is placed upon a couch of blankets and robes, with the head towards the west and the feet to the east ; the Valuables belonging to the deceased are placed with the body in the grave. With the man are deposited his bows and arrows or gun, and with the woman her cooking utensils and other implements of her toil. Over the body sticks are placed six or eight inches deep and grass over these, so that when the earth is filled in, it need not come in contact with the body or its trappings. After the grave is filled with earth, a pen of poles is built around it, or, as is frequently the case, stakes are driven so that they cross each other from either side about midway over the grave, thus forming a complete protection from the invasion of wild animals. After all this is done, the grass ... is carefully scraped from about the grave for several feet, so that the ground is left smooth and clean. It is seldom the case that the relatives accompany the remains to the grave, but they more often employ others to bury the body for them, usually women. Mourning is similar in this tribe as in others, and it consists in cutting off the hair, fasting, &c. Horses are also killed at the grave." *(Yarrow, ow, H. C. A Further Contribution to the Study of the Mortuary Customs of the North American Indians. In First Annual Report Bureau of Ethnology, 1879-1880. Washington, 1881. pp. 102-103.)*

The graves were probably grouped in the vicinity of the village, similar to the cemeteries of the Pawnee. And like the latter the graves of the dead were undoubtedly visited by the mourners who would " cry," and lament their loss.

Dr Fordyce Grinnell, physician to the Wichita Agency, Indian Territory, furnishes the following description of the burial ceremonies of the Wichita Indians, who call themselves. "*Kitty-la- tats*" or those of the tattooed eyelids.

"When a Wichita dies the town-crier goes up and down through the village and announces the fact. Preparations are immediately made for the burial, and the body is taken without delay to the grave prepared for it reception. If the grave is some distance from the village the body is carried thither on the back of a pony, being first wrapped in blankets and then laid prone across the saddle, one walking on either side to support it. The grave is dug from 3 to 4 feet deep and of sufficient length for the extended body. First blankets and buffalo robes are laid in the bottom of the grave, then the body, being taken from the horse and unwrapped, is dressed in its best apparel and with ornaments is placed upon a couch of blankets and robes, with the head towards the west and the feet to the east; the valuables belonging to the deceased are placed with the body in the grave. With the man are deposited his bows and arrows or gun, and with the woman her cooking utensils and other implements of her toil. Over the body sticks are placed six or eight inches deep and grass over these, so that when the earth is filled in it need not come in contact with the body or its trappings. After the grave is filled with earth a pen of poles is built around it, or, as is frequently the case, stakes are driven so that they cross each other from either side about midway over the grave, thus forming a complete protection from the invasion of wild animals. After all this is done, the grass or other *debris* is carefully scraped from about the grave for several feet, so that the ground is left smooth and clean. It is seldom the case that the relatives accompany the remains to the grave, but they more often employ others to bury the body for them, usually women. Mourning is similar in this tribe as in others, and consists in cutting off the hair, fasting, &c. Horses are also killed at the grave."

Caddoe

Origin: East Texas, southern Arkansas, western Louisiana, and southeastern Oklahoma.

The Caddoes, *Ascena*, or Timber Indians, as they call themselves, follow nearly the same mode of burial as the Wichitas, but one custom prevailing is worthy of mention.

"If a Caddo is killed in battle, the body is never buried, but is left to be devoured by beasts or birds of prey and the condition of such individuals in the other world is considered to be far better than that of persons dying a natural death.

Hopi

Origin: Northeast Arizona

For obvious reasons grave digging is not a profitable pastime for ethnologists, whose chief object may be gained only through friendliness with the Indian group. Moreover, as Southwestern funerals are usually private affairs and as informants are loath to speak on a subject so fearful to them, data on modern disposal of the dead has been scanty. Consequently, we were interested in the details of one Hopi and of two Navajo children's burials which had been removed by an anthropological hobbyist whom we chanced to meet.

The Hopi bury their dead in the talus slope of the cliffs leading down to a bench on the mesa. From reluctant informants, the Beagleholes' obtained our best description of Hopi burial customs. According to their two informants, men from the Second Mesa, the Hopi are very much afraid of their dead and avoid being in the room with a corpse or taking part in the funeral proceedings if possible. The clothing worn at death is left on the body, which is flexed after the hair has been washed and tied in place.

The father, or some member of the clan of the deceased, makes prayer feathers, one of which is tied to the hair of the corpse. One of the plumes is placed under each foot, one in each hand, and one over the navel. Cotton, symbol of the future existence of the dead as a cloud, is placed over the face. Food for the death journey consists of wafer bread and a gourd of water; these are placed where the thighs flex against the body. The corpse of a man is wrapped, preferably in a buckskin, but if that is lacking a woman's white wedding dress is used. The body of a woman is wrapped in her large or small wedding blanket, or in both. The burial bundle of either sex is then tied up in a blanket belonging to the deceased and is carried to the burial ground, to be placed, facing west, in a shallow grave, quickly covered with sand, and marked with a stick which serves "as a ladder for the soul (breath) to depart westward." On the next day a bowl of corn meal and five prayer sticks are placed on the grave, a prayer is said, and four parallel marks are drawn on the trail to close it so that the spirit may not return to haunt the village.

The Beagleholes' information on child burials consisted merely of the statement that children were buried in the children's cemetery and that infants were placed in graves in the same cemetery or in fissures in the cliffs. The burial procedure is the same as for adults except that the infant is wrapped in a "cradle quilt" provided by the maternal aunt. The spirit of of an infant is believed to be reborn in another child of the opposite sex.

The Hopi child burial for which we have data had been taken from the children's cemetery on the bench at the eastern point of the Second Mesa, below Mishongnovi. The sites were heaped with low mounds of stones, and a short stick protruded a foot or two from the top of each. If the burial was in a crevice the stick projected from the earth filled crack. On top of the graves were placed pottery bowls, granite pans, and baskets of food. Other funerary offerings placed on the graves were personal belongings of the dead. Offerings, bowls, sherds, granite pans, and baskets in various states of decomposition were found scattered over the talus slope, where they had been washed by the water which pours over the cliffs above after heavy rains.

The burial was that of an infant, probably about six months old. Below the pile of rocks on the surface was a covering of earth. Below the earth a sheepskin protected the burial bundle itself. This pelt probably took the place of the buckskin used in adult male burials. The bundle was wrapped with two small hand-pieced quilts, inside of which was a wrapping of old coarse muslin. Beneath this was another quilt like the others, securely tied by the corners. Another quilt was beneath, and inside it a cloth which had to be pealed away to find the mummified body of the baby.

The legs were drawn up and the arms were pulled down to the sides, in the flexed burial position. A prayer plume had been tied to a lock of hair on the forehead, and one was beneath each arm and each foot. Another was laid over the navel, The child was naked, except for a pair of moccasins made of rabbit skin with the fur turned to the inside. A small black, white, and green plaque, about four inches in diameter and of the coiled type made on the Second Mesa, was placed upon the abdomen over the prayer plume. Two folded cloth diapers were among the wrappings. A pair of knitted bootees tied together by a ribbon was laid under the legs of the child, and a homemade cloth baby bonnet, decorated with blue feather- stitching and tied with ribbons, was under the head. Coarsely ground corn was heaped under the upper part of each arm. The face and front section of the head was covered with a piece of fine cotton cloth in which a mouth slit and two nasal apertures had been cut. The hair was covered with finely ground meal. There was no evidence of cotton over the face or head, but it is possible that the mask of cloth was intended to replace it.

No surface offerings were found with this burial, but on top of one rock pile marking a grave in the cemetery was found a weather-dried rubber ball, a crudely carved wooden duck about four inches long, a wooden peg- top, a celluloid comb such as are used by women at the back of their hair, and a handful of tiny blue and pink glass beads, evidently the remnants of a modern necklace. On top of another pile of stones was a small bundle tied up in white cloth. Within the covering was a calico elephant from which the sawdust stuffing was leaking, an empty Post Toasties box, an empty milk can with two holes at the top indicating that the can had been emptied by intention or at least had been opened and left to evaporate on the grave, a pair of rubber baby pants, a tiny white dress of commercial make, a pair of baby stockings, and a white stocking cap, home-made, with a pink tassel of crochet thread at the peak.

The type of offerings left with these child burials makes it difficult to believe that the Hopi picture their dead ancestors, relatives, and children only as animate cloud beings or katcinas, who certainly would not need food-to say nothing of rubber pants. For at least a short period after death, the spirit apparently requires not only clothing and sustenance for the death journey but also personal treasurers, such as toys.

A comparison of Navajo and Hopi burials with those of the prehistoric Southwest should provide data on the rate of acculturation in customs which are sometimes considered as among the last to be affected by outside influence. Kroeber, in 1927, aid out data from various parts of the world to show that burial customs are far less deeply rooted in a culture complex and hence are more changeable than hitherto has been supposed. He pointed out, however, that in dynastic Egypt and in the Southwestern Pueblo area mortuary customs had remained approximately stable over long periods of time. The Hopi and Navajo child burials examined confirm this by suggesting little change since prehistoric times in major traits of funerary custom, but they likewise show an appreciable influence from white culture contact in minor characteristics. *A. L. Kroeber, Disposal of the Dead (American Anthropologist, Vol. 29, pp. 308-15, 1927).*

Origin: northeastern Arizona and northwestern New Mexico.

The following interesting account of burial among the Pueblo Indians of San Geronimo de Taos, New Mexico, furnished by Judge Anthony Joseph, will show in a manner how civilized customs have become grafted upon those of a more barbaric nature. It should be remembered that the Pueblo people are next to the Cherokees, Choctaws, and others in the Indian Territory, the most civilized of our tribes.

According to Judge Joseph, these people call themselves *Wee-ka-nahs*.

These are commonly known to the whites as *Piros*. The manner of burial by these Indians, both ancient and modern, as far as I can ascertain from information obtained from the most intelligent of the tribe, is that the body of the dead is and has been always buried in the ground in a horizontal position with the flat bottom of the grave. The grave is generally dug out of the ground in the usual and ordinary manner, being about 6 feet deep, 7 feet long, and about 2 feet wide. It is generally finished after receiving its occupant by being leveled with the hard ground around it, never leaving, as is customary with the whites, a mound to mark the spot. This tribe of Pueblo Indians never cremated their dead, as they do not know, even by tradition, that it was ever done or attempted. There are no utensils or implements placed in the grave, but there are a great many Indian ornaments, such as beads of all colors, sea-shells, hawk-bells, round looking-glasses, and a profusion of ribbons of all imaginable colors; then they paint the body with red vermilion and white chalk, giving it a most fantastic as well as ludicrous appearance. They also place a variety of food in the grave as a wise provision for its long journey to the happy hunting-ground beyond the clouds.

The funeral ceremonies of this tribe are very peculiar. First, after death, the body is laid out on a fancy buffalo robe spread out on the ground, then they dress the body in the best possible manner in their style of dress; if a male, they put on his beaded leggings and embroidered *saco*, and his fancy dancing-moccasins, and his large brass or shell ear-rings; if a female, they put on her best manta or dress, tied around the waist with a silk sash, put on her feet her fancy dancing-moccasins; her *rosario* around her neck, her brass or shell ear-rings in her ears, and with her tressed black hair tied up with red tape or ribbon, this completes her wardrobe for her long and happy chase. When they get through dressing the body, they place about a dozen lighted candles around it, and keep them burning continually until the body is buried. As soon as the candles are lighted, the *veloris*, or wake, commences; the body lies in state for about twenty-four hours, and in that time all the friends, relatives, and neighbors of the deceased or "*difunti*" visit the wake, chant, sing, and pray for the soul of the same, and tell one another of the good deeds and traits of valor and courage manifested by the deceased during his earthly career, and at intervals in their praying, singing,& c., some near relative of the deceased will step up to the corpse and every person in the room commences to cry bitterly and express aloud words of endearment to the deceased and of condolence to the family of the same in their untimely bereavement.

At about midnight supper is announced, and every person in attendance marches out into another room and partakes of a frugal Indian meal, generally composed of wild game; Chilé Colorado or red-pepper tortillas, and guayaves, with a good supply of mush and milk, which completes the festive board of the *veloris* or wake. When the deceased is in good circumstances, the crowd in attendance is treated every little while during the wake to alcoholic refreshments.

This feast and feasting is kept up until the Catholic priest arrives to perform the funeral rites.

When the priest arrives, the corpse is done up or rather baled up in a large and well-tanned buffalo robe, and tied around tight with a rope or lasso made for the purpose; then six or eight men act as pall-bearers, conducting the body to the place of burial, which is in front of their church or chapel. The priest conducts the funeral ceremonies in the ordinary and usual way of mortuary proceedings observed by the Catholic church all over the world. While the grave-diggers are filling up the grave, the friends, relatives, neighbors, and, in fact, all persons that attend the funeral, give vent to their sad feelings by making the whole pueblo howl; after the tremendous uproar subsides, they disband and leave the body to rest until Gabriel blows his trumpet. When the ceremonies are performed with all the pomp of the Catholic church, the priest receives a fair compensation for his services; otherwise he officiates for the yearly rents that all the Indians of the pueblo pay him, which amount in the sum total to about $2,000 per annum.

These Pueblo Indians are very strict in their mourning observance, which last for one year after the demise of the deceased. While in mourning for the dead, the mourners do not participate in the national festivities of the tribe, which are occasions of state with them, but they retire into a state of sublime quietude which makes more civilized people sad to observe; but when the term of mourning ceases, at the end of the year, they have high mass said for the benefit of the soul of the departed; after this they again appear upon the arena of their wild sports and continue to be gay and happy until the next mortal is called from this terrestrial sphere to the happy hunting-ground, which is their pictured celestial paradise. The above cited facts, which are the most interesting points connected with the burial customs of the Indians of the pueblo San Geronimo de Taos, are not in the least exaggerated, but are the absolute facts, which I have witnessed myself in many instances for a period of more than twenty years that I have resided but a short distant from said pueblo, and, being a close observer of their peculiar burial customs, am able to give you this true and undisguised information relative to your circular on "burial customs."

Moquis (Pueblo)

Origin:northeastern part of Arizona, near the borders of New Mexico

G. K. Gilbert, of the United States Geological Survey, informs the writer that in 1878 he had a conversation with an old Moquis chief as to their manner of burial, which is as follows: The body is placed in a receptacle or cist of stone slabs or wood, in a sitting posture, the hands near the knees, and clasping a stick (articles are buried with the dead), and it is supposed that the soul finds its way out of the grave by climbing up the stick, which is allowed to project above the ground after the grave is filled in.

Origin: Texas, Oklahoma, and and New Mexico.

From Dr. O. G. Given, physician to the Kiowa and Comanche Agency, Indian Territory, the following description of burial ceremonies was received. According to this gentleman the Kiowas call themselves Kaw-a-wāh, the Comanches Nerm, and the Apaches Tāh-zee.

They bury in the ground or in crevices of rocks. They do not seem to have any particular rule with regard to the position. Sometimes prone, sometimes supine, but always recumbent. They select a place where the grave is easily prepared, which they do with such implements as they chance to have, viz, a squaw-axe, or hoe. If they are traveling, the grave is often very hastily prepared and not much time is spent in finishing. I was present at the burial of Black Hawk, an Apache chief, some two years ago, and took the body in my light wagon up the side of a mountain to the place of burial. They found a crevice in the rocks about four feet wide and three feet deep. By filling in loose rocks at either end they made a very nice tomb. The body was then put in face downwards, short sticks were put across, resting on projections of rock at the sides, brush was thrown on this, and flat rocks laid over the whole of it.

The body of the deceased is dressed in the best clothing, together with all the ornaments most admired by the person when living. The face is painted with any colored paint they may have, mostly red and yellow, as I have observed. The body is then wrapped in skins, blankets, or domestic, with the hands laid across the breast, and the legs placed upon the thighs. They put into the grave their guns, bows and arrows, tobacco, and if they have it a blanket, moccasins, and trinkets of various kinds. One 143or more horses are killed over or near the grave. Two horses and a mule were killed near Black Hawk's grave. They were led up near and shot in the head. At the death of a Comanche chief, some years ago, I am told about seventy horses were killed, and a greater number than that were said to have been killed at the death of a prominent Kiowa chief a few years since.

The mourning is principally done by the relatives and immediate friends, although any one of their own tribe, or one of another tribe, who chances to be passing, will stop and moan with the relatives. Their mourning consists in a weird wail, which to be described must be heard, and once heard is never forgotten, together with the scarifying of their faces, arms, and legs with some sharp instrument, the cutting off of the hair, and oftentimes the cutting off of a joint of a finger, usually the little finger (Comanches do not cut off fingers). The length of time and intensity of their mourning depends upon the relation and position of the deceased in the tribe. I have known instances where, if they should be passing along where any of their friends had died, even a year after their death, they would mourn.

The Comanches of Indian Territory (*Nem, we, or us, people*), according to Dr. Fordyce Grinnell, of the Wichita Agency, Indian Territory, go to the opposite extreme, so far as the protection of the dead from the surrounding earth is concerned. The account as received is given entire, as much to illustrate this point as others of interest.

When a Comanche is dying, while the death-rattle may yet be faintly heard in the throat, and the natural warmth has not departed from the body, the knees are strongly bent upon the chest, and the legs flexed upon the thighs. The arms are also flexed upon each side of the chest, and the head bent forward upon the knees. A lariat, or rope, is now used to firmly bind the limbs and body in this position. A blanket is then wrapped around the body, and this again tightly corded, so that the appearance when ready for burial is that of an almost round and compact body, very unlike the composed pall of his Wichita or Caddo brother. The body is then taken and placed in a saddle upon a pony, in a sitting posture; a squaw usually riding behind, though sometimes one on either side of the horse, holds the body in position until the place of burial is reached, when the corpse is literally tumbled into the excavation selected for the purpose. The deceased is only accompanied by two or three squaws, or enough to perform the little labor bestowed upon the burial. The body is taken due west of the lodge or village of the bereaved, and usually one of the deep washes or heads of cañons in which the Comanche country abounds is selected, and the body thrown in, without special reference to position. With this are deposited the bows and arrows; these, however, are first broken. The saddle is also placed in the grave, together with many of the personal valuables of the departed. The body is then covered over with sticks and earth, and sometimes stones are placed over the whole.

Funeral ceremonies.—the best pony owned by the deceased is brought to the grave and killed, that the departed may appear well mounted and caparisoned among his fellows in the other world. Formerly, if the deceased were a chief or man of consequence and had large herds of ponies, many were killed, sometimes amounting to 200 or 300 head in number.

The Comanches illustrate the importance of providing a good pony for the convoy 100of the deceased to the happy-grounds by the following story, which is current among both Comanches and Wichitas:

"A few years since, an old Comanche died who had no relatives and who was quite poor. Some of the tribe concluded that almost any kind of a pony would serve to transport him to the next world. They therefore killed at his grave an old, ill-conditioned, lop-eared horse. But a few weeks after the burial of this friendless one, lo and behold he returned, riding this same old worn-out horse, weary and hungry. He first appeared at the Wichita camps, where he was well known, and asked for something to eat, but his strange appearance, with sunken eyes and hollow cheeks, filled with consternation all who saw him, and they fled from his presence. Finally one bolder than the rest placed a piece of meat on the end of a lodge-pole and extended it to him. He soon appeared at his own camp, creating, if possible, even more dismay than among the Wichitas, and this resulted in both Wichitas and Comanches leaving their villages and moving *en mass* to a place on Rush Creek, not far distant from the present site of Fort Sill.

"When the troubled spirit from the sun setting world was questioned why he thus appeared among the inhabitants of earth, he made reply that when he came to the gates of paradise the keepers would on no account permit him to enter upon such an ill-conditioned beast as that which bore him, and thus in sadness he returned to haunt the homes of those whose stinginess and greed permitted him no better equipment. Since this no Comanche has been permitted to depart with the sun to his chambers in the west without a steed which in appearance should do honor alike to the rider and his friends."

The body is buried at the sun setting side of the camp, that the spirit may accompany the setting sun to the world beyond. The spirit starts on its journey the following night after death has taken place; if this occur at night, the journey is not begun until the next night.

Mourning observances.—All the effects of the deceased, the tents, blankets, clothes, treasures, and whatever of value, aside from the articles which have been buried with the body, are burned, so that the family is left in poverty. This practice has extended even to the burning of wagons and harness since some of the civilized habits have been adopted. It is believed that these ascend to heaven in the smoke, and will thus be of service to the owner in the other world. Immediately upon the death of a member of the household, the relatives begin a peculiar wailing, and the immediate members of the family take off their customary apparel and clothe themselves in rags and cut themselves across the arms, breast, and other portions of the body, until sometimes a fond wife or mother faints from loss of blood. This scarification is usually accomplished with a knife, or, as in earlier days, with a flint. Hired mourners are employed at times who are in no way related to the family, but who are accomplished in the art of crying for the dead. These are invariably women. Those nearly related to the departed, cut off the long locks from the entire head, while those more distantly related, or special friends, cut the hair only from one side of the head. In case of the death of a chief, the young warriors also cut the hair, usually from the left side of the head.

After the first few days of continued grief, the mourning is conducted more especially at sunrise and sunset, as the Comanches venerate the sun; and the mourning at these seasons is kept up, if the death occurred in summer, until the leaves fall, or, if in the winter, until they reappear.

Great Basin

Shoshone

Origin: Utah, Nevada, Wyoming, Idaho

Dr. W. J. Hoffman writes as follows regarding the burial lodges of the Shoshones of Nevada:

The Shoshones of the upper portion of Nevada are not known to have at any time practiced cremation. In Independence Valley, under a deserted and demolished *wickeup* or "brush tent," I found the dried-up corpse of a boy, about twelve years of age. The body had been here for at least six weeks, according to information received, and presented a shriveled and hideous appearance. The dryness of the atmosphere prevented decomposition. The Indians in this region usually leave the body when life terminates, merely throwing over it such rubbish as may be at hand, or the remains of their primitive shelter tents, which are mostly composed of small branches, leaves, grass, &c.

The Shoshones living on Independence Creek and on the eastern banks of the Owyhee River, upper portion of Nevada, did not bury their dead at the time of my visit in 1871. Whenever the person died, his lodge (usually constructed of poles and branches of *Salix*) was demolished and placed in one confused mass over his remains, when the band removed a short distance. When the illness is not too great, or death sudden, the sick person is removed to a favorable place, some distance from their temporary camping ground, so as to avoid the necessity of their own removal. Coyotes, ravens, and other carnivores soon remove all the flesh so that there remains nothing but the bones, and even these are scattered by the wolves. The Indians at Tuscarora, Nevada, stated that when it was possible and that they should by chance meet the bony remains of any Shoshone, they would bury it, but in what manner I failed to discover as the were very reticent, and avoided giving any information regarding the dead. One corpse was found totally dried and shriveled, owing to the dryness of the atmosphere in this region.

The Shoshones, of Nevada, generally concealed their dead beneath heaps of rocks, according to H. Butterflied, of Tyho, Nye County, Nevada, although occasionally they either burn or bury them. He gives as reasons for rock burial: 1st, to prevent coyotes eating the corpses; 2d, because they have no tools for deep excavations; and 3d, natural indolence of the Indians—indisposition to work any more than can be helped.

Ute Indians

Origin: Colorado, Utah, New Mexico, and Nevada.

While in the Territory of Utah, in 1872, the writer discovered a natural cave not far from the House Range of mountains, the entrance to which resembled the shaft of a mine. In this the Gosi-Ute Indians had deposited their dead, surrounded with different articles, until it was quite filled up; at least it so appeared from the cursory examination made, limited time preventing a careful exploration. In the fall of the same year another cave was heard of, from an Indian guide, near the Nevada border, in the same Territory, and an attempt made to explore it, which failed for reasons to be subsequently given. This Indian, a Gosi-Ute, who was questioned regarding the funeral ceremonies of his tribe, informed the writer that not far from the very spot where the party were encamped was a large cave in which he had himself assisted in placing dead members of his tribe. He described it in detail and drew a rough diagram of its position and appearance within. He was asked if an entrance could be effected, and replied that he thought not, as some years previous his people had stopped up the narrow entrance to prevent game from seeking a refuge in its vast vaults, for he asserted that it was so large and extended so far under ground that no man knew its full extent. In consideration, however, of a very liberal bribe, after many refusals, he agreed to act as guide. A rough ride of over an hour and the desired spot was reached. It was found to be almost upon the apex of a small mountain apparently of volcanic origin, for the hole which was pointed out appeared to have been the vent of the crater. This entrance was irregularly circular in form and descended at an angle. As the Indian had stated, it was completely stopped up with large stones and roots of sage brush, and it was only after six hours of uninterrupted, faithful labor that the attempt to explore was abandoned. The guide was asked if many bodies were therein, and replied "Heaps, heaps," moving the hands upwards as far as they could be stretched. There is no reason to doubt the accuracy of the information received, as it was voluntarily imparted.

In a communication received from Dr. A. J McDonald, physician to the Los Pinos Indian Agency, Colorado, a description is given of crevice or rock-fissure burial, which follows.

"As soon as death takes place the event is at once announced by the medicine-man, and without loss of time the squaws are busily engaged in preparing the corpse for the grave. This does not take long; whatever articles of clothing may have been on the body at the time of death are not removed. The dead man's limbs are straightened out, his weapons of war laid by his side, and his robes and blankets wrapped securely and snugly around him, and now everything is ready for burial. It is the custom to secure, if possible, for the purpose of wrapping up the corpse, the robes and blankets in which the Indian died. At the same time that the body is being fitted for interment, the squaws having immediate care of it, together with all the other squaws in the neighborhood, keep up a continued chant or dirge, the dismal cadence of which may, when the congregation of women is large, be heard for quite a long distance. The death song is not a mere inarticulate howl of distress; it embraces expressions eulogistic in character, but whether or not any particular formula of words is adopted on such occasion is a question which I am unable, with the materials at my disposal, to determine with any degree of certainty.

"The next duty falling to the lot of the squaws is that of placing the dead man on a horse and conducting the remains to the spot chosen for burial. This is in the cleft of a rock, and, so far as can be ascertained, it has always been customary among the Utes to select sepulchers of this character. From descriptions given by Mr. Harris, who has several times been fortunate enough to discover remains, it would appear that no superstitious ideas are held by this tribe with respect to the position in which the body is placed, the space accommodation of the sepulcher probably regulating this matter; and from the same source I learn that it is not usual to find the remains of more than one Indian deposited in one grave. After the body has been received into the cleft, it is well covered with pieces of rock, to protect it against the ravages of wild animals. The chant ceases, the squaws disperse, and the burial ceremonies are at an end. The men during all this time have not been idle, though they have in no way participated in the preparation of the body, have not joined the squaws in chanting praises to the memory of the dead, and have not even as mere spectators attended the funeral, yet they have had their duties to perform. In conformity with a long-established custom, all the personal property of the deceased is immediately destroyed. His horses and his cattle are shot, and his wigwam, furniture, &c., burned. The performance of this part of the ceremonies is assigned to the men; a duty quite in accord with their taste and inclinations. Occasionally the destruction of horses and other property is of considerable magnitude, but usually this is not the case, owing to a practice existing with them of distributing their property among their children while they are of a very tender age, retaining to themselves only what is necessary to meet every-day requirements.

"The widow 'goes into mourning' by smearing her face with a substance composed of pitch and charcoal. The application is made but once, and is allowed to remain on until it wears off. This is the only mourning observance of which I have any knowledge.

"The ceremonies observed on the death of a female are the same as those in the case of a male, except that no destruction of property takes place, and of course no weapons are deposited with the corpse. Should a youth die while under the superintendence of white men, the Indians will not as a rule have anything to do with the interment of the body. In a case of the kind which occurred at this agency some time ago, the squaws prepared the body in the usual manner; the men of the tribe selected a spot for the burial, and the employees at the agency, after digging a grave and depositing the corpse therein, filled it up according to the fashion of civilized people, and then at the request of the Indians rolled large fragments of rocks on top. Great anxiety was exhibited by the Indians to have the employees perform the service as expeditiously as possible."

Goshute

Origin: Utah

"Skull Valley, which is a part of the Great Salt Lake Desert, and which we have crossed to-day, Mr. George W. Bean, my guide over this route last fall, says derives its name from the number of skulls which have been found in it, and which have arisen from the custom of the Goshute Indians burying their dead in springs, which they sink with stones or keep down with sticks. He says he has actually seen the Indians bury their dead in this way near the town of Provo, where he resides."

Skull Valley photo taken by the Bureau of Land Management.

As corroboration of this statement, Captain Simpson mentions in another part of the volume that, arriving at a spring one evening, they were obliged to dig out the skeleton of an Indian from the mud at the bottom before using the water.

This peculiar mode of burial is entirely unique, so far as known, and but from the well-known probity of the relater might well be questioned, especially when it is remembered that in the country spoken of water is quite scarce and Indians are careful not to pollute the streams or springs near which they live. Conjecture seems useless to establish a reason for this disposition of the dead.

Blackfoot

Origins: Montana, Idaho, and Alberta, Canada.

John Young, Indian agent at the Blackfeet Agency, Montana, sends the following account of tree-burial among this tribe:

"Their manner of burial has always been (until recently) to enclose the dead body in robes or blankets, the best owned by the departed, closely sewed up, and then, if a male or chief, fasten in the branches of a tree so high as to be beyond the reach of wolves, and then left to slowly waste in the dry winds. If the body was that of a squaw or child, it was thrown into the underbrush or jungle, where it soon became the prey of the wild animals. The weapons, pipes, &c., of men were enclosed, and the small toys of children with them. The ceremonies were equally barbarous, the relatives cutting off, according to the depth of their grief, one or more joints of the fingers, divesting themselves of clothing even in the coldest weather, and filling the air with their lamentations. All the sewing up and burial process was conducted by the squaws, as the men would not touch nor remain in proximity to a dead body.

"When an Indian of any importance is departing, the squaws assemble in the lodge or tepee and sing the death-song, recounting the prowess and virtues of the dying one, and the oldest man at hand goes into the open air and solemnly addresses the 'Great Spirit,' bespeaking a welcome for him into the happy hunting grounds. Whatever property the deceased has—lodge, arms, or ponies—if a will was made, it was carefully carried out; if not, all was scrambled for by the relatives. I have often had, when a man wanted to go out of mourning, to supply the necessary clothing to cover his nakedness.

"Further mourning observances were and are, the women relatives getting on some elevated spot near where the body rests, and keeping up a dismal wail, frequently even in extreme cold weather, the greater part of the night, and this is kept up often for a month. No cremation or burying in a grave was practiced by them at any time. Pained by often coming on skeletons in trees and the stench of half-consumed remains in the brush, and shocked by the frequent mutilations visible, I have reasoned with the poor savages. In one case, when a woman was about to cut off a finger in evidence of her grief for the loss of a child, she consented on entreaty to cut off only one joint, and on further entreaty was brought to merely making a cut and letting out some blood. This much she could not be prevailed upon to forego…. Their mourning and wailing, avoiding the defilement of touching a dead body, and other customs not connected with burial observances, strongly point to Jewish origin."

This painting was being sold on "auction zip" with the following description. "This is an original oil on canvas work of art. This is a folk art in style. This features 5 Blackfoot Indians preparing the body for burial. The female Indian on the left is offering a prayer well the kneeling Indian is cutting off one of her fingers on a log along with the man. The standing male Indian sings the death song while the male Indian on the far right is bending over readying to cut his left leg to let blood. This is a fantastic work of a very private ceremony that only a few could witness. Most likely painted from the Blackfoot People."

Keating [Footnote: Long's Exped. to the St. Peter's River, 1834, p. 392.] thus describes burial scaffolds:

"On these scaffolds, which are from 8 to 10 feet high, corpses were deposited in a box made from part of a broken canoe. Some hair was suspended, which we at first mistook for a scalp, but our guide informed us that these were locks of hair torn from their heads by the relatives to testify their grief. In the center, between the four posts which supported the scaffold, a stake was planted in the ground; it was about six feet high, and bore an imitation of human figures, five of which had a design of a petticoat, indicating them to be females; the rest, amounting to seven, were naked, and were intended for male figures; of the latter four were headless, showing that they had been slain; the three other male figures were unmutilated, but held a staff in their hand, which, as our guide informed us, designated that they were slaves. The post, which is an usual accompaniment to the scaffold that supports a warrior's remains, does not represent the achievements of the deceased; but those of the warriors that assembled near his remains danced the dance of the post, and related their martial exploits. A number of small bones of animals were observed in the vicinity, which were probably left there after a feast celebrated in honor of the dead.

"The boxes in which the corpses were placed are so short that a man could not lie in them extended at full length, but in a country where boxes and boards are scarce this is overlooked. After the corpses have remained a certain time exposed, they are taken down and buried. Our guide, Renville, related to us that he had been a witness to an interesting, though painful, circumstance that occurred here. An Indian who resided on the Mississippi, hearing that his son had died at this spot, came up in a canoe to take charge of the remains and convey them down the river to his place of abode, but on his arrival he found that the corpse had already made such progress toward decomposition as rendered it impossible for it to be removed. He then undertook, with a few friends, to clean off the bones. All the flesh was scraped off and thrown into the stream, the bones were carefully collected into his canoe, and subsequently carried down to his residence."

Maximilian, who came in contact with these tribes during the summer of 1833, wrote regarding the customs of the people at the time of the death of one of their number : " "When a Blackfoot dies, they do not bury him in the ground if they can avoid it, but sew him up in a buffalo robe, dressed in his best clothes, his face painted red, but without his weapons, and lay him in some retired place, in

ravines, rocks, forests, or on a high, steep bank, and often cover the body with wood or stones, that the wolves may not get at it. Frequently, when they cannot find a solitary spot, the corpse remains above ground in a kind of wooden shed, and they were often obliged to bury it, or to give it to the Whites as a desirable present, which cannot be refused. The relations cut off their long hair, smear it, as well as their faces and clothes,with whitish-grey clay, and, during the time of mourning, and wear their worst clothing. Often, too, they cut off a joint of a finger. They believe the dead go into another country, where they will have lack of nothing; and that they have often been heard when they were summoned to smoke a pipe together. At the funeral of rich Indians, several horses are often killed upon the spot; and we were told of instances when twelve or fifteen horses were killed in this manner at the funeral of a celebrated chief . . . The relations assemble at the residence of the deceased, and even the men lament and wail. The corpse is generally buried on the first day, and in case of death during the night, it is removed on the following morning." He likewise referred briefly to the treatment of the sick: "The medicine men or physicians of the Blackfeet are very unskillful. We always saw them take water in their mouths, which they spit out over the wounded . . . Drums and rattles were daily used in their attendance on the sick, in the closed tent . . . These Indians have some efficacious remedies derived from the vegetable kingdom, one of which is a whitish root from the Rocky Mountains, which is called, by the Canadians, rhubarb, which is said to resemble our rhubarb in its effect and taste, and likewise to act as an emetic. Another root is esteemed to be a powerful remedy against the bite of serpents. In all cases they have recourse to the drum and the rattle, and have great confidence in the intolerable noise caused by those instruments. The Blackfeet make their rattles of leather, wood, or bladder."

The burial and mourning customs of the Blackfeet were interestingly described by another observer a few years later : "The Blackfeet do not place their dead on scaffolds but either in a hole well covered to keep off the wolves, or they leave them in the lodge with everything just as it is when they die. In that case the wolves of course eat their bodies very soon ; and I am told that in this way the body of nearly every Blackfoot is disposed of. When one of them is in mourning he puts white earth on his head and goes out before his lodge wailing most piteously; as soon as the neighbors see that they all rush to his lodge and take it and everything it contains, leaving him nothing but his horse. The death of a relation is therefore a very serious affair, since a man loses all his property as well as his friend." (Culbertson, p. 126.)

The two preceding accounts contain rather conflicting statements, but they may refer to different groups of the Blackfoot confederacy. Possibly the tribal customs have undergone a change within a comparatively short time. This would be suggested by the following quotation: "Their manner of burial has always been (until recently) to enclose the dead body in robes or blankets, the best owned by the departed, closely sewed up, and then, if a male or chief, fasten in the branches of a tree so high as to be beyond the reach of wolves, and then left to slowly waste in the dry winds. If the body was that of a squaw or child, it was thrown into the underbrush or jungle, where it soon became the prey of the wild animals. The weapons, pipes, &c., of men were enclosed, and the small toys of children with them. The ceremonies were equally barbarous, the relatives cutting off, according to the depth of their grief, one or more joints of the fingers, divesting themselves of clothing even in the coldest weather, and filling the air with their lamentations. All the sewing up and burial process was conducted by the squaws, as the men would not touch nor remain in proximity to a dead body." The preceding notes were prepared by John Young at the Blackfoot Agency, and tell of conditions as they existed some 50 years ago, but it is doubtful if he was acquainted with local customs of the more distant villages, where the older methods of disposing of the dead may still have been practiced.

Another and what is intended to be a general account of the burial customs of these tribes written only a few years later is very interesting as it contains references to certain customs not mentioned by other writers. It begins : "Their funeral and burial ceremonies indicate their belief in the immortality of the soul. These forms are of a similar type among all the tribes composing the nation. They place

their dead, dressed in gaudiest apparel, within a tent, in a sitting posture, or occasionally fold them in skins and lay them on high scaffolds out of the reach of wild beasts, under which the relatives weep and wail. The arms and horses are buried with them, to be used in the long journey to the spirit land, showing the possession of the idea of the dual nature of matter and spirit." And the same writer continues and relates a curious custom following the death of a child : "Immediately upon its decease, the whole village rush into the lodge and take possession of what ever portable property they can seize upon, until the grief-stricken parents are stripped of all their worldly possessions, not even excepting their clothing. The only method of evading the custom is to secrete the most valuable property beforehand, generally a matter difficult of accomplishment." Evidently the death of a child caused much sorrow among the people, and as told by one who as well acquainted with the ways of life of Blackfeet : "Late one afternoon as I was pursuing my way through the outskirts of the camp, I heard a low sad wail, and on looking up, saw a poor woman meanly clad, the beautiful garments of yesterday, having been taken from her. Her legs from the knees to the feet had been gashed with a knife and the blood was clotted upon them. Her hair had been cut off, and one of the fingers on the left hand had been severed at the first joint. A piece of wood lay in the palm of the injured hand, the clotted blood was mingled with ashes, which had been sprinkled over it. I spoke to her and she pointed to a tree, where hidden within the branches lay a little bundle, the darling of her bosom, recently dead. She turned from me and sang her coronach, mentioning the name of her babe and calling upon it to come back to her. Deeply and tender these Indian mothers love their children, and no suffering is too great for them to bear on their behalf."

In the same account is a reference to the placing of the dead "in the crotches of trees, or raised platforms, and in lodges," the latter probably resembling the similar form of burial as mentioned among the Crow and Oglala. The writer whose work has just been quoted continues and gives a brief description of the treatment of the sick, and likewise of conditions that exist after death. He says:

"When anyone is sick a part of the garments of the sick person is placed upon the top of the lodge, that being shaken by the wind the prairie spirits may be induced to stop upon their journey, and the medicine man earnestly performs his incantations and giving of medicines, assisted by the friends of the sick person, and the gods, listening to the prayers, will aid in the overthrow of the evil genius which dwells in the body. During a severe time of sickness in one of the camps, as I sat beside the medicine man in one of the lodges, a large number of children were brought in, and the medicine man, taking the dress from the top of the lodge, rubbed the children's persons with it, as a protection against the attack of the disease. When anyone dies, he is said to have gone to the Sand Hills.

" The people are afraid of the spirits of the dead, and at once they remove the lodge, and sometimes even tear down the house, lest the spirit of the deceased return and inflict injury upon the living. They believe that the spirits of the dead hold communion with each other, and require food and clothing like the living, only as they 'are spiritual, they need the spiritual part, and not the material, for their sustenance. *The Smithsonian Bureau of Ethnology, Bulletin 83, 1927*

Yakima

Origin: Idaho, Oregon, Washington

Long before my time, perhaps in my grandmother's time, they rubbed pitch over the face e if the widow woman, to which they added a coating of charcoal. The face was covered all over in this way and she had to wear it for five years. The hair was cut out and sometimes it was cut almost as close as if it was shaved from the head. Our tribes have not done this for many years, but about twenty years ago I saw an old woman of the Pitt River, California, with pitch on their faces. I asked them why this pitch, and they answered: "Our grandson was in school to a white teacher, They ran and will see him no more. He is dead."

They mourned him every day, but he was not dead as they though. He and this teacher had married, but after about three years they parted and the young man came back. The old people then discarded the pitch and no longer mourned.

The custom of burying the dead in housed among the Yakima, was recent and borrowed by them from the Wascos and Wishoms, about the time they came into the Yakima nation by right of treaty 1855. The Yakima buried the dead in the rocks along the bluff and rock slides.

Pacific Northwest

Achomawi

Origin: Northeast California

Achomawi Indians of California, who "bury the body in the ground in a standing position, the shoulders nearly even with the ground. The grave is prepared by digging a hole of sufficient depth and circumference to admit the body, the head being cut off. In the grave are placed the bows and arrows, bead-work, trappings, &c., belonging to the deceased; quantities of food, consisting of dried fish, roots, herbs, &c., were placed with the body also. The grave was then filled up, covering the headless body; then a bundle of fagots was brought and placed on the grave by the different members of the tribe, and on these fagots the head was placed, the pile fired, and the head consumed to ashes; after this was done, the female relatives of the deceased, who had appeared as mourners with their faces blackened with a preparation resembling tar or paint, dipped their fingers in the ashes of the cremated head and made three marks on their right cheek. This constituted the mourning garb, the period of which lasted until this black substance wore off from the face. In addition to this mourning, the blood female relatives of the deceased (who, by the way, appeared to be a man of distinction) had their hair cropped short. I noticed while the head was burning that the old women of the tribe sat on the ground, forming a large circle, inside of which another circle of young girls were formed standing and swaying their bodies to and fro and singing a mournful ditty. This was the only burial of a male that I witnessed. The custom of burying females is very different, their bodies being wrapped or bundled up in skins and laid away in caves, with their valuables, and in some cases food being placed with them in their mouths. Occasionally money is left to pay for food in the spirit land."

Karuk

Origin: northwestern corner of the state of California, in Humboldt and Siskiyou Counties.

Stephen Powers in his valuable work so often quoted, gives a number of examples of superstitions regarding the

EMMA MILLET LUSCIER

dead of which the following relates to the Karuk of California.

"How well and truly the Karuk reverence the memory of the dead is shown by the fact that the highest crime one can commit is the *pet- chi-e-ri*, the mere mention of the dead relative's name. It is a deadly insult to the survivors and can be atoned for only by the same amount of blood money paid for willful murder. In default of that they will have the villain's blood.... At the mention of his name the moldering skeleton turns in his grave and groans. They do not like stragglers even to inspect the burial place.... They believe that the soul of a good Karok goes to the 'happy western land' beyond the great ocean. That they have a well grounded assurance of an immortality beyond the grave is proven, if not otherwise, by their beautiful and poetical custom of whispering a message in the ear of the dead.... Believe that dancing will liberate some relative's soul from bonds of death and restore him to earth" *First Annual Report of the Bureau of Ethnology to the Secretary of the Smithsonian Institution, 1879-80,*

Shanel Indians

Origins: Northern California

According to Stephen Powers, [Footnote: Contrib. to N. A. Ethnol., 1877, vol. iii, p. 169.] cremation was common among the Se-nel of California. He thus relates it—

"The dead are mostly burned. Mr. Willard described to me a scene of incremation that be once witnessed which was frightful for its exhibitions of fanatic frenzy and infatuation. The corpse was that of a wealthy chieftain, and as he lay upon the funeral pyre they placed in his mouth two gold twenties, and other smaller coins in his ears and hands, on his breast, etc., besides all his finery, his feather mantles, plumes, clothing, shell money, his fancy bows, painted arrows, etc. When the torch was applied they set up a mournful ululation, chanting and dancing about him, gradually working themselves into a wild and ecstatic raving, which seemed almost a demoniacal possession, leaping, howling, lacerating their flesh. Many seemed to lose all self-control. The younger English-speaking Indians generally lend themselves charily to such superstitious work, especially if American spectators are present, but even they were carried away by the old contagious frenzy of their race. One stripped off a broadcloth coat, quite new and fine, and ran frantically yelling and cast it upon the blazing-pile. Another rushed up and was about to throw on a pile of California blankets, when a white man, to test his sincerity, offered him $16 for them, jingling the bright coins before his eyes, but the savage (for such he had become again for the moment), otherwise so avaricious, hurled him away with a yell of execration and ran and threw his offering into the flames. Squaws, even more frenzied, wildly flung upon the pyre all they had in the world—their dearest ornaments, their gaudiest dresses, their strings of glittering shells. Screaming, wailing, tearing their hair, beating their breasts in their mad and insensate infatuation, some of them would have cast themselves bodily into the flaming ruins and perished with the chief had they not been restrained by their companions. Then the bright, swift flames with their hot tongues licked this 'cold obstruction' into chemic change, and the once 'delighted spirit' of the savage was borne up…

"It seems as if the savage shared in Shakespeare's shudder at the thought of rotting in the dismal grave, for it is the one passion of his superstition to think of the soul of his departed friend set free and purified by the swift purging heat of the flames, not dragged down to be clogged and bound in the moldering body, but borne up in the soft, warm chariots of the smoke toward the beautiful sun, to bask in his warmth and light, and then, to fly away to the Happy Western Land. What wonder if the Indian shrinks with unspeakable horror from the thought of *burying his friend's soul!*—of pressing and ramming down with pitiless clods that inner something which once took such delight in the sweet light of the sun! What wonder if it takes years to persuade him to do otherwise and follow our custom! What wonder if even then he does it with sad fears and misgivings! Why not let him keep his custom! In the gorgeous landscapes and balmy climate of California and India incremation is as natural to the savage as it is for him to love the beauty of the sun. Let the vile Esquimaux and the frozen Siberian bury their dead if they will; it matters little, the earth is the same above as below, or to them the bosom of the earth may seem even the better; but in California do not blame the savage if he recoils at the thought of going under ground! This soft, pale halo of the lilac hills—ah, let him console himself if he will with the belief that his lost friend enjoys it still! The narrator concluded by saying that they destroyed full $500 worth of property. 'The blankets,' said he with a fine Californian scorn of such absurd insensibility to a good bargain, 'the blankets that the American offered him $16 for were not worth half the money.'

"After death the Se-nel hold that bad Indians return into coyotes. Others fall off a bridge which all souls must traverse, or are hooked off by a raging bull at the further end, while the good escape across. Like the Yokaia and the Konkan, they believe it necessary to nourish the spirits of the departed for the space of a year. This is generally done by a squaw, who takes pinole in her blanket, repairs to the scene of the incremation, or to places hallowed by the memory of the dead, where she scatters it over the ground, meantime rocking her body violently to and fro in a dance and chanting the following chorus:

Hel-lel-li-ly,
Hel-lel-lo,
Hel-lel-lu.

"This refrain is repeated over and over indefinitely, but the words have no meaning whatever."

Yuki

Origin: Northwest California

Stephen Powers describes a similar mode of grave preparation among the Yuki of California: The Yuki bury their dead in a sitting posture. They dig a hole six feet deep sometimes and at the bottom of it "*coyote*" under, making a little recess in which the corpse is deposited. *Contributions to the Bureau of Ethnology., 1877, vol. iii, p. 133.*

Tolowa

Taa-laa-wa Dee-ni Tolowa woman with facial tattoos, circa 1900

Origin: Northwest California

 "The Tolowa share in the superstitious observance for the memory of the dead which is common to the Northern Californian tribes When I asked the chief Tahhokolli to tell me the Indian words for 'father' and 'mother' and certain others similar, he shook his head mournfully and said 'all dead,' 'all dead,' 'no good.' They are forbidden to mention the name of the dead, as it is a deadly insult to the relatives,"… and that the "Mat-toal hold that the good depart to a happy region somewhere southward in the great ocean, but the soul of a bad Indian transmigrates into a grizzly bear, which they consider of all animals the cousin-german of sin. *Annual Report of the Bureau of American Ethnology to the Smithsonian Institution 1881*

Yokayo

Yokayo Indian Village, Ukiah, Cal.

Yokayo Indians circa 1916

Origin: Near Ukiah California

The interesting account which now follows is by Stephen Powers, [Footnote: Cont. to North American Ethnol., 1878, iv, p. 164.] and relates to the Yo-kai-a [Yokayo] of California, containing other matters of importance pertaining to burial.

"I paid a visit to their camp four miles below Ukiah, and finding there a unique kind of assembly-house, desired to enter and examine it, but was not allowed to do so until I had gained the confidence of the old sexton by a few friendly words and the tender of a silver half dollar. The pit of it was about 50 feet in diameter and 4 or 5 feet deep, and it was so heavily roofed with earth that the interior was damp and somber as a tomb. It looked like a low tumulus, and was provided with a tunnel-like entrance about 10 feet long and 4 feet high, and leading down to a level with the floor of the pit. The mouth of the tunnel was closed with brush, and the venerable sexton would not remove it until he had slowly and devoutly paced several times to and fro before the entrance.

"Passing in I found the massive roof supported by a number of peeled poles painted white and ringed with black and ornamented with rude devices. The floor was covered thick and green with sprouting wheat, which had been scattered to feed the spirit of the captain of the tribe, lately deceased. Not long afterward a deputation of the Senel came up to condole with the Yo-kai-a on the loss of their chief, and a dance or series of dances was held which lasted three days. During this time of course the Senel were the guests of the Yo-kai-a, and the latter were subjected to a considerable expense. I was prevented by other engagements from being present, and shall be obliged to depend on the description of an eye-witness, Mr. John Tenney, whose account is here given with a few changes.

"There are four officials connected with the building, who are probably chosen to preserve order and to allow no intruders. They are the assistants of the chief. The invitation to attend was from one of them, and admission was given by the same. These four wore black vests trimmed with red flannel and shell ornaments. The chief made no special display on the occasion. In addition to these four, who were officers of the assembly-chamber, there was an old man and a young woman, who seemed to be priest and priestess. The young woman was dressed differently from any other, the rest dressing in plain calico dresses. Her dress was white covered with spots of red flannel, cut in neat figures, ornamented with shells. It looked gorgeous and denoted some office, the name of which I could not ascertain. Before the visitors were ready to enter, the older men of the tribe were reclining around the fire smoking and chatting. As the ceremonies were about to commence, the old man and young woman were summoned, and, standing at the end opposite the entrance, they inaugurated the exercises by a brief service, which seemed to be a dedication of the house to the exercises about to commence. Each of them spoke a few words, joined in a brief chant, and the house was thrown open for their visitors. They staid at their post until the visitors entered and were seated on one side of the room. After the visitors then others were seated, making about 200 in all, though there was plenty of room in the center for the dancing.

"Before the dance commenced the chief of the visiting tribe made a brief speech, in which he no doubt referred to the death of the chief of the Yo-kai-a, and offered the sympathy of his tribe in this loss. As he spoke, some of the women scarcely refrained from crying out, and with difficulty they suppressed their sobs. I presume that he proposed a few moments of mourning, for when he stopped the whole assemblage burst forth into a bitter wailing, some screaming as if in agony. The whole thing created such a din that I was compelled to stop my ears. The air was rent and pierced with their cries. This wailing and shedding of tears lasted about three or five minutes, though it seemed to last a half hour. At a given signal they ceased, wiped their eyes, and quieted down.

"Then preparations were made for the dance. One end of the room was set aside for the dressing-room. The chief actors were five men, who were muscular and agile. They were profusely decorated with paint and feathers, while white and dark stripes covered their bodies. They were girt about the middle with cloth of bright colors, sometimes with variegated shawls. A feather mantle hung from the shoulder, reaching below the knee; strings of shells ornamented the neck, while their heads were covered with a crown of eagle feathers. They had whistles in their mouths as they danced, swaying their heads, bending and whirling their bodies; every muscle seemed to be exercised, and the feather ornaments quivered with light. They were agile and graceful as they bounded about in the sinuous course of the dance.

"The five men were assisted by a semicircle of twenty women, who only marked time by stepping up and down with short step; they always took their places first and disappeared first, the men making their exit gracefully one by one. The dresses of the women were suitable for the occasion. They were white dresses trimmed heavily with black velvet. The stripes were about three inches wide, some plain and others edged like saw-teeth. This was an indication of their mourning for the dead chief in whose honor they had prepared that style of dancing. Strings of haliotis and pachydesma shell beads encircled their necks, and around their waists were belts heavily loaded with the same material. Their head-dresses were more showy than those of the men. The head was encircled with a bandeau of otters' or beavers' fur, to which were attached short wires standing out in all directions, with glass or shell beads strung on them, and at the tips little feather flags and quail plumes. Surmounting all was a pyramidal plume of feathers, black, gray, and scarlet, the top generally being a bright scarlet bunch, waving and tossing very beautifully. All these combined gave their heads a very brilliant and spangled appearance.

"The first day the dance was slow and funereal, in honor of the Yo- kai-a chief who died a short time before. The music was mournful and simple being a monotonous chant in which only two tones were used, accompanied with a rattling of split sticks and stamping on a hollow slab. The second day the dance was more lively on the part of the men, the music was better, employing airs which had a greater range of tune and the women generally joined in the chorus. The dress of the women was not so beautiful as they appeared in ordinary calico. The third day if observed in accordance with Indian custom the dancing was still more lively and the proceedings more gay just as the coming home from a Christian funeral is apt to be much more jolly than the going out."

A Yo-kai-a widow's style of mourning is peculiar. In addition to the usual evidences of grief she mingles the ashes of her dead husband with pitch making a white tar or unguent, with which she smears a band about two inches wide all around the edge of the hair (which is previously cut off close to the head) so that at a little distance she appears to be wearing a white chaplet.

It is their custom to feed the spirits of the dead for the space of one year by going daily to places which they were accustomed to frequent while living, where they sprinkle pinole upon the ground. A Yo-kai-a mother who has lost her babe goes every day for a year to some place where her little one played when alive or to the spot where the body was burned and milks her breasts into the air. This is accompanied by plaintive mourning and weeping and piteous calling upon her little one to return and sometimes she sings a hoarse and melancholy chant and dances with a wild ecstatic swaying of her body.

Round Valley

Origin: Northern California

J. L. Burchard, agent to the Round Valley Indians, of California, furnishes an account of burial somewhat resembling that of the Navajos:

When I first came here the Indians would dig a round hole in the ground, draw up the knees of the deceased Indian, and wrap the body into as small a bulk as possible in blankets, tie them firmly with cords, place them in the grave, throw in beads, baskets, clothing, everything owned by the deceased, and often donating much extra; all gathered around the grave wailing most pitifully, tearing their faces with their nails till the blood would run down their cheeks, pull out their hair, and such other heathenish conduct. These burials were generally made under their thatch houses or very near thereto. The house where one died was always torn down, removed, rebuilt, or abandoned. The wailing, talks, &c., were in their own jargon; none else could understand, and they seemingly knew but little of its meaning (if there was any meaning in it); it simply seemed to be the promptings of grief, without sufficient intelligence to direct any ceremony; each seemed to act out his own impulse.

Yurok

Yurok Indians in ceremonial costumes circa 1905.

Origin: They lived in northwestern California near the Klamath River and Pacific coast.

"Stephen Powers [Footnote: Cont. to N. A. Ethnol., 1877, ii, p.58] gives a tradition current among the Yurok of California as to the use of fires.

"After death they keep a fire burning certain nights in the vicinity of the grave. They hold and believe, at least the 'Big Indians' do, that the spirits of the departed are compelled to cross an extremely attenuated greasy pole, which bridges over the chasm of the debatable land, and that they require the fire to light them on their darksome journey. A righteous soul traverses the pole quicker than a wicked one, hence they regulate the number of nights for burning a light according to the character for goodness or the opposite which the deceased possessed in this world." Dr. Emil Bessels, of the Polaris expedition, informs the writer that a somewhat similar belief obtains among the Esquimaux.

Klamath

Origin: Northern California and southern Oregon

George Gibbs [Footnote: Schoolcraft's Hist. Indian Tribes of the United States Pt. 3, 1853, p. 140] gives the following account of burial among the Klamath and Trinity Indians of the Northwest coast.

The graves which are in the immediate vicinity of their houses exhibit very considerable taste and a laudable care. The dead are inclosed in rude coffins formed by placing four boards around the body and covered with earth to some depth; a heavy plank often supported by upright head and foot stones is laid upon the top or stones are built up into a wall about a foot above the ground and the top flagged with others. The graves of the chiefs are surrounded by neat wooden palings, each pale ornamented with a feather from the tail of the bald eagle. Baskets are usually staked down by the side according to the wealth or popularity of the individual and sometimes other articles for ornament or use are suspended over them. The funeral ceremonies occupy three days during which the soul of the deceased is in danger from *O-mah- u* or the devil. To preserve it from this peril a fire is kept up at the grave and the friends of the deceased howl around it to scare away the demon. Should they not be successful in this the soul is carried down the river, subject, however, to redemption by *Peh-ho wan* on payment of a big knife. After the expiration of three days it is all well with them.

The question may well be asked, is the big knife a "sop to Cerberus"?

Tolkotins

Origin: Oregon

Ross Cox [Footnote: Adventures on the Columbia River, 1831, vol. ii, p. 387] gives an account of the process as performed by the Tolkotins "The ceremonies attending the dead are very singular, and quite peculiar to this tribe of Oregon:

The body of the deceased is kept nine days laid out in his lodge, and on the tenth it is buried. For this purpose a rising ground is selected, on which are laid a number of sticks, about seven feet long, of cypress, neatly split, and in the interstices is placed a quantity of gummy wood. During these operations invitations are dispatched to the natives of the neighboring villages requesting their attendance at the ceremony. When the preparations are perfected the corpse is placed on the pile, which is immediately ignited, and during the process of burning, the bystanders appear to be in a high state of merriment. If a stranger happen to be present they invariably plunder him, but if that pleasure be denied them, they never separate without quarreling among themselves. Whatever property the deceased possessed is placed about the corpse, and if he happened to be a person of consequence, his friends generally purchase a capote, a shirt, a pair of trousers, etc., which articles are also laid around the pile. If the doctor who attended him has escaped uninjured, he is obliged to be present at the ceremony, and for the last time tries his skill in restoring the defunct to animation. Failing in this, he throws on the body a piece of leather, or some other article, as a present, which in some measure appeases the resentment of his relatives, and preserves the unfortunate quack from being maltreated. During the nine days the corpse is laid out the widow of the deceased is obliged to sleep along side it from sunset to sunrise; and from this custom there is no relaxation even during the hottest days of summer! While the doctor is performing his last operations she must lie on the pile, and after the fire is applied to it she cannot stir until the doctor orders her to be removed, which, however, is never done until her body is completely covered with blisters. After being placed on her legs, she is obliged to pass her hands gently through the flame and collect some of the liquid fat which issues from the corpse, with which she is permitted to wet her face and body! When the friends of the deceased observe the sinews of the legs and arms beginning to contract they compel the unfortunate widow to go again on the pile, and by dint of hard pressing to straighten those members.

"If during her husband's lifetime she has been known to have committed any act of infidelity or omitted administering to him savory food or neglected his clothing, etc, she is now made to suffer severely for such lapses of duty by his relations, who frequently fling her in the funeral pile, from which she is dragged by her friends; and thus between alternate scorching and cooling she is dragged backwards and forwards until she falls into a state of insensibility.

"After the process of burning the corpse has terminated, the widow collects the larger bones, which she rolls up in an envelope of birch bark, and which she is obliged for some years afterwards to carry on her back. She is now considered and treated as a slave, all the laborious duties of cooking, collecting fuel, etc., devolve on her. She must obey the orders of all the women, and even of the children belonging to the village, and the slightest mistake or disobedience subjects her to the infliction of a heavy punishment. The ashes of her husband are carefully collected and deposited in a grave, which it is her duty to keep free from weeds; and should any such appear, she is obliged to root them out with her *fingers*. During this operation her husband's relatives stand by and beat her in a cruel manner until the task is completed or she falls a victim to their brutality. The wretched widows, to avoid this complicated cruelty, frequently commit suicide. Should she, however, linger on for three or four years, the friends of her husband agree to relieve her from her painful mourning. This is a ceremony of much consequence, and the preparations for it occupy a considerable time, generally from six to eight months. The hunters proceed to the various districts in which deer and beaver abound, and after collecting large quantities of meat and fur return to the village. The skins are immediately bartered for guns, ammunition, clothing, trinkets, etc. Invitations are then bent to the inhabitants of the various friendly villages, and when they have all assembled the feast commences, and presents are distributed to each visitor. The object of their meeting is then explained, and the woman is brought forward, still carrying on her back the bones of her late husband, which are now removed and placed in a covered box, which is nailed or otherwise fastened to a post twelve feet high. Her conduct as a faithful widow is next highly eulogized, and the ceremony of her manumission is completed by one man powdering on her head the down of birds and another pouring on it the contents of a bladder of oil. She is then at liberty to marry again or lead a life of single blessedness; but few of them, I believe, wish to encounter the risk attending a second widowhood.

"The men are condemned to a similar ordeal, but they do not bear it with equal fortitude, and numbers fly to distant quarters to avoid the brutal treatment which custom has established as a kind of religious rite."

Skokomish

Origin: Washington State

From a number of examples, the following, relating to the Clallams and furnished by the Rev. M. Eells, missionary to the Agency, Washington Territory, is selected:

"The deceased was a woman about thirty or thirty-five years of age, dead of consumption. She died in the morning, and in the afternoon I went to the house to attend the funeral. She had then been placed in a Hudson's Bay Company's box for a coffin, which was about 3 1/2 feet long, 1 3/4 wide, and 1 1/2 high. She was very poor when she died, owing to her disease, or she could not have been put in this box. A fire was burning near by, where a large number of her things had been consumed, and the rest were in three boxes near the coffin. Her mother sang the mourning song, sometimes with others, and often saying. 'My daughter, my daughter, why did you die?' and similar words. The burial did not take place until the next day, and I was invited to go. It was an aerial burial, in a canoe. The canoe was about 25 feet long. The posts, of old Indian hewed boards, were about a foot wide. Holes were cut in these, in which boards were placed, on which the canoe rested. One thing I noticed while this was done which was new to me, but the significance of which I did not learn. As fast as the holes were cut in the posts green leaves were gathered and placed over the holes until the posts were put in the ground. The coffin-box and the three others containing her things were placed in the canoe and a roof of boards made over the central part, which was entirely covered with white cloth. The head part and the foot part of her bedstead were then nailed on to the posts, which front the water, and a dress nailed on each of these. After pronouncing the benediction, all left the hill and went to the beach except her father, mother, and brother, who remained ten or fifteen minutes, pounding on the canoe and mourning. They then came down and made a present to those persons who were there—a gun to me, a blanket to each of two or three others, and a dollar and a half to each of the rest, there being about fifteen persons present. Three or four of them then made short speeches, and we came home.

"The reason why she was buried thus is said to be because she is a prominent woman in the tribe. In about nine months it is expected that there will be a '*pot-latch*' or distribution of money near this place, and as each tribe shall come they will send a delegation of two or three men, who will carry a present and leave it at the grave; soon after that shall be done she will be buried in the ground. Shortly after her death both her father and mother cut off their hair as a sign of their grief."

Chinook Indians

Origin: They lived in what is now Washington and Oregon, mainly around the Columbia River and Pacific Ocean

George Gibbs [Footnote: Cont. N. A. Ethnol. 1877, I, p. 200.] gives a most interesting account of the burial

177

ceremonies of the Indians of Oregon and Washington Territory, which is here reproduced in its entirety, although it contains examples of other modes of burial besides that in canoes; but to separate the narrative would destroy the thread of the story:

"The common mode of disposing of the dead among the fishing tribes was in canoes. These were generally drawn into the woods at some prominent point a short distance from the village, and sometimes placed between the forks of trees or raised from the ground on posts. Upon the Columbia River the Tsinuk had in particular two very noted cemeteries, a high isolated bluff about three miles below the mouth of the Cowlitz, called Mount Coffin, and one some distance above, called Coffin Rock. The former would appear not to have been very ancient. Mr. Broughton, one of Vancouver's lieutenants, who explored the river, makes mention only of *several* canoes at this place; and Lewis and Clarke, who noticed the mount, do not speak of them at all, but at the time of Captain Wilkes's expedition it is conjectured that there were at least 3,000. A fire caused by the carelessness of one of his party destroyed the whole, to the great indignation of the Indians.

It is hardly necessary to say that such a practice is altogether foreign to Indian character. The bones of the adults had probably been removed and buried elsewhere. The corpses of children are variously disposed of; sometimes by suspending them, at others by placing in the hollows of trees, A cemetery devoted to infants is, however, an unusual occurrence. In cases of chiefs or men of note much pomp was used in the accompaniments of the rite. The canoes were of great size and value—the war or state canoes of the deceased. Frequently one was inverted over that holding the body, and in one instance, near Shoalwater Bay, the corpse was deposited in a small canoe, which again was placed in a larger one and covered with a third. Among the *Tsinuk* and *Tsihalis* the *tamahno-us* board of the owner was placed near him. The Puget Sound Indians do not make these *tamahno-us* hoards, but they sometimes constructed effigies of their chiefs, resembling the person as nearly as possible, dressed in his usual costume, and wearing the articles of which he was fond. One of these, representing the Skagit chief Sneestum, stood very conspicuously upon a high bank on the eastern side of Whidbey Island The figures observed by Captain Clarke at the Cascades were either of this description or else the carved, posts which had ornamented the interior of the houses of the deceased, and were connected with the superstition of the *tamahno-us*. The most valuable articles of property were put into or hung up around the grave, being first carefully rendered unserviceable, and the living family were literally stripped to do honor to the dead. No little self-denial must have been practiced in parting with articles so precious, but those interested frequently had the least to say on the subject. The graves of women were distinguished by a cup, a Kamas stick, or other implement of their occupation, and by articles of dress.

"Slaves were killed in proportion to the rank and wealth of the deceased. In some instances they were starved to death, or even tied to the dead body and left to perish thus horribly. At present this practice has been almost entirely given up, but till within a very few years it was not uncommon. A case which occurred in 1850 has been already mentioned. Still later, in 1853, Toke, a Tsinuk chief living at Shoalwater Bay, undertook to kill a slave girl belonging to his daughter, who, in dying, had requested that this might be done. The woman fled, and was found by some citizens in the woods half starved. Her master attempted to reclaim her, but was soundly thrashed and warned against another attempt.

"It was usual in the case of chiefs to renew or repair for a considerable length of time the materials and ornaments of the burial- place. With the common class of persons family pride or domestic affection was satisfied with the gathering together of the bones after the flesh had decayed and wrapping them in a new mat. The violation of the grave was always regarded as an offense of the first magnitude and provoked severe revenge. Captain Belcher remarks, 'Great secrecy is observed in all their burial ceremonies, partly from fear of Europeans, and as among themselves they will instantly punish by death any violation of the tomb or wage war if perpetrated by another tribe, so they are inveterate and tenaciously bent on revenge should they discover that any act of the kind has been perpetrated by a white man. It is on record that part of the crew of a vessel on her return to this port (the Columbia) suffered because a person who belonged to her (but not then in her) was known to have taken a skull, which, from the process of flattening, had become an object of curiosity.' He adds, however, that at the period of his visit to the river 'the skulls and skeletons were scattered about in all directions; and as I was on most of their positions unnoticed by the natives, I suspect the feeling does not extend much beyond their relatives, and then only till decay has destroyed body, goods, and chattels. The chiefs, no doubt, are watched, as their canoes are repainted, decorated, and greater care taken by placing them in sequestered spots.'

"The motive for sacrificing or destroying property on occasion of death will be referred to in treating of their religious ideas. Wailing for the dead is continued for a long time, and seems to be rather a ceremonial performance than an act of spontaneous grief. The duty, of course, belongs to the woman, and the early morning is usually chosen for the purpose. They go out alone to some place a little distant from the lodge or camp, and in a loud, sobbing voice repeat a sort of stereotyped formula, as, for instance, a mother, on the loss of her child, *'Ah seahb shed-da bud-dah ah ta bud! ad-de- dah,* Ah chief!' 'My child dead, alas!' When in dreams they see any of their deceased friends this lamentation is renewed."

With most of the Northwest Indians it was quite common, as mentioned by Mr. Gibbs, to kill or bury with the dead a living slave, who, failing to die within three days was strangled by another slave, but the custom has also prevailed among other tribes and peoples, in many cases the individuals offering themselves as voluntary sacrifices. Bancroft states "that in Panama, Nata, and some other districts, when a cacique died those of his concubines that loved him enough, those that he loved ardently and so appointed, as well as certain servants, killed themselves and were interred with him. This they did in order that they might wait upon him in the land of spirits." It is well known to all readers of history to what an extreme this revolting practice has prevailed in Mexico, South America, and Africa.

March 29th [1847]
"We came to another Indian burial ground, which seemed to be highly decorated. I wished my Indians to put ashore, but they would not do so. I was obliged therefore, to put them out of the canoe on the opposite side of the river, and paddle the canoe over by myself. I have no doubt that they would have opposed my doing so had it not been for the name which I had already acquired amongst the Indians, of being a great medicine-man, on account of the likenesses which I had taken.

My power of portraying the feature of individuals was attributed entirely to supernatural agency, and I found that, in looking at my pictures, they always covered their eyes with their hands and looked through the fingers; this being also the invariable custom when looking at a dead person.

On arriving at the place I found it lavishly decorated with numerous articles, of supposed utility and ornament, for the convenience of the defunct in the journey to the world of spirits. These articles consisted of blankets, tin cups, pots, pans, kettles, plates, baskets, horn bowls, and spoons, with shreds of cloth of various colors. One canoe, which was decorated more highly than the rest, I examined particularly. All the articles appended to it were rendered useless for this world by either tearing, breaking, or boring holes in them, the Indians believing that they would be made whole again by the Great Spirit.

On examining the interior of a canoe I found a great number of ioquas and other shells, together with beads and rings: even the mouth of the deceased was filled with these articles. The body itself was carefully enveloped in numerous folds of matting made of rushes. At the bottom of the canoe lay a bow and arrow, a paddle, a spear, and a kind of pick, made of horn, for digging the camas roots; the top of the canoe immediately over the body, had a covering of bark, and holes were bored in the bottom to allow the water to run out. These canoes are always placed on wooden supports, suspended in branches of trees, or placed upon isolated rocks in the river, to keep them beyond the reach of ravenous animals.

METHOD OF BURIAL.

"During my stay the Indians watched me closely from the opposite bank, and, on my return, they examined me as minutely as they well could with their eyes to see that I had not brought anything away with me. Had I been so imprudent as to have done so I should probably have answered for the sacrilege with my life, death being the certain penalty to the most trifling violation of the sanctity of the coffin canoe. I endeavored to discover who was buried in the richly decorated canoe, but the only information I could get from them was that the deceased was the daughter of a Chinook chief.

The Indians here have a superstitious dread of mentioning the name of any person after death, nor will they tell you their own names, which can only be found out from a third party. One of the men asked me if my desire to know his name proceeded from a wish to steal it. It is not an uncommon thing for a chief, when he wishes to pay you a very high compliment, to give and call you by his own name, and adopt some other for himself" (Kane: 1925).

The second example is by *Catlin [Footnote: Hist. North American Indians, 1844, II, p. 141]* and relates to the Chinook.

"… This little cradle has a strap which passes over the woman's forehead whilst the cradle rides on her back, and if the child dies during its subjection to this rigid mode its cradle becomes its coffin, forming a little canoe, in which it lie floating on the water in some sacred pool, where they are often in the habit of fastening their canoes containing the dead bodies of the old and young, or, which is often the case, elevated into the branches of trees, where their bodies are left to decay and their bones to dry whilst they are bandaged in man skins and ominously packed in their canoes, with paddles to propel and ladles to bail them out, and provisions to last and pipes to smoke as they are performing their 'long journey after death to their contemplated hunting grounds,' which these people think is to be performed in their canoes."

Aleut

Origin: Aleutian Islands

Martin Sauer, secretary to Billings' Expedition [Footnote: Billings' Exped. 1802, p. 167.] in 1802, speaks of the Aleutian Islanders embalming their dead, as follows:

"They pay respect, however, to the memory of the dead, for they embalm the bodies of the men with dried moss and grass; bury them in their best attire, in a sitting posture, in a strong box, with their darts and instruments; and decorate the tomb with various colored mats, embroidery, and paintings. With women, indeed, they use less ceremony. A mother will keep a dead child thus embalmed in their hut for some months, constantly wiping it dry; and they bury it when it begins to smell, or when they get reconciled to parting with it."

Regarding these same people, a writer in the San Francisco Bulletin gives this account-

"The schooner William Sutton, belonging to the Alaska Commercial Company, has arrived from the seal islands of the company with the mummified remains of Indians who lived on an island north of Ounalaska one hundred and fifty years ago. This contribution to science was secured by Captain Henning, an agent of the company, who has long resided at Ounalaska. In his transactions with the Indians he learned that tradition among the Aleuts assigned Kagamale, the island in question, as the last resting-place of a great chief, known as Karkhayahouchak. Last year the captain was in the neighborhood of Kagamale, in quest of sea-otter and other furs and he bore up for the island, with the intention of testing the truth of the tradition he had heard. He had more difficulty in entering the cave than in finding it, his schooner having to beat on and off shore for three days. Finally, he succeeded in effecting a landing, and clambering up the rocks he found himself in the presence of the dead chief, his family and relatives.

"The cave smelt strongly of hot sulfurous vapors. With great care the mummies were removed, and all the little trinkets and ornaments scattered around were also taken away.

"In all there are eleven packages of bodies. Only two or three have as yet been opened. The body of the chief is enclosed in a large basket- like structure, about four feet in height. Outside the wrappings are finely-wrought sea-grass matting, exquisitely close in texture, and skins. At the bottom is a broad hoop or basket of thinly-cut wood, and adjoining the center portions are pieces of body armor composed of reeds bound together. The body is covered with the fine skin of the sea-otter, always a mark of distinction in the interments of the Aleuts, and round the whole package are stretched the meshes of a fish-net, made of the sinews of the sea lion; also those of a bird-net. There are evidently some bulky articles enclosed with the chief's body, and the whole package differs very much from the others, which more resemble, in their brown-grass matting, consignments of crude sugar from the Sandwich Islands than the remains of human beings. The bodies of a papoose and of a very little child, which probably died at birth or soon after it, have sea-otter skins around them. One of the feet of the latter projects, with a toe-nail visible. The remaining mummies are of adults.

"One of the packages has been opened, and it reveals a man's body in tolerable preservation, but with a large portion of the face decomposed. This and the other bodies were doubled up at death by severing some of the muscles at the hip and knee joints and bending the limbs downward horizontally upon the trunk. Perhaps the most peculiar package, next to that of the chief, is one which encloses in a single matting, with sea-lion skins, the bodies of a man and woman. The collection also embraces a couple of skulls, male and female, which have still the hair attached to the scalp. The hair has changed its color to a brownish red. The relics obtained with the bodies include a few wooden vessels scooped out smoothly; a piece of dark, greenish, flat stone, harder than the emerald, which the Indians use to tan skins; a scalp-lock of jet-black hair; a small rude figure, which may have been a very ugly doll or an idol; two or three tiny carvings in ivory of the sea-lion, very neatly executed, a comb, a necklet made of birds' claws inserted into one another, and several specimens of little bags, and a cap plaited out of sea-grass and almost water-tight."

With the foregoing examples as illustration, the matter of embalment may be for the present dismissed, with the advice to observers that particular care should be taken, in case mummies are discovered, to ascertain whether the bodies have been submitted to a regular preservative process, or owe their protection to ingredients in the soil of their graves or to desiccation in arid districts.

Gwich'in

Origin: Northeast Alaska

W. L. Hardisty [Footnote: Rep. Smithsonian Inst., 1866, p. 319] gives a curious example of log-burial in trees, relating to the Loucheux [Gwich'in] of British America:

"They enclose the body in a neatly-hollowed piece of wood, and secure it to two or more trees, about six feet from the ground. A log about eight feet long is first split in two, and each of the parts carefully hollowed out to the required size. The body is then enclosed and the two pieces well lashed together, preparatory to being finally secured, as before stated, to the trees"

Origin: Alaska, Canada, Siberia, and Greenland

The next description of cave burial, described by W. H. Dall [Footnote: Contrib. to N. A. Ethnol., 1877, vol 1, p 62.], is so remarkable that it seems worthy of admittance to this paper. It relates probably to the Innuit of Alaska.

"The earliest remains of man found in Alaska up to the time of writing I refer to this epoch [Echinus layer of Dall]. There are some crania found by us in the lowermost part of the Amaknak cave and a cranium obtained at Adakh, near the anchorage in the Bay of Islands. These were deposited in a remarkable manner, precisely similar to that adopted by most of the continental Innuit, but equally different from the modern Aleut fashion. At the Amaknak cave we found what at first appeared to be a wooden enclosure, but which proved to be made of the very much decayed supra-maxillary bones of some large cetacean. These were arranged so as to form a rude rectangular enclosure covered over with similar pieces of bone. This was somewhat less than 4 feet long, 2 feet wide, and 18 inches deep. The bottom was formed of flat pieces of stone. Three such were found close together, covered with and filled by an accumulation of fine vegetable and organic mold. In each was the remains of a skeleton in the last stages of decay. It had evidently been tied up in the Innuit fashion to get it into its narrow house, but all the bones, with the exception of the skull, were reduced to a soft paste, or even entirely gone. At Adakh a fancy prompted me to dig into a small knoll near the ancient shell-heap; and here we found, in a precisely similar sarcophagus, the remains of a skeleton, of which also only the cranium retained sufficient consistency to admit of preservation. This enclosure, however, was filled with a dense peaty mass not reduced to mold, the result of centuries of sphagnous growth, which had reached a thickness of nearly 2 feet above the remains. When we reflect upon the well-known slowness of this kind of growth in these northern regions, attested by numerous Arctic travelers, the antiquity of the remains becomes evident."

The practice of preserving the bodies of those belonging to the whaling class—a custom peculiar to the Kadiak Innuit—has erroneously been confounded with the one now described. The latter included women as well as men, and all those whom the living desired particularly to honor. The whalers, however, only preserved the bodies of males, and they were not associated with the paraphernalia of those I have described. Indeed, the observations I have been able to make show the bodies of the whalers to have been preserved with stone weapons and actual utensils instead of effigies, and with the meanest apparel, and no carvings of consequence. These details, and those of many other customs and usages of which the shell heaps bear no testimony.

Figure 5, copied from Dall, represents the Alaskan mummies.

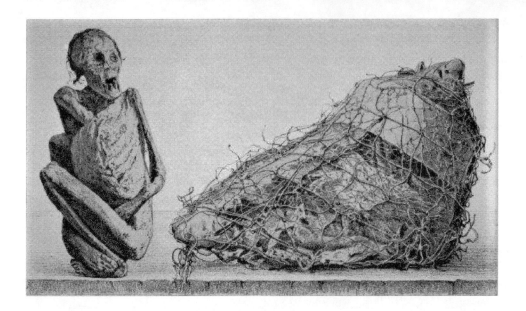

Martin Sauer, secretary to Billings' Expedition, speaks of the Aleutian Islanders embalming their dead, as follows:

They pay respect, however, to the memory of the dead, for they embalm the bodies of the men with dried moss and grass; bury them in their best attire, in a sitting posture, in a strong box, with their darts and instruments; and decorate the tomb with various colored mats, embroidery, and paintings. With women, indeed, they use less ceremony. A mother will keep a dead child thus embalmed in their hut for some months, constantly wiping it dry; and they bury it when it begins to smell, or when they get reconciled to parting with it.

Regarding these same people, a writer in the San Francisco Bulletin gives this account:

The schooner William Sutton, belonging to the Alaska Commercial Company, has arrived from the seal islands of the company with the mummified remains of Indians who lived on an island north of Ounalaska one hundred and fifty years ago. This contribution to science was secured by Captain Henning, an agent of the company who has long resided at Ounalaska. In his transactions with the Indians he learned 136that tradition among the Aleuts assigned Kagamale, the island in question, as the last resting-place of a great chief, known as Karkhayahouchak. Last year the captain was in the neighborhood of Kagamale in quest of sea-otter and other furs, and he bore up for the island, with the intention of testing the truth of the tradition he had heard. He had more difficulty in entering the cave than in finding it, his schooner having to beat on and off shore for three days. Finally he succeeded in affecting a landing, and clambering up the rocks he found himself in the presence of the dead chief, his family and relatives.

The cave smelt strongly of hot sulfurous vapors. With great care the mummies were removed, and all the little trinkets and ornaments scattered around were also taken away.

In all there are eleven packages of bodies. Only two or three have as yet been opened. The body of the chief is enclosed in a large basket-like structure, about four feet in height. Outside the wrappings are finely wrought sea-grass matting, exquisitely close in texture, and skins. At the bottom is a broad hoop or basket of thinly cut wood, and adjoining the center portions are pieces of body armor composed of reeds bound together. The body is covered with the fine skin of the sea-otter, always a mark of distinction in the interments of the Aleuts, and round the whole package are stretched the meshes of a fish-net, made of the sinews of the sea lion; also those of a bird-net. There are evidently some bulky articles enclosed with the chief's body, and the whole package differs very much from the others, which more resemble, in their brown-grass matting, consignments of crude sugar from the Sandwich Islands than the remains of human beings. The bodies of a papoose and of a very little child, which probably died at birth or soon after it, have sea-otter skins around them. One of the feet of the latter projects, with a toe-nail visible. The remaining mummies are of adults.

One of the packages has been opened, and it reveals a man's body in tolerable preservation, but with a large portion of the face decomposed. This and the other bodies were doubled up at death by severing some of the muscles at the hip and knee joints and bending the limbs downward horizontally upon the trunk. Perhaps the most peculiar package, next to that of the chief, is one which encloses in a single matting, with sea-lion skins, the bodies of a man and woman. The collection also embraces a couple of skulls, male and female, which have still the hair attached to the scalp. The hair has changed its color to a brownish red. The relics obtained with the bodies include a few wooden vessels scooped out smoothly: a piece of dark, greenish, flat stone, harder than the emerald, which the Indians use to tan skins; a scalp-lock of jet-black hair; a small rude figure, which may have been a very ugly doll or an idol; two or three tiny carvings in ivory of the sea-lion, very neatly executed; a comb, a necklet made of bird's claws inserted into one another, and several specimens of little bags, and a cap plaited out of sea-grass and almost water-tight.

In Cary's translation of Herodotus (1853, p. 180) the following passage occurs which purports to describe the manner in which the Macrobrian Ethiopians preserved their dead. It is added, simply as a matter of curious interest, nothing more, for no remains so preserved have ever been discovered.

After this, they visited last of all their sepulchers, which are said to be prepared from crystal in the following manner. When they have dried the body, either as the Egyptians do, or in some other way, they plaster it all over with gypsum, and paint it, making it as much as possible resemble real life; they then put round it a hollow column made of crystal, which they dig up in abundance, and is easily wrought. The body being in the middle of the column is plainly seen, nor does it emit an unpleasant smell, nor is it in any way offensive, and it is all visible as the body itself. The nearest relations keep the column in their houses for a year, offering to it the first-fruits 137of all, and performing sacrifices; after that time they carry it out and place it somewhere near the city.

Eskimo

Origin: Alaska, Canada, Greenland

Capt. F. W. Beechey describes a curious mode of burial among the Esquimaux on the west coast of Alaska, which appears to be somewhat similar to lodge burial. Figure 11, after his illustration, affords a good idea of these burial receptacles.

Eskimo lodge burial.

Near us there was a burying ground, which in addition to what we had already observed at Cape Espenburg furnished several examples of the manner in which this tribe of natives dispose of their dead. In some instances a platform was constructed of drift-wood raised about two feet and a quarter from the ground, upon which the body was placed, with its head to the westward and a double tent of drift-wood erected over it, the inner one with spars about seven feet long, and the outer one with some that were three times that length. They were placed close together, and at first no doubt sufficiently so to prevent the depredations of foxes and wolves, but they had yielded at last, and all the bodies, and even the hides that covered them, had suffered by these rapacious animals.

In these tents of the dead there were no coffins or planks, as at Cape Espenburg, the bodies were dressed in a frock made of eider duck skins, with one of deer skin over it, and were covered with a sea horse hide, such as the natives use for their *baidars*. Suspended to the poles, and on the ground near them, were several Esquimaux implements, consisting of wooden trays, paddles, and a tamborine, which, we were informed as well as signs could convey the meaning of the natives, were placed there for the use of the deceased, who, in the next world (pointing to the western sky) ate, drank, and sang songs. Having no interpreter, this was all the information I could obtain, but the custom of placing such instruments around the receptacles of the dead is not unusual, and in all probability the Esquimaux may believe that the soul has enjoyments in the next world similar to those which constitute their happiness in this.

Haida

Origin: Alaska and northwest British Columbia

A Weird Mourning Song of the Haidas

During a fourteen-months' stay on the Queen Charlotte islands in the years 1869-70, connected with coast mining, we had to employ a large number of Indians, who, in order to be nearer their work and also to have homes, added house to house, until there was quite a village. In the center of this village stood two large houses, one being a store and trading post, the other dwelling and boarding house for the white people employed on the works, which at the time numbered fifteen. A little to the north of the latter was an Indian house of considerable dimensions. In this house, three or four times every week, all the Indians met for what appeared to be some sort of amusement. They seated themselves in an oval around a fire, which was all the light they had. While thus squatted on the floor, they all together sung, and beat time with sticks on a board laying before each one. After singing and beating a while, one of their number would begin to speak, then all would stop and listen. As soon as the speaker stopped, all would again sing until the speaker, who had been sitting passive, again began to speak. Thus they kept on until one or two o'clock in the morning. One thing I noticed, they always ended with the same song every night. And such a song! Anything so weird in the midnight hours I never before heard in all my life. So weird, so sad and mournful was it, that I never forgot it. When it was sung I could not help shedding tears, let me do my best. After two or three nights' experience, I asked the Indians what they were doing and what they were singing. In answer to my request, I received the following. Before I begin it will be necessary, in order to understand clearly the cause of these meetings, to give a few facts.

Early in the spring of 1868, the smallpox broke out amongst our Indian population. The Haidas, in order to escape the fell destroyer of their race, left to the number of three hundred. They started in twenty-five large canoes, hoping, after a few weeks' sailing at farthest, to reach their island home. But oh, vain hope ! In less than two days' sailing they found with dismay that six or seven of their number had the dreaded smallpox and could go no further. Here they anchored in a small harbor on an island. Here they stayed by their companions until they died, and then left, leaving behind them the bodies wrapped in blankets where they died, and beside them all their belongings. Thus one by one they were left behind, until one boy alone of all that number, reached home. At first they broke up the canoes when there was none left to sail them; afterwards, when there were few to break them, they were left on shore, where their owners lay, rotting in the timber.

To hold communion with the spirits of their relations who thus fell by the way, my informant said, they met, and to learn what progress they were making in the other life — which they considered to be one of unending progression — and if satisfactory the women, who are the mourners, would wash their faces and leave off their lamentations. When the Haidas mourn the passing away of their relations, they paint their faces black, which so remains for one year. As the year of mourning draws to a close, regular seances are held in one or the other of the houses. Those of their number who are mediumistic would give tests under spirit control. Sometimes a Skaga (who is a good medium) would be brought from his home in a distant village to give them communications from the shady side of life. The Skaga thus brought was always paid handsomely, as the following will show. My informant further said that after ten or twelve days were past a famous Skaga named, I think, Tow-ah-tee, living at Gumshewa. had been sent for to give them who had lost relations in the village, words of comfort from the dark be yond, and that each person had agreed to pay a number of blankets according to their ability. He said that when the Skaga came I had to come also, and see for myself by taking part in the ceremony. The Skaga came and I went to see.

Entering the house I found at least twenty-five people, men, women and children, seated as before mentioned in an oval form, with a small fire at one end and the Skaga at the other, both within its circuit. All were seated on the floor. While the singing and beating were going on, I noticed the Skaga's body making spasmodic movements, which ceased when he began to speak, while all listened without a word or a move. To my surprise, his voice would change every time he spoke — now like a man's, then like a woman's or a young person's. Amongst the number who subscribed to pay the Skaga was a man named Scielass (dirty), who with his wife took part in the sitting, they being anxious to hear from their two sons, nice boys, who both fell by the smallpox. These boys both came that night, and gave their experience. A young woman, a relation to some one in the company, one who had been well known to all present while in the body, came and through the Skaga medium; and through him gave a most excellent discourse. Thus they kept on, the hours passing unheeded until near two o'clock, when all left for home after singing the same weird song with its mournful numbers. From what I heard that night and what I learned the next morning, the past night's work was highly satisfactory, as was apparent. Next morning all the women appeared in clean clothes and with clean faces. After remaining amongst these people a few days, the Skaga got his fee and left for home.

As I have gone so far from my original subject, I may as well say a few words on what was said by the visitors from the other side through their medium, the Skaga. While on this part of the subject, I shall only give a summary of the whole, instead of taking each one in detail. Some said that when they awoke to consciousness, they were glad to find that, instead of their old bodies all covered with the loathsome smallpox, they not only had clean and beautiful bodies, but were in a beautiful country, where the skies were ever clear and the loveliest of flowers were ever in bloom, All said they were so happy that if they could come back to live again on earth they would not do so. Some of them gave messages for other spirits, who were unable to control the Skaga. Most of them told their relations not to grieve for them any more, because they were not dead, and their grief only rendered them (the spirits) unhappy. Thus they all kept on until morning, giving and receiving messages, which in the estimation of these people were strictly honest. To me it was something new, something I had never seen nor heard of before. After seriously considering the matter, I concluded that what the spirits of the dead, after throwing off their earthly bodies, were able to communicate with their friends and relations still on earth, through a medium, was the matter embraced in this song. *American Antiquarian and Oriental Journal Vol. 13 1891*

Made in United States
Troutdale, OR
04/04/2024

18940290R00113